Canto is an imprint offering a range of titles, classic and more recent, across a broad spectrum of subject areas and interests. History, literature, biography, archaeology, politics, religion, psychology, philosophy, and science are all represented in Canto's specially selected list of titles, which now offers some of the best and most accessible of Cambridge publishing to a wider readership.

The English Languages

Hundreds of millions of people use English every day everywhere in the world, but may or may not succeed in understanding each other. Despite the success of its standard form (or forms) in many countries, the complex called 'English' is immensely diverse – probably more diverse than any single language has ever been – and is likely to become even more so in the next century. This book is a compelling and broad-ranging invitation to consider the variety, the options, and the implications of this vast system. *The English Languages* looks at the 'pluralism' of English, especially the 'Englishes' that have been discussed in the last twenty years or so, and addresses the question of whether or not English can be considered a family of languages in its own right, like the Romance languages.

Tom McArthur studied at both Glasgow and Edinburgh universities. He is founder editor of the quarterly *English Today: The International Review of the English Language* (Cambridge University Press, 1984–   ) and of *The Oxford Companion to the English Language* (1992). He has published some 20 books on language, language teaching, lexicography, and Indian philosophy. A former Head of English at Cathedral School, Bombay, and Associate Professor of English at the Université du Québec, he has since 1984 been an independent writer, editor, consultant, and broadcaster, and Honorary University Fellow at the Dictionary Research Centre, the University of Exeter.

The English Languages

Tom McArthur

CAMBRIDGE
UNIVERSITY PRESS

PUBLISHED BY THE PRESS SYNDICATE OF THE UNIVERSITY OF CAMBRIDGE
The Pitt Building, Trumpington Street, Cambridge CB2 1RP, United Kingdom

CAMBRIDGE UNIVERSITY PRESS
The Edinburgh Building, Cambridge CB2 2RU, United Kingdom
40 West 20th Street, New York, NY 10011–4211, USA
10 Stamford Road, Oakleigh, Melbourne 3166, Australia

First published 1998

Printed in the United Kingdom at the University Press, Cambridge

Typeset in 9.5pt/11.5pt Charter

A catalogue record for this book is available from the British Library

Library of Congress cataloguing in publication data

McArthur, Tom (Thomas Burns)
    The English languages / Tom McArthur
        p.   cm.
    Includes index.
    ISBN 0 521 48582 7 (paperback)   ISBN 0 521 48130 9 (hardback)
    1. English language – Variation – English-speaking countries.
2. English language – Variation – Foreign countries. 3. English
language – Variation – Great Britain. 4. Communication,
International. I. Title.
PE2751.M38   1998
427–dc21   97-42227   CIP

ISBN 0 521 48130 9 hardback
ISBN 0 521 48582 7 paperback

To Sidney Greenbaum (1929–1996),
the first grammarian of International Standard English

Contents

3 Cracks in the academic monolith

4 Models of English

Introduction

English spoken; American understood.

(The *Daily Chronicle*, London, 10 June 1908)

English and French spoken; Australian understood.

(a notice in Turkey, quoted in O. Hogue's
Trooper Bluegum at Dardanelles,
London, 1916)

English understood?

Although the writers of the gems quoted above were essentially amusing themselves at other people's expense, they were also pointing to something significant that received little official or scholarly attention at the time. The early years of the twentieth century were marked by the worldwide spread not only of English at large but also of an increasingly prestigious *Standard* English. As a result, more and more people throughout both the British Empire and the United States were sensitive to any perceived failure – individual or collective – to live up to that standard. At the same time, the many marked differences in usage around the world had been obvious for decades, as demonstrated for example by comments from two writers in the 1880s, one from each side of the Atlantic:

○ When I speak my native tongue in its utmost purity in England, an Englishman can't understand me at all.

(Sam Clemens (Mark Twain), *The Stolen White Elephant*, 1882)

○ The American I have heard up to the present is a tongue as distinct from English as Patagonian.

(Rudyard Kipling, *From Sea to Sea*, 1889)

Wry hyperbole in both cases, certainly, but again, something serious behind the smile. If officialdom or the scholarly world in the late nineteenth century commented on kinds of alienness and incomprehension *inside* English, it was usually to advocate more efficient schooling and a greater exposure to the language of schools and books, so that such deficiencies might be reduced. By and large, the only English-speaking scholars of the period who took on diversity every day were the dialectologists, but they pursued their cataloguing and commentary under the vast shadow of standardization. As a result, they considered that, in the face of universal education, the dialects of the British and Irish islands and of North America were dying out, and so worked with a sense of urgency. Soon, they supposed, there would be nothing left to describe, apart from a few fossils embedded here and there in an otherwise smoothly standard medium, a state of affairs which had been the dream of British and American opinion-formers since the eighteenth century.

Monolithic and pluralist models

In more recent times, Randolph Quirk has observed (with a scarcely veiled allusion to Empire) that English is 'a language – *the* language – on which the sun does not set, whose users never sleep' (*English in the World*, co-edited with H. G. Widdowson, Cambridge University Press, 1985, p. 1). This observation, it seems to me, implies that all such users understand one another all or a great part of the time and wherever they may find themselves. Yet incomprehension (whether mutual or in one direction) is a common state within English as a world language, despite the relative success of more or less universal education and a vast and growing programme of instruction for foreign learners.

Such incomprehension often leads to an insistence that what the other person is speaking *can't* be English – although the other person knows it is. In recent years, some observers have coped with this difficulty (among other things) by proposing not one monolithic English but a range of 'Englishes', each with its distinctive history and characteristics, such as American English, British English, Canadian English, Indian English, Irish English, New Zealand English, Malaysian English, Nigerian English, Singapore English, and Zimbabwean English (each indeed with their *sub*-varieties). These observers also note that, without the bridge of yet another English (increasingly nowadays called 'International Standard English'), many who speak English cannot communicate easily or at all with one another. And, while making their communicative compromises, and learning to understand one another, they all the time come up against usages that strike them as seriously strange: either as straightforward 'broken' or 'fractured' English, or 'not quite English, really', or at the least 'not part of *my* English'.

It is not my intention here, in a post-modernist rampage, to undermine all traditional assumptions about something that appears to be as straightforward as English; there is too much of the traditionalist in me for that. But it *is* my intention to consider how the 'straightforward' monolithic model (one English, century after century, continent upon continent) came into existence and how in recent years pluralist counter-models (many Englishes down the centuries and around the world) have emerged. I will also argue that rather than weakening or destroying the 'establishment' view, such new models complement and indeed augment it, because they offer other perspectives on what many (but by no means all) users of English have regarded as a suitable and *true* view of things. The subject is in reality too large to fit one model – *any* model, revered or radical, singular or plural – and benefits from our having a wide and flexible range of descriptions available to us.

In addition, and importantly, what one can say in this regard about English is also relevant for other widely used languages, past and present. The issue is not just how the vast English language complex is currently perceived and used worldwide, but also how human beings, operating on any large geopolitical stage at any point in time, have perceived and used *any* 'world language'.

A personal note

Since the mid-1980s, I have been fortunate enough to edit two publications concerned with what is now variously called: 'English as a world language' or 'world English'; 'English as an international language' or 'international English'; and 'English as a global language' or 'global English'. The first of these is the quarterly *English Today: The international review of the English language*, published by Cambridge University Press since 1985; the second is *The Oxford Companion to the English Language*, published by Oxford University Press in 1992.

Though very different, these publications have drawn on or exhibited the views of hundreds of academic and other commentators worldwide, granting me in the process a privileged position in which to meditate on – and at times brood over – the vast and intricate condition of 'English'. From time to time, I have added some of my own observations and views to those published in *English Today*, and in the *Companion* have sought to discuss and interpret as objectively as possible the many facets of this enormous 'language'. But increasingly in the course of this two-fold undertaking I have wanted to take certain matters farther, and am grateful to Cambridge University Press for the opportunity to do so here.

While writing something called *The English Languages* I have been well aware of how one can stir up emotions by offering new linguistic lamps for old. Yet I am also aware that these new vessels are not really so new. Their informal, populist roots (as Clemens, Kipling, and the others indicate) lie in soil over a century old, while their formal, academic roots can be found in a mass of comment since the 1960s. (See especially chapter 3.) My wish

has been to display and discuss here both the nature of the language models involved and the many versions of them now available, both old and
new. (See especially chapter 4.)

The result, I freely admit, is intricate, kaleidoscopic, and at times dizzy-
ing. The monolithic linear model that takes us from Old English through
Middle English to Modern English (culminating with Darwinian elegance in
the standard international language of newspapers and airports) has, it
seems to me, been asked to bear more weight than it can reasonably support.
The emergence therefore of plural, non-linear models is a positive development, among whose advantages are a more accurate depiction of the diversity in which we are embedded and also a more democratic approach to the
social realities of English at the end of the twentieth century.

One necessarily becomes personal, even political, at this point. But I
have long doubted whether academic reports, especially in the humanities
and social sciences, can ever be free of the predispositions of the writer;
there is ideology everywhere. In addition, I have no wish to divorce my
academic interests and aims from my personal experiences, needs, and
values, even if I could do so. All my thinking life I have had a profound personal investment in the study of 'English', to help me decide whether –
having grown up a tridialectal Scot – I was really born to this language at
all (my mother tongue that wasn't my mother's tongue, though the resemblances were close). In the past, I have often felt (and been helped to feel)
that I was half a foreign learner. And as a student of French, Latin, and
Greek at school in Glasgow, I was astonished and intrigued by how much
of English *isn't* English. For such reasons, I have allowed the flesh and
blood of language into this book, including at times my own. (See especially chapters 5, 6, and 8.)

Terminology and presentation

The traditional monolithic view of English provides us with, and is buttressed by, a mix of both everyday and technical vocabulary that presents
English as a single entity. An example is the quasi-singular uncountable
noun *English* itself, which represents a single mass comparable to *bread*
and *wine*. Another is how the words *dialect* and *language* are used as
everyday expressions and in technical terminology. *Dialect* as used by linguists is more or less neutral, but its wider lay use is generally negative:
for most people, a dialect is a 'non-' or 'sub-'standard variety of a language
(which is generally represented by its standard variety, located somewhere apart from and 'above' those dialects). For other people, however,
especially recently, *dialect* may refer to both a non-standard and a standard variety, as in the phrases *Yorkshire dialect* and *standard dialect*, the
latter being for many traditionalists a contradiction in terms. In addition,

and very technically, a language can sometimes be a dialect, as for example when English is referred to as a dialect of Germanic or French as a dialect of the Romance family.

The moment one writes such words as *English, the language,* and *the English language* one adopts (or re-adopts, by default) the traditional model, confirming a primacy that is built into usage itself. If, however, to counter this from the start, one immediately uses such exotic alternatives as *the Englishes, the English languages, the English language complex,* and *the English language family,* one both fails to present one's argument sensibly and appears to be using clumsy new jargon to no good end. To limit the damage, I have tried to keep the older and newer terms as distinct as possible, and to limit my use of the newer terminology until the need for it has been established. Where I resort to traditional usage (as I do, for various reasons, throughout the book), I do so because it is appropriate in the context, not because it is a kind of Platonic default mode. Models at the end of the day are just models, however powerful or entrenched they may be.

In addition, although I believe that my use of the terminology of linguistics in this study is generally straightforward, I have more or less systematically stretched several terms in order to make them cover more ground than usual. Three linked examples of this are *acrolect, mesolect* and *basilect,* which originated in the 1960s as terms describing only creole languages. I have used them here to cover not only creoles, but also language forms in a continuum of usage from any low, often stigmatized language or variety of a language (the *basilect*) to a high, prestigious language or variety of a language (the *acrolect*), with an often unstable form or range of forms between them (the *mesolect* or *mesolects*). I have done this here because the three terms seem to me to fit the more general situation I am trying to describe: morphologically, they refer to any kind of low (*basi-*), high (*acro-*), or middling (*meso-*) language form (*-lect*) and not only to such aspects of creole languages. (See especially chapter 7.)

Finally, I have arranged the kinds of information in this book in two ways: the text, divided into chapters, and numbered panels accompanying those chapters. Each chapter starts with an epigraph drawn from the world of lexicography, in ways that I hope remind us what tricky things words can be. The discussions, quotations, and stories in each chapter successively develop my main theme, but at the same time each chapter is an end in itself, dealing with a particular aspect of the English-language conundrum in its own right. As a result, sometimes a line of thought that starts in one chapter may be dropped in the next, but taken up again later, once a range of additional material has been assimilated into the discussion. Part of this range of additional material is presented in panels, which augment the main text with such things as lists of territories, citations, and samples of different usage round the world. I have not provided a general bibliography; instead, the sources of all quotations are given immediately, in as full a form as possible each time, and specific bibliographies appear in various panels.

The development of this book

The material in this book has been developing since the mid-1980s, taking the form of a series of lectures and published papers, etc.:

○ 'The English languages?', article in *English Today* 11, July 1987.
○ 'The English language or the English languages?', closing chapter in *The English Language*, the tenth and last volume of the *Sphere History of Literature*, edited by W. F. Bolton and David Crystal, London: Sphere Books, 1987.
○ 'Standard English, the English language, and the English languages', a paper presented at the conference 'What is Standard English?', organized by the Oxford University Department for External Studies, Rewley House, December 1989. Unpublished.
○ 'English in tiers', an article in *English Today* 23, July 1990, discussing Vernacular, Latin, and Greek words and word elements in the vocabulary of Standard English.
○ 'The English languages?', a lecture at the Department of English of the University of Georgia, Park Hall, Athens, May, 1991. A development of the 1987 *English Today* article and the 1989 Oxford talk. Unpublished.
○ 'The Scots – bilingual or just confused?', a paper in the festschrift issue for Braj B. Kachru of *World Englishes*, 11: 2/3, 1992.
○ 'One language or many languages? – English at the end of the twentieth century', a double plenary address to the Sixth Annual International Conference on Pragmatics and Language Learning and the Conference on World Englishes, organized by the Division of English as an International Language, the University of Illinois, Urbana-Champaign, April 1992. Published as 'Models of English' in *English Today* 32, October 1992.
○ 'The Coming Hybrids', an article in *Verbatim: The Language Quarterly*, Diamond Jubilee Issue, Winter 1993.
○ 'Learning whose English?', opening address to a symposium for teachers of English at the University of Coimbra, Portugal, to celebrate the 25th anniversary of the International House English language school in the city, March, 1993, on speech styles and pronunciation targets in English as a world language. Unpublished.
○ 'Language used as a loaded gun', an article in the *Education Guardian*, London, on the national curriculum and Standard English, 20 April 1993. Reprinted in *English Today* 38, April 1994.
○ 'English Tomorrow', a position paper presented to a British Council ELT

staff conference concerned with the promotional theme English 2000, at Alston Hall, Lancashire, July, 1993. Unpublished.

o 'The spread of English', a lecture to graduate students at the Centre for Applied Language Studies, the University of Reading, October 1993. Unpublished.

o 'The English languages', a lecture to the English Society of the University of Uppsala, Sweden, October 1993. Unpublished.

o 'English: the shape of things to come', a lecture at an in-service training seminar for teachers at the University of Uppsala, Sweden, October 1993. Unpublished.

o 'Organized Babel: English as a global lingua franca', a plenary paper at *GURT '94* (Georgetown University Round Table on Language and Linguistics, 1994): *Educational Linguistics, Crosscultural Communication, and Global Interdependence*, whose proceedings were edited by James E. Alatis and published in 1995.

o 'The Printed Word in the English-speaking World', a plenary session at Style Council 96, in Adelaide, South Australia, March 1996: printed in *English Today* 49, January 1997 (and to appear in the proceedings of the conference).

o 'The Changing Face of English', the 1996 SAAL Lecture (Singapore Association for Applied Linguistics), given at the National University, Singapore, March, on recent developments in English as a world language. Unpublished.

o 'Models of International English and what teachers can do with them', closing plenary at the conference 'Language Analysis and Description: applications in language teaching', held at the Hong Kong University of Science and Technology, June 1996.

o 'International Standard English – Fact or fiction?', a lecture given at the City University, Hong Kong, October 1996. Unpublished.

o 'The English Languages', a lecture and discussion at the English Seminar at the University of Heidelberg, Germany, November 1996. Unpublished.

o 'Ten Models of International English', the closing session at the symposium 'Standard, Nonstandard, Substandard', at the University of Heidelberg, Germany, November 1996. Unpublished.

o 'English in the World and in Europe', second chapter of Reinhard Hartmann (ed.), *English Language in Europe*, Europa 2:3, 1996. Exeter: Intellect.

o 'World English, Classroom English: The Question of a Standard', double lecture at an in-service training course for teachers at the University of Uppsala, Sweden, March 1997. Unpublished.

o 'English as a World Language', lecture at the British Teachers' Centre, Kuala Lumpur, March 1997. Unpublished.

o 'Varieties of English or English languages?', a plenary session at a conference for university teachers of English, the University of Sfax, Tunisia, April 1997. Unpublished.

o 'On the Origin and Nature of Standard English', forthcoming, for a special issue on Standard English in the journal *World Englishes*, edited by Anne Pakir and Saran Gill.

Acknowledgements

Pre-eminently, I would like to acknowledge my colleague Sidney Greenbaum of University College London, who died suddenly, at the height of his renown, in 1996, not long after completing his masterwork, *The Oxford English Grammar*. This book is respectfully and affectionately dedicated to his memory and his work.

I must also thank the following colleagues and friends for the many ways in which they have made my work easier, better, and more secure, enabled me to try out my thoughts on various captive audiences, and helped me in this project and with the ideas that animate it: John Algeo of the University of Georgia, USA; David Blair, Pam Peters, and Colin Yallop of Macquarie University, Sydney, Australia; John D. Battenburg of California Polytechnic, San Luis Obispo, USA; Mongi Bahloul of the University of Sfax, Tunisia; Loga Baskaran of the University of Malaya, Kuala Lumpur, Malaysia; François Chevillet of Grenoble III (Université Stendhal), France; Reinhard Hartmann of the University of Exeter, England; Gregory James of the Hong Kong University of Science and Technology, HK SAR; Braj B. Kachru of the University of Illinois, Urbana-Champaign, USA; Alan S. Kaye of California State University at Fullerton, USA; Alan Kirkness of the University of Auckland, New Zealand; Donald MacQueen of Uppsala University, Sweden; Beat Glauser and Volker Mohr of the University of Heidelberg, Germany; Anne Pakir of the National University of Singapore; and, for support well and truly beyond the call of duty, Loreto Todd of the University of Leeds, England.

Finally, it is a special pleasure to thank the team at Cambridge University Press who ultimately brought this book to life, most particularly Canto editors Vicki Cooper and Pauline Graham, designer Peter Ducker (who also looks after my journal *English Today* and has lived with my foibles for years), copy-editor Hazel Brooks, and indexer Barbara Hird.

1   Organized Babel

babel /ˈbeɪb(ə)l/ *n. & a.* Also B-. E16.
[*Babel*, the city and tower where the confusion of tongues took place (*Gen.* 11), = Heb.
babel Babylon, f. Akkadian *bab ili* gate of
God.] A *n.* **1** A confused medley of sounds;
meaningless noise. E16. **2** A scene of confusion; a noisy assembly. E17. **3** (B-) A lofty
structure; a visionary project. M17...

(definition, in Leslie Brown (ed.), *The New
Shorter Oxford English Dictionary*, 1993)

[E16/17 = early 16th/17th century;
M17 = mid-17th century]

Together yet separate: *Is English we speakin'*

The Bible is not so widely read as once it was, nor are its stories, laws,
admonitions, and prophecies so well known as once they were, but such
phrases as *Adam and Eve, the Garden of Eden, Noah's Ark*, and *the Tower of
Babel* continue to resonate in those languages which have ancient links
with Christianity and Judaism. The original account of Babel, which takes
up less than half of one brief chapter of the Book of Genesis, opens with
the assertion that 'the whole earth was of one language', then reports that
in the land of Shinar (Sumer, now southern Iraq) humankind undertook a
project so vast and arrogant that it brought down upon them the very
wrath of God:

> **4** And they said; Goe to, let vs build vs a city and a tower, whose top
> may reach vnto heauen, and let vs make vs a name, lest we be scattered
> abroad vpon the face of the whole earth. **5** And the LORD came downe
> to see the city and the tower, which the children of men builded. **6** And
> the LORD said; Behold, the people is one, and they haue all one
> language: and this they begin to doe: and now nothing will be restrained
> from them, which they haue imagined to doe. **7** Goe to, let vs goe
> downe, and there confound their language, that they may not
> vnderstand one anothers speech. **8** So the LORD scattered them abroad
> from thence, vpon the face of all the earth: and they left off to build the
> Citie. **9** Therefore is the name of it called Babel [marginal note: 'that is,

Confusion'], because the LORD did there confound the language of all the earth.

(King James Bible, 1611: Genesis 11:4–9.)

People still call a bedlam of tongues a *Babel*, and some have used the term *Babelization* for the mixing of their own cherished language with other tongues – which is not at all what happened in Genesis. But for such commentators the divine dismembering of a single pure language is not the issue: humanity nowadays confounds its tongues very well on its own. Yet the ancient Hebrew word and image remain attractive to language conservatives when commenting on such latter-day Babylons as London and Los Angeles, where (as they see it) proper English is beset by a host of multicultural demons.

Nowadays, wherever people go (conservatives and liberals alike), they find that a means of communication which they could once safely and sufficiently call 'English' – without even dividing it into British and American – has been caught up in rapid and unprecedented global change. And has also, apparently, been beset by an academic jargon using terms like *sociolinguistic, creolization, acrolect,* and *basilect* as well as, increasingly, the plural form *Englishes*. In addition, many people are aware of a paradox in the use of English everywhere: that stability and flux go side by side, centripetal and centrifugal forces operating at one and the same time.

The stability and the centripetal tendencies relate largely to Standard English, while the flux and the centrifugal tendencies involve all the other 'non-' or 'substandard' forms, whose nature and interplay with standard usage pose all kinds of social, cultural, and communicative problems. Generally, when we say that people 'speak English', we mean that they can – to a greater or less extent – manage the pronunciation, grammar, and vocabulary of the standard form (or, more accurately, one of the standard forms) of the language. Such speakers may also, to a greater or lesser degree, be fluent in a dialect, creole, or whatever but standardness remains the central issue, even though the number of primarily dialect- and creole-speakers, etc., in Anglophone territories is greater than the number of people who function wholly or mostly in Standard English: broadly speaking, the English of the educational world, the news and documentary media, government, administration, law, and high-level business.

Indeed, if people are regarded as speaking 'only' a dialect or (more exotically) a creole, there may be doubt – in practical terms, relating for example to certain kinds of employment – about whether they 'really' speak English, and this doubt may be present as much in liberal as in conservative minds, although liberals might be uncomfortable about conceding the point. In many instances, it may be assumed that people in the traditional English-speaking world can and do use the standard when they have to, because of schooling and exposure to the media, but 'broad' dialect- and creole-speakers do not – cannot, by definition? – come high on any social, cultural, economic, or linguistic scale. In sociolinguistic terms (especially as applied to creoles), such people are said to speak a *basilect*, while those who mix local with standard usage speak a *mesolect* (and *are* higher up the ladder), and speakers of something more or less standard (the *acrolect*) come highest of all – a state of affairs which I would argue also holds true for the traditional regional dialects of English in the British Isles and North America.

This is an intricate and thorny issue among scholars of language, but by and large it is something that people understand – whether they like it or not, and whether they freely acknowledge it or not. We do not in our more tactful moments discuss possible pecking orders within the global English language complex, but we frequently reveal our attitudes and perceptions in such off-the-cuff remarks as:

○ 'Yes, he speaks English, but it's *American* English. *And New York*.'
○ 'Well, yes, she speaks English, if *that*'s what they do in Scotland.'
○ 'Sometimes I'm not sure they *really* speak English in London – the ordinary people, I mean. I can't make head nor tail of them. I think they do it *deliberately*.'
○ 'You know, his Irish (or Yorkshire or Ozark or Newfoundland) dialect is impenetrable. I don't understand *a word he says*.'
○ 'Well, Jamaican isn't English at all, is it?'

Or, to quote lines which have become a sociocultural cliché:

> An Englishman's way of speaking absolutely classifies him.
> The moment he talks he makes some other Englishman despise him.
> One common language I'm afraid we'll never get.
> Oh, why can't the English learn to set
> A good example to people whose English is painful to your ears?
> The Scotch and the Irish leave you close to tears.
> There even are places where English completely disappears.
> In America, they haven't used it for years!

> (from the play *My Fair Lady*, 1956 (film version 1964), based on George Bernard Shaw's play *Pygmalion*, 1912. The phonetician Henry Higgins (who was probably based on the real-life scholars Henry Sweet and Daniel Jones) is speaking to his friend Colonel Pickering.)

Although such comments are often made wryly, in short-lived exasperation, or with good humour, they have sharp edges. Millions who have grown up in the confident belief that they are native speakers of English have been brought up short by the snap judgements of other native speakers. 'Is English we speaking', insists the title of an article by the Caribbean poet and academic Mervin Morris. The phrase says it all (using the standard form *speaking* too, rather than *speakin'*, which would better represent what West Indians actually say). But when Morris looks closely at his mother tongue(?s) he can also note:

> For most West Indians the language of feeling, their most intimate language, is creole. It has been observed that West Indians who seem entirely comfortable in standard English often break into creole in moments of excitement or agitation.
>
> ('Is English we speaking', a lecture given in London in 1992, organized by the British Library's Centre for the Book, and published both as a booklet by the Centre and in *English Today 36*, October 1993. p. 23.)

Togetherness and separateness co-exist here. Morris has already observed at an earlier point in his lecture that many investigators doubt whether the continuum of West Indian usage *is* English from one end to the other: that is, from international standard through acrolect and mesolect to basilect. Some scholars and social activists indeed argue (with passion) that Creole – capital 'C' – is a different language altogether from English, with its own range of dialects around the islands and coasts of the Caribbean, no matter how closely it meshes with English and how strong the historical links may be with it. Morris in fact quotes Peter A. Roberts in this regard:

> The wide spectrum in Jamaica challenges the definition of a language in that it calls into question the extent to which two speech varieties in a society can differ and still be treated as belonging to the same language.
>
> (Roberts, *West Indians and Their Language*, Cambridge University Press, 1988, p. 33)

But whether Jamaican Patois/Patwa is part of English or distinct from it, the problems of perception, performance, and self-confidence remain, as is inadvertently made clear by the comment of a woman in Kingston, when asked by the sociolinguist Peter Patrick if she preferred English to Patwa:

> Yes. Mi jos laik di inglish. Fa, yu si wen mi ina de konchri, an mi jos a taak di patwa den... yu fiil so imbaris.
>
> (quoted by Barbara Rosen in 'Is English Really a Family of Languages?', in the *International Herald Tribune*, 15 October 1994. (See also chapter 9.) NOTE: The woman's remarks were apparently rendered in the *Tribune* in a distinctive Patwa orthography so as to underline – ironically? – its distance from what might be called 'conventional English'.)

Behind such claims, queries, and observations lie vast, hard-to-describe continuums of language behaviour, in which the centre does not quite hold and people who speak 'peripheral' varieties find it difficult – often embarrassing – to communicate beyond their immediate milieux, and sometimes even within them. Indeed, there has long been a Babelish confounding of tongues inside what we call English, regardless of how convinced we may all be that it *is* English we speakin'.

Vertical imagery: *Basilects, mesolects, and acrolects*

Current interest in (and concern about) variation within English can to a
large extent be attributed to greater awareness – through easier worldwide travel and communication – of the paradox touched on above: that
stability and flux, homogeneity and heterogeneity, run everywhere side by
side. By and large, the dialects and creoles of English are resistant strains,
many of them at least as old as the standard language, which began to
take on its present form towards the end of the seventeenth century. By
then, this incipient spoken and especially written standard could be found
not only among the social and scholarly élite of metropolitan south-east
England (where it originated) but also increasingly among their peers
throughout Britain and Ireland, on ships at sea, and in colonies and trading posts in North America, Africa, and Asia – where it kept company with
dialects from England, Scotland, Wales, and Ireland and maritime pidgins
and trade jargons ancestral to the present-day creoles of the Atlantic and
Pacific. English was not particularly homogeneous at that time either.

At the end of the twentieth century, linguists, lexicographers, language
teachers, journalists, publishers, and others tend to agree that several
Anglophone nations have their own Standard English. The first standard
variety, in the United Kingdom and its Empire, was paramount at the end
of the nineteenth century, was widely regarded as unique, and most commonly called the King's or Queen's English. The second long-established
standard, in the United States and its dependencies, began to assert itself
internationally in the early twentieth century – sometimes to the aston-
ishment, amusement, or chagrin not only of those Britons who cared
about such things but of many Americans as well. Joint entitlement was,
however, harder to deny by mid-century: both the UK and US had fully-
developed educational systems, publishing industries, dictionaries, grammars, and manuals of style and usage, and radio broadcasting with rec-
ommended language styles for newsreaders and continuity staff. As a
result, for many people only these two standard varieties are legitimate,
just as a century earlier only one was broadly accepted. (For further discussion, see chapter 5.)

In recent decades, however, it has become clear that Australia, Canada,
New Zealand, and South Africa (pretty much in that order) also have – or
are in the process of acquiring – institutions and publications which
enable them to be less dependent on the norms of the UK and US: that is,
they are *endonormative* rather than *exonormative*. Indeed, there were by
the mid-1990s three clear-cut national standards, Standard Australian by
that time being buttressed with a comparable range of dictionaries and
other such services to those that support Standard British and Standard
American. In addition, and despite stormy argument, it is becoming clear
that standardizing processes have begun in at least India, Nigeria,

Singapore, and Malaysia. And finally, these standard and standardizing varieties have begun to constitute something nebulous yet nonetheless real that to date has had at least four names: 'International Standard English', 'Standard International English', 'World Standard English', and 'Standard World English' (with or without the capital 'S').

All English-speaking territories appear to have a continuum of usage from their 'broad' vernacular(s) through the local standard (or near-standard: endonormative or exonormative or mixed) to the international standard (or near-standard, often mixing elements of British and American) – and all of them, as it were, fuzzy at the edges. The new global 'acrolect' (to stretch the original sense of that term) has in recent years become the *de facto* target of teachers and learners of English as a foreign language worldwide, whether or not the immediate focus of the teaching is Standard British or Standard American.

All native speakers (however we understand that term) are located somewhere on the above continuum, able to a greater or less extent to shift from the more local and vernacular to the more standard and global, and maybe back again: to be, as it were, to some degree 'bidialectal' or 'bilingual' within the language. For some, the limits of linguistic flexibility are tight, and focused on one point on the spectrum; for others, they are wider, allowing considerable dexterity, but few are so flexible that they can operate with ease from one end of the available continuum to the other. The reason for this may be more social than linguistic: people can be doubtful about the communal credentials of someone who is too flexible. Usually, if people have gone to school for enough years and begun to move in 'higher' social circles with enough success, they are constrained by circumstance and practice to stay close to the acrolect rather than slide back 'down' to mesolect or basilect – all of which Greek-derived terms are just as socially loaded as the more transparently class-related 'upper', 'middle', and 'lower'. However, since its beginnings, Standard English has unarguably been 'up' in social and educational terms and all other varieties 'down', a state of affairs with parallels in many languages, and one which has always caused tension.

Only in the last quarter of this century has an alternative to the vertical and hierarchical model become possible: a 'sideways' view in which the standard and the rest are conceived as occupying much the same level, equal but different, each legitimately and appropriately serving its own social purposes – and each subject to greater or lesser consistency in and accuracy of performance. This broadly egalitarian metaphor, however, has a long way to go before it becomes the 'commonsense' view of things, if indeed it ever does. In the meantime, the traditional up/down, high/low imagery continues to hold sway worldwide, as a consequence of which it features strongly in this study.

English that isn't English: *Dialects and creoles*

Whatever the social realities within English worldwide, far more people speak 'non-standard' – until recently often called 'substandard' – varieties than use the standard language in a way deemed consistent (and respectable) by teachers, editors, and language professionals. Most traditional dialects have obvious enough links with the standard language, and since the mid-nineteenth century have been greatly affected by it, but several remain so distinct that, in the opinion of some observers, they meet the criteria for separate languagehood. Thus, the criterion of having its own typographic conventions has long been met by Scots (also known at various times as Inglis, Broad Scots, Braid Scóts, Lowland Scots, the guid Scóts tongue, Lallans, and the Doric), which has had a print tradition since the sixteenth century – not far short of English in England (late fifteenth century). The following is a passage of Scots composed however not in the 1500s but the second half of the twentieth century:

> Sae they wan atowre the Loch tae the kintra o the Gerasenes. As shune as he cam aff the boat, a man wi an onclean spírit cam out frae the graffs tae meet him. This man howffed i the graff chaumers, an the day wis by whan onie-ane could siccar him, een wi a chein. Monitime they hed bund him wi aa kin o shackles an cheins, but the cheins he rave them sindrie, an the shackles he dang them asmash; an he wis as stour as nae man could maister him. Day an nicht he wis ey thereout amang the graffs or on the braesides, rairin an haggin himsel wi stanes.

('Mark's Gospel', 5:1–5, *The New Testament in Scots*)

This work, a translation directly from Greek by the clergyman William Lorimer, was completed in 1967 and published by Penguin in 1985, becoming an international bestseller. Its Scots usage, however, is so unlike the standard language of school and university anywhere that most non-Scots have difficulty following it, and many Scots (accustomed to reading only Standard English and unpractised in their own literary tradition) need help with it – many of them in the process rejecting it as *passé*, irrelevant, and even embarrassing. A synchronic neighbour of Lorimer's translation is *The Revised English Bible*, published jointly by Oxford and Cambridge in 1989. Its Standard English version of the same passage is:

> So they came to the country of the Gerasenes on the other side of the lake. As he stepped ashore, a man possessed of an unclean spirit came up to him from among the tombs where he had made his home. Nobody could control him any longer; even chains were useless, for he had often been fettered and chained up, but had snapped his chains and broken the fetters. No one was strong enough to master him. Unceasingly, night and day, he would cry out aloud among the tombs and on the hillsides and gash himself with stones.

('The Gospel according to Mark', 5:1–5, verse numbers omitted)

For further comparison, the pre-standard King James version (1611) of the passage is:

> **1** And they came ouer vnto the other side of the sea, into the countrey of the Gadarenes. **2** And when hee was come out of the ship, immediatly there met him out of the tombes, a man with an vncleane spirit, **3** Who had his dwelling among the tombs, and no man could binde him, no not with chaines: **4** Because that he had bene often bound with fetters and chaines, and the chaines had bene plucked asunder by him, and the fetters broken in pieces: neither could any man tame him. **5** And alwayes night and day, he was in the mountaines, and in the tombes, crying, and cutting himselfe with stones.

('The Gospel according to S. Marke', 5:1–5)

Lorimer and Oxbridge are as different from one another as each is from the Authorized Version. Thus, Lorimer has *howffed i the graff chaumers*, a direct translation of which in Standard English is 'lived in the tomb chambers' – very different renderings of the Greek from both the Authorized 'had his dwelling among the tombs' and the Oxbridge 'the tombs where he had made his home'. Discussion has proceeded for generations in literary, scholarly, and other circles regarding the nature and status of Scots, some arguing that it is no more and no less than a northern dialect of English, others that it is a language in its own right, and still others swithering between the two positions. There are few objective yardsticks for such matters, but one does now exist. The European Bureau of Lesser Used Languages, established in Dublin by the European Community in 1982, lists Scots alongside Gaelic, Welsh, Breton, Basque, and various others as a minority language (of what is now the European Union).

In contrast to all of the above is the following passage from the *Tok Pisin Nupela Testamen*, published in Canberra, Australia, and Port Moresby, Papua-New Guinea in 1969, translating Mark as follows:

> Ol i kamap long hapsait bilong raunwara, long graun bilong ol Gerasa. Em i lusim bot pinis, na kwiktaim wanpela man i gat spirit doti i stap long en, em i kam painim Jisas. Dispela man i stap nabaut long ples matmat na i kam. Em i save slip long ples matmat. Na i no gat wanpela man inap long pasim em. Sen tu i no inap. Planti taim ol i bin pasim em long hankap na sen. Tasol em i save brukim sen no hankap tu. Em i strongpela tumas, na i no gat man inap long holim pas em. Oltaim long san na long nait em i stap long matmat na long maunten. Na em i save singaut no gut na katim skin bilong em yet long ston.

('Gutnius Mak i raitim', 5:1–5)

The pidgin-cum-creole called Tok Pisin ('Talk Pidgin') is so different from both Standard English and the traditional dialects that it is easy to perceive it as a separate language, yet the greater part of its wordstock is English – with such exceptions as *save* ('know': compare *savvy*) from Portuguese and *bembe* ('butterfly') from Tolai. Thus, *hapsait bilong raun-*

wara (above) may seem in sound and print to be entirely non-English, but can be glossed as 'halfside belong roundwater' and translated as 'on the other side of the lake'. The equally alien-looking *Sen tu i no inap* can be glossed element for element as 'Chain too he not enough' and means here 'Even chains were useless'. Both pronunciation and orthography are therefore massively different from conventional English, but if the orthography were closer to it, printed Tok Pisin would be much easier to follow, although in the process it would look more like 'debased' English (as many have regarded it, and some continue to regard it) than a means of communication in its own right. With its distinctive orthography, however, Tok Pisin successfully stands apart. (See panel 1.1 and chapter 7.)

Indeed, it has so successfully stood apart that it is one of the three official languages of Papua New Guinea along with Standard English and the indigenous pidgin Hiri Motu, and has among its other institutions a newspaper called *Wantok* ('One Talk', meaning variously one language, one community, someone who speaks the same language, a compatriot, and a neighbour – a range of senses utterly distinct from anything in conventional English). For the people of PNG, therefore, as well as for linguists, Tok Pisin is categorically distinct, whatever its relationship with 'English' as the term is usually understood. Paradoxically, we may say that Tok Pisin is in large part English-derived (much as French is Latin-derived), but in a narrower sense it is not English at all (just as French is not Latin). Or, put in a way which I think more comfortably addresses the realities, Tok Pisin is *'an* English language' without being part of what I am calling here 'conventional English' (by which I intend Standard English and those dialects and non-standard usages that belong in the same broad area of intelligibility). In the same way, French is a Latin or Romance language without being in any sense 'conventional Latin' (which would include such varieties as Classical, Medieval, and present-day Vatican Latin).

Scots and Tok Pisin are of equivalent but different significance in this discussion, Scots because it is a markedly distinct ancient entity close to but not within the traditional home of conventional English, and Tok Pisin because it is one of a number of more recent but unarguably distinct forms far from that home, whose independent status linguistically and legally is beyond dispute. The linked yet distinct histories of traditional Scots and conventional English date from the Early Middle Ages. Whereas English arose out of the Anglo-Saxon dialects of Old English at large, Scots emerged only from the northernmost Anglian (Northumbrian) dialects. If a case can be made for Scots as a distinct language from conventional English (and the European Union has accepted such a case), it is nonetheless 'an English language', because among other things the Scots themselves referred to it for centuries as *Inglis* (English, pronounced /ˈɪŋlz/), often used in contrast with *Southron* (Southern), one of their words for the speech of England. The ancient distinction of 'Inglis' and 'English' is like that between 'Dutch' and 'Deutsch' (German), words which refer to two Germanic languages without anyone needing to suppose that Dutch is therefore *really* Deutsch, despite the similarity and common ancestry of the names and many of the usages.

Whereas Scots (with its sole overseas offshoot Ulster Scots) is unique among traditional other-than-standard forms of English, there are many English-related pidgins and creoles comparable to Tok Pisin, while at the same time being markedly different from it and from one another. Their number depends on what varieties one counts in an area and how one relates them to each other, but most notably includes Krio in Sierra Leone, Kamtok in Cameroon, Sranan and Saramaccan in Surinam, Creolese in Guyana, and Patwa in Jamaica. All are wholly or largely unintelligible to speakers of conventional English who have not been brought up with them, and are for this and other reasons regarded by most creolists (and many other people) as languages in their own right – however their relationship with conventional English may then be described, and regardless of the fact that most are in a continuum relationship with conventional English. Already therefore, without advancing far into the discussion of variability in English, we have eight entities that are often called kinds of English while being very distinct from 'English' as conventionally understood: Scots, Tok Pisin, Krio, Kamtok, Sranan, Saramaccan, Creolese, and Patwa. (For further specimens of dialectal and creole 'Englishes', see panel 1.2, for Scots see chapter 6, and for pidgins and creoles see chapter 7.)

English that isn't English: *Nativized varieties and Anglo-hybrids*

In addition to dialects and creoles, there are two further categories of usage so distinct from conventional English that they pose problems of intelligibility. The first is generally called *nativized English* (sometimes *indigenized English*), and occurs in territories where it was not originally present, but English has been present for some time, and may or may not be the primary language of the majority of people using it. Typically, such a variety incorporates features of the regional language(s) concerned, including rhythm, accent, intonation, grammatical structures, and words. The dialogue below, which is a specimen of the nativized English of Malaysia at an acrolectal level, comes from a recorded conversation between two women lawyers in Kuala Lumpur, neither of whom is a native speaker of English or Malay. Chandra is a Tamil and Lee Lian is Chinese, and both have learned Malay and English as second or third languages.

CHANDRA:　Lee Lian, you were saying you wanted to go shopping, nak perga tak? [Malay: 'Want to go, not?']

LEE LIAN:　Okay, okay, at about twelve, can or not?

CHANDRA:　Can lah, no problem one! My case going to be adjourned anyway.

LEE LIAN:　What you looking for? Furnitures or kitchenwares? You were saying, that day, you wanted to beli some barang-barang [Malay: 'buy... things'].

CHANDRA:　Yes lah! Might as well go window-shopping a bit at least. No chance to ronda [Malay: 'patrol, loaf'] otherwise. My husband, he got no patience one!

LEE LIAN:　You mean you actually think husbands got all that patience ah? No chance man! Yes or not?

CHANDRA:　Betul juga [Malay: 'True also']. No chance at all! But if anything to do with their stuff – golf or snooker or whatever, then dia pun boleh sabar one [Malay: 'he too can be patient'].

> (Loga Baskaran, 'The Malaysian English Mosaic',
> in *English Today* 37, January 1994, p. 28)

　　This variety, nicknamed *Malenglish* and *Manglish*, is marked by such grammatical forms as (above) *furnitures, can or not?* and *He got no patience one*, and such borrowings as the lexical items *lah* (an emphatic particle), *beli,* and *barang,* and the stock phrases *nak perga tak* and *betul juga*. People who know English but not Malay may get the gist of the lawyers' conversation, but all in all the faster and more relaxed the conversation the harder it is for outsiders to follow – and to see it in print is most unusual. In addition, if the speakers move farther towards the Malay end of their shared continuum, they will soon reach a point beyond which non-Malaysians cannot go, despite the fact that much that remains is still manifestly English. Baskaran, of the Faculty of Language and Linguistics at the University of Malaya, Kuala Lumpur, demonstrates this state of affairs cogently in a second study, one of whose recorded conversations takes place at a London University postgraduate hall of residence between two Malaysian women, Vimala, a Tamil, and Zainab, a Malay:

VIMALA:　Apa ini? What happened to you pagi tadi? I tunggu tunggu sampai dah fed-up! Mana you pergi, joker you!

ZAINAB:　Nowhere-lah! I was stuck in the computer room. Big queue there. Hanya three computer, thirteen orang line-up! If I keluar, I go back to the end of the line. Jadi, sampai sekarang pun, I'll still be there! Mana lah!

VIMALA:　Okay, now you dah makan?

ZAINAB:　Not yet! Sampai nak pengsan. Come let's go to Nahar. Dekat saja, much easier, faster pun!

VIMALA:　Okay-lah, no choice! I tengok you tengah famished. No breakfast also, isn't it?

ZAINAB:　Jangan buang masa lah! Nanti, Nahar close. Then must trot to Satay House pula(k)!

[*Translation (with the original English shown in angle brackets)*: What's this? <What happened to you> morning just now (= this morning)? I waited waited still already <fed-up>! Where <you> went, <joker you>! – <Nowhere> *emphatic particle*! <I was stuck in the computer room. Big queue there>. Only <three computer, thirteen> people <line-up!> – <If I> move out, <I go back to the end of the line.> Therefore till now also <I'll still be there!> Where *emphatic particle*! – <Okay, now you> already eaten? – <Not yet!> Nearly wanting to faint! <Come, let's go to Nahar.> Near only (=It's very near), <much easier, faster> too! – Okay *emphatic particle* <no choice! I> see <you (=you are)> half <famished>. <No breakfast also, isn't it? (= You haven't had breakfast either, have you?)> – Don't waste time *emphatic particle*. Wait. <Nahar close (= is closed). <Then must trot to> Kebab <House> instead!]

(Loga Baskaran, 'International and national perspectives:
The Malaysian English tapestry', unpublished paper presented at the
1st IAWE (International Association of World Englishes) conference,
University of Illinois, Urbana, April 1994)

People in such situations have more than simply two languages at their disposal. Because they can fluently switch systems, from A to B and back again, they have in fact a third system available to them, and in two forms: AB (in which A dominates) and BA (in which B dominates). And this hybrid, which they use only among themselves, may well be their most natural linguistic condition – unless indeed they have additional languages at their disposal, in which case their hybridizing capacities are greater still (as is indeed the case in territories like Malaysia). Comparably, in the Texas–Mexican borderlands, Latinos routinely mix Spanish and English in what is locally called *Tex-Mex* or *Border Lingo* – part of the large and varied complex called *Spanglish*, which is spoken in California, Florida, New Mexico, New York, Puerto Rico, Texas, and elsewhere. In the following recorded dialogue, a Mexican-American husband and wife and a sales clerk are talking in a Texan convenience store in much the same style as the two Malaysians in London:

HUSBAND: Que necesitamos?
WIFE: Hay que comprar pan, con thin slices. [She turns to the sales clerk.]
    Donde está el thin-sliced bread?
CLERK: Está en aisle three, sobre el second shelf, en el wrapper rojo.
WIFE: No lo encuentro.
CLERK: Tal vez out of it.

[Translation: What do we need? – We have to buy bread with <thin slices>. Where is <the thin-sliced bread>? – It is on <aisle three>, on the <second shelf>, in the red <wrapper>. – <I can't find it>. – Maybe we're <out of it>.]

(Lorraine Goldman, 'Tex-Mex', *English Today* 5, January 1986,
p. 23.)

Such routine blending may often surprise, amuse, and even charm visitors, but it also commonly alarms purists on both sides of the linguistic divide – especially because such interaction occurs at all social levels. (See also chapter 9.)

Developments of this kind constitute a massive shift in the way such languages as English, Malay, and Spanish have traditionally been used, understood, discussed, and described. In the Philippines, the comparable Anglo-hybrid to Malenglish and Spanglish is called both *Mix-Mix* (for obvious reasons) and *Taglish* (because it blends English and Tagalog, the main indigenous language of Metro Manila). The sample which follows is taken from a leaflet issued by the HongkongBank in 1994 for Filipino workers in Hong Kong who regularly send money home to their families. The leaflet is avowedly bilingual, English and Tagalog, but the bilingualism is unequal. In the Tagalog section, English is strongly present, often occurring in uneven chunks, but in the English section no Tagalog appears.

(1) Part of the Tagalog column:

Arrange to pay in regular amounts
May tatlong paraan para maisaayos ang paghulog ng pera sa inyong Cash Card account:
a. Mag-deposito ng pera mula sa ibang HongkongBank account, at any Hongkongbank ATM, using your Cash Card.
b. Mag-transfer ng regular amount bawa't buwan (by Standing Instruction) galang sa inyong Current o Savings Account, whether the account is with HongkongBank or not. Ito ang pinakamahusay na paraan to make sure na sapat ang pera sa inyong Cash Card account pag kailangan, lalo na kung maiaarange ninyo sa inyong employer na sueldohan kayo sa pamamagitan din ng Standing Instruction. At wala nang pila!
c. Magbayad in cash or cheques at any branch.
Puwede n'yo ring i-check kung magkano ang laman ng inyong Cash Card account, free of charge, at any HongkongBank ATM.

(2) The equivalent part of the English column:

Arrange to pay in regular amounts
You can arrange to pay money into your Cash Card account in three ways.
a. By depositing cash or cheques, or transferring money from another HongkongBank account, at any HongkongBank ATM, using your Cash Card.
b. By transferring a regular amount every month (by Standing Instruction) from your Current or Savings account, whether the account is with HongkongBank or not. This is the best way to make sure that you have the right amount of money in your Cash Card account when it's needed, particularly if you can arrange for your employer to pay you by Standing Instruction as well. And it saves queuing!
c. By paying in cash or cheques at any Branch.

You can always check how much money you've got in your Cash Card account, free of charge, at any HongkongBank ATM.

Many blend-names have been coined for such hybrids, usually in patterns comparable to *Spanglish* and *Taglish*. Such names started out as (and generally continue to be) informal, humorous, and often dismissive, but many – for convenience or the lack of anything more academically respectable – are now virtually technical terms. They do not, however, necessarily refer only to hybridization, often being labels for kinds of English spoken by people from particular backgrounds, but if hybridization occurs it is usually given such a name, as with: *Anglikaans; Arablish; Chinglish; Frenglish, franglais; Gerlish, Engleutsch, Deutschlish; Hindlish; Italglish, itangliano; Japlish, Japalish, Janglish; Swenglish* (pronounced 'Swinglish'); *Russlish; Taglish; Spanglish, englañol.*

This hybridization of English and an indefinite range of other languages is the most extensive of its kind ever known. Various observers have talked and written about an 'imperialist', 'hegemonic', or 'killer' English which displaces and destroys other languages (such as Gaelic, Welsh, and many Amerindian languages), but few have predicted that under certain circumstances English would simply flow into rather than supplant so many tongues – much as, almost a thousand years ago, the blending of Anglo-Saxon and Norman-French produced something new: compare the Anglo-Saxon poem *Beowulf*, the French poem the *Chanson de Roland*, and Chaucer's hybrid *Canterbury Tales*. (See also chapter 7.) Although Anglo-hybrids are generally unstable, the hybridness itself is stable enough, and if past forms such as Middle English are representative, the languages affected will undergo irreversible change in territories where such massive code-mixing occurs. And while the hybridization is taking place, certain 'epiphytic' phenomena, apparently beginning in Japan but now found throughout East Asia and even elsewhere, have begun to add their mite to the general impression of Babel.

Decorative English: *'A talisman of modernity'*

At the end of the 1980s, a line of black leather pilots' jackets was manufactured in the Chinese province of Guangxi, with the following string of letters on the back of each: *nnehirpitothuihdronjfemtyouovhreuorhwhehpt.* Not long before this, a similar jacket was produced in Guangzhou province (and sold there and in Guangdong), the letters on the back reading *neveriputbofftlhtomorohowhatyoucnotforyaetsspot.* Some time earlier still, the source of inspiration for both of these developments appeared in Hong Kong. On the back of this original garment was the less opaque advice-cum-invitation: *Never put off til tomorrow what you can do today. Let's sport.* Reporting in 1991 from Hong Kong on these jackets and related matters, Mark N. Brock observed:

> The message printed on the copy of the jacket produced near Hong Kong in Guangzhou is somewhat garbled yet still recognizable, even though the letters are run together in a rather haphazard manner. Copies of the jacket produced in the more interior province (Guangxi), however, pay even less attention to the configuration of letters. The apparent popularity of these jackets demonstrates that it is not the message that matters but rather the medium, the letters, and what their presence suggests. In many parts of Asia, English, even when it is scarcely recognizable as such, serves as a status marker, a talisman of modernity.... Of the many students and strangers I've queried about the English words adorning their jackets, notebooks, and pencil boxes, only a handful had ever paid any attention at all to what was printed. The fact that English words ornamented their possessions seemed satisfaction enough for most.
>
> (Brock, 'The Good Feeling of Fine: English for Ornamental Purposes', *English Today* 26, April 1991, p. 51.)

Brock was discussing a phenomenon that appears to have begun in Japan some years earlier. In 1987, John Dougill (writing in Japan) made the following points about such decorative usage:

> The widespread use of English in Japan is a reflection of the country's desire to internationalise and of its fascination with the world of the *gaijin* (literally, 'outsider' or 'alien'), particularly America.... Compared with the Chinese characters used for everyday purposes, the *romaji* (Roman alphabet) of English seems smart, sophisticated and modern. Indeed, such is the difference between the scripts that merely the appearance of romaji is enough to suggest glamorous associations. One company recognises this by printing on their writing paper, 'The very best stationery for people who get excited when they see English all over everything.' Apparently, the English is never even read, even by students and teachers of the language: it is purely decorative.
>
> (Dougill, 'English as a decorative language', *English Today* 12, October 1987, p. 33.)

Brock in 1991 was unaware of Dougill's article in 1987 (until as editor of *English Today* I informed him), and so it is significant that, on a matter that has received little attention, both writers have accounted for the absence of concern over content in the same McLuhanesque vein: that the medium is indeed the message. Dougill expresses some puzzlement that so many misspellings, errors of grammar, and other wayward usage have appeared on so many products manufactured in Japan, a country with a reputation for efficient and accurate work. This puzzlement is especially appropriate because Japan has been exporting Decorative English widely, in the process creating a minor global trend. Such constructions appear as far afield as Switzerland where, as Dougill points out, shopping bags from

Japan have been sold with statements on them like *A is for Ambrella* (with a picture alongside).

He suggests a reason for such creations: that, in the companies which produce them, the ingrained respect among younger people for their seniors – whose English is likely to be shaky – could prevent corrections and improvements being adopted: better to be wrong in public than lose face in private. He notes that 'despite the huge number of native speakers working and teaching in the country, none are asked to do the simple matter of proof-reading'. Japanese Decorative English is a *wasei* ('made-in-Japan') matter affected by local pronunciation and style, from *l-r* transposition (*flesh meat* for 'fresh meat' and *a heathery life* for 'a healthy life') to such koan-like invitations as *Joyful, let us dash in a sky*. (See panel 1.3 for further details.) Dougill compares such usage to the Mad Hatter's Tea Party in *Alice in Wonderland*. Suspecting that the Hatter would have appreciated the formulations *Good time Bunbun* and *Dusk times mind is a beginning*, he notes Lewis Carroll's observation, 'The Hatter's remark seemed to [Alice] to have no meaning in it, and yet it was certainly English.'

This is the crux of the matter. Whatever one may think or feel about such usage, however gross its grammar or strange its semantics, and however marginal it may be in the great Anglophone scheme of things, as a social and commercial fad it is widespread and spreading further. Although it is a sort of nonsense created in Asia for mainly Asian purposes, it is *English* nonsense – not Japanese, Chinese, Korean, Portuguese or Spanish nonsense. If, as may happen, English-speaking and other manufacturers climb on this bandwagon – in the same way as Western vehicle manufacturers have begun to mimic the off-beat computer-created names for Japanese cars – then Mad Hatter English will, like so many other things, go global. Let's sport.

Domesticated English: *Gairaigo* and *wasei eigo*

Providing a kind of international commercial ambience is only one way in which the Japanese have put English to use. A vastly more significant area is the mass of English words adopted in recent years into Japanese – comparable in scale to the shift of Latin words into English in the sixteenth century. However, in contrast to the programmed efficiency with which Malaysia has been officially adopting and adapting English technical terms into its standard variety of Malay (Bahasa Malaysia), the Japanese acquisition of English words has been largely haphazard.

The earliest Japanese linguistic borrowing from abroad was the writing system known as Kanji, adopted from China over a thousand years ago along with many Chinese words. The earliest borrowings from the languages of Europe took place in the sixteenth century, and were often borrowings of borrowings. Thus, *tabako* came from Portuguese *tabaco*, which like English *tobacco* came from Carib or Taino, languages of Central America; *kohii* was from Dutch *koffie*, a word which like *coffee* in English came originally from Arabic. When Japan re-opened to the West in the nineteenth century, further words were adapted from European sources, this time mainly German, French, and English. The generic Japanese term for such adoptions is *gairaigo* (from *gai* 'outside', *rai* 'come', and *go* 'language': compare *gaijin*, 'outside person, foreigner').

The Japanese have used such words freely for decades, often without knowing or recalling that they are foreign, even though they are generally written in a special shorthand-like syllabic script called *katakana* (as opposed to the more traditional syllabic script *hiragana*). In the American-style menus of Japanese fast-food outlets, many items consist of English-derived *gairaigo* printed in katakana script alongside Decorative English in roman letters (such as *All take out OK!*). Gillian S. Kay, writing from Japan on such matters in 1986, made the following comment:

> Such loan-words, or *gairaigo* ('language from abroad') have an important function in modern Japanese life. They can be used where there is no Japanese word, especially to name things introduced into Japan from other countries, such as *foku* (fork), *katen* (curtain) and *sukato* (skirt), or for modern machines such as *terebi* (television) and *konpyuta* (computer). Imported foreign culture, too, brings or generates its own vocabulary. Western sports such as baseball, boxing and wrestling are very popular in Japan, and have lent such expressions as *hitto endo ran* (hit and run), *nokku auto* (knock out) and *surikaunto* (three count) to the Japanese language.

> ('The English in Japanese', in *English Today* 6, April 1986, p. 25)

Decorative English and *gairaigo* are of course different in kind from dialects, creoles, nativized varieties, and hybrids, and are also different from each other. On the one hand, Decorative English uses a limited and often distorted range of English both alongside and apart from Japanese (and other languages), without anyone being concerned about whether its messages make much sense. *Gairaigo*, on the other hand, occurs inside Japanese – the opposite of Malay words and phrases used in Malaysian English but strictly comparable to English expressions used in Malay. The words make complete sense, because they represent concepts and items for which, in most cases, no prior Japanese or Malay word existed. However, *gairaigo* can be recognized as part of a hybridizing process, in that so much English-derived material is now used in Japan that many older people do not understand what is going on. (See panels 1.4 and 1.5 for further specimens.) Something comparable is happening in Japan in our time to the massive presence of French words in Chaucer's *Canterbury Tales* and Latinate words in scholarly books generally after *c.*1550.

There is no nativized English in Japan on anything like the scale of Malaysia, Singapore, and the Philippines, but a strong interest in English has led to its use as both Brock's 'talisman of modernity' and a quarry for useful and fashionable vocabulary and word-play in Japanese. The present-day English component in *gairaigo* is often used in novel ways, as for example *imejiappu* ('image up'), 'improving one's image', and *besuappu* ('base up'), 'pay rise'. The Japanese call such usages *wasei eigo* ('Made-in-Japan English'), and when they employ such terms as *Japanese English* and *Japlish* they usually intend not English spoken or written by Japanese but this innovative English-derived material inside the language itself.

Gairaigo and *wasei eigo* are the Japanese part of a process currently under way in many languages and territories, as younger people learn Standard English formally at educational institutions, then probably use it in their work, and also informally absorb it from the media and other sources. A single diffuse phenomenon may therefore include in varying degrees in different places the nativization of English, its hybridization with local languages, and the (often massive) absorption of English material into those languages. Phenomena like *gairaigo* and *wasei eigo* cannot be sharply separated from either the production of Decorative English or enthusiasm for US movies, pop music with lyrics in English, and use of the Internet in English and Japanese. Although they do not use English as such to any great extent among themselves, younger people in Japan are otherwise much the same as their peers in the Philippines, Malaysia, and elsewhere, and the choices they make will powerfully shape their own languages and their English far into the next century.

Near-English: *Getting things done – somehow*

The phenomena discussed above include dialects, creoles, nativized varieties, hybrids, decorative adaptations, and a massive adoption of English words into other languages. But matters hardly end there. Within this worldwide complex there is also what is often called 'fractured English', specimens of which are regularly culled by journalists and others from hotel notices, restaurant menus, etc., and listed under jokey titles like 'English as she is spoke'. Such lists often contain classics of misuse that have become cliché-like, deriving (often without acknowledgement or even awareness) from a small number of early articles on the subject. One such article is 'Fractured "Inglish"', by the American writer Nino lo Bello (in *The New Gazette* of February/March 1981), in which he personally attests most of the items he lists, six of which are:

○ *In Istanbul*
American Dentist. 2th floor – Teeth extracted by latest Methodists.

○ *In a Romanian hotel*
  The lift is being fixed for the next days. During that time we regret that you will be unbearable.

○ *On a Moscow hotel room door*
  If this is your first visit to the USSR you are welcome to it.

○ *From a physician's sign in Rome*
  Specializing in women and other diseases.

○ *In Prague (at the office of Cedok, the Czechoslovak state tourist agency)*
  Take one of our horse-driven city tours – We quarantee no miscarriages.

○ *In Thailand, at the Temple of the Reclining Buddha*
  It is forbidden to enter a woman even a foreigner if dressed as a man.

However risible and risqué they may be, and unlike the Decorative English on consumer goods, such constructions are serious attempts to communicate, in the same spirit as the following directions on a packet of cannelloni:

> Important: Albadoro Cannelloni do not ought to boil.
> 1 Bring in Cannelloni, as they are, a stuffing maked with: beef, eggs, cheese, parmigiano, papper or spices, as you like, all well amalgamated ad juicy.
> 2. Besmear a backing-pan, previously buttered, with a good tomato-sauce and after, dispose the Cannelloni, lightly distanced between them, in a only couch.
>   At last, for a safe success in cooking, shed the remnant sauce, possibly diluted with broth, as far as to cover the surface of Cannelloni.
> 3. Add puffs of butter and grated cheese, cover the backing-pan, and put her into the oven, previously warmed at 180/200 centigrade degrees above zero.
> 4. Cook for about an half of hour at the same temperature without to uncover the backing-pan and after, to help at table,

> (Glyn Hughes, 'English on dis-play: a fractured language',
> *English Today* 31, July 1992, p. 45.)

Such English is widely assumed to be the work of people who have been inadequately prepared for writing in the language. However, the following samples from my own files indicate that restaurateurs, hoteliers, and writers of culinary instructions are hardly alone. People involved in academic and other high-level communication are also part of this worldwide tendency:

○ *Saudi Arabia*
  I find your E-Mail address in magazine tolking about english

langueg in the world and in the British Council library in Riyadh...
and your address was an artecal tolking abut english in the
Enternet.

○ *Zaire*
We are thankful to the professors of the English Department for
their educational actions on us.

○ *China*
Different countries have different idiomatic expressions which
can't be explained by why.

○ *Iran*
It is my pleasure to provide you with an article entitled 'Present
Perfect Simple and Progressive Tenses in English and Persian'....
Your any considerative in this regad would be my best appreciative.

○ *Iraq*
Please direct my letter to whom it may concern as soon as it is
possible, because, indeed, I am in desperate need. Thanks for your
gracious helps; and for your nice attention.

Such usage is widespread and spreading wider, in a continuum which
stretches from the nearly standard to the barely comprehensible. In 1995,
the US journalist Barry Newman published an amusing yet serious article
called 'Global chatter: the reality of "business English"', in which he
demonstrates that the useful – even vital – fracturing of English now
occurs on a vast daily basis. When researching his article, Newman discussed with me who he might talk to and where he might go to find out
what is *really* happening to English in the hands and on the tongues of
non-Anglophones doing business around the world. Although at the end
of his review he drew no direct conclusion, he made it clear that what I
will call 'near-English' is being massively used every day to cut deals and
run businesses, as for example in a Japanese car company in the Czech
Republic, in which English is the only shared medium. Talking to some of
the managers of the company, Newman impishly asked if they had managed to 'get the hang of it' all:

'I am getting hang?' asks Satoshi Nishide, managing director of Daihatsu
Auto in Prague. Mr Nishide, 31, studied English for 10 years and has done
business in it for nine. He and his Czech staff sit at a table in their office
behind the showroom, groping for the hang of it.
'Means... I depend on it?' wonders technical manager Vladimir Moravec.
Spare-parts manager Milan Jandak: 'I'd like to have it?' Sales manager
Arnost Barna: 'I'd like to stop it?'
'I know this phrase,' Mr. Nishide says. 'But I don't know.'

(*The Wall Street Journal*, 22 March 1995, front page.)

People who think of a state of affairs like this as a re-play of Babel are not necessarily wrong-headed. From one point of view bedlam does abound where all was once (apparently) good order and discipline. Yet as Newman makes clear there is method in this mayhem, even though no individual, group, or government can seriously influence it or even adequately catalogue it.

The dialects and creoles of English are not deficient systems, and the nativized varieties and Anglo-hybrids are effective and creative phenomena, however deplorable they may be to purists on both sides of the language divide. And their users are not beyond the pale of education and professionalism, as the two Malaysian lawyers (above) demonstrated. Indeed, perpetrators of such usages include traditionalists themselves – when they let down their guard and behave like everyone else. Nor, finally, are the people who fracture the language knaves and vandals. As Newman puts it:

> The vocabulary may be deficient and the grammar defective, but when foreigners speak English to foreigners, they communicate. [The linguist Alan Firth], who is 34 and hails from Yorkshire, works at the University of Aalborg, in Denmark. A local dairy lets him record its overseas calls. He knows all about 'cheese talk.' A classic example:
> 'So I told him,' says an importer in Cairo, 'not to send the cheese after the, the blowing in customs.'
> The Danish exporter says, 'I see, yes.'
> 'So I don't know what we can do with the order now.'
> 'I'm not, er, blowing, er, what is this, er, too big or what?'
> 'No, the cheese is *bad*. It is, like, fermenting in the customs' cool rooms.'
> 'Ah! It's gone off!'
> 'Yes, it's gone off.'
> Both knew what 'bad' meant. Now the Egyptian knows what 'gone off' means to the Dane, and the Dane what 'blowing' means to the Egyptian. But what interests Prof. Firth is the semantic two-step. First, the Dane acts as if he understands 'blowing.' Only when his sale seems at risk does he demand a definition. Then he provides a definition of his own, and the Egyptian acts as if he knew what 'gone off' meant all along.
> After dissecting this dialogue and many others, Prof. Firth has an idea of what makes foreigners so good at getting points across in English. They don't joke. They ignore gaffes. They pay no attention to grammar. They don't mind pauses. They don't care if two people speak at once. They aim for normality, and live with confusion.... 'Once you get the contract, you go back, clear things up and 5,000 tons of cheese are on their way to Egypt.'

(as above)

This is today's – and tomorrow's – world. One morning, in Singapore in 1996, I went into the tourist information centre in the Raffles Hotel. Inside, four young women (two Chinese, two Malay) were efficiently dealing with inquiries that came at them in both fluent and fractured English from people of all kinds of backgrounds. After some time I was the only visitor left in the centre, and since I was looking at leaflets on a rack the staff left me alone, beginning to chat and joke among themselves. I looked at my leaflets but listened closely, because linguistically everything had changed. Where I had understood them before as they dealt with their clientele, now I didn't, *couldn't*. I duly went over with an inquiry about car rentals to one of the Chinese women, and when I'd got the information I wanted I risked a further question:

> 'When you were all talking together, some of it was in Malay, wasn't it?'
> She smiled. 'Yes.'
> 'And some of it was Chinese?'
> She laughed. 'Yes.'
> 'And a lot of it was English.'
> 'Yes. But all mixed up. That's what we do. We all do it.'

Ay, there's the rub. What she says is true for so many people. Worldwide communication centres on Standard English, which however radiates out into many kinds of English and many other languages, producing clarity here, confusion there, and novelties and nonsenses everywhere. The result can be – often is – chaotic, but despite the blurred edges, this latter-day Babel manages to work. *Is* English we speakin', but not as we once thought we knew it.

Panel 1.1 Papua-New Guinea: a selection of expressions in Tok Pisin

As indicated in chapter 1, the vast majority of the words of Tok Pisin derive from English but in their pronunciation, spelling, and use they may well differ from it more markedly than do Anglicisms in Japanese and Bahasa Malaysia.

(1) Vocabulary items
bebi baby
belhat ('belly hot') angry, impatient
grasop grasshopper
grisman ('grease man') flatterer, fat man
grisim ('grease him') to grease, oil, lubricate
kontrak a contract, an agreement
kopi coffee
makim ('mark him') to mark, sketch, appoint, assign, promise in marriage, point at, aim at, imitate, copy, represent
manki ('monkey') boy, errand boy, male servant
papamama parents
paradais paradise
pasis passage, bay, harbour
pastaim ('past time') first, at first
pepa paper, contract, legal agreement
 haus pepa ('house paper') office
 niuspepa newspaper
 pepa bilong rait ('paper belong write') writing paper
 strongpela pepa ('strong-fellow paper') cardboard, wrapping paper
 mekim pepa ('make him paper') sign a contract
 brukim pepa ('break him paper') break a contract, tear or fold a sheet of paper

(2) Sentences, phrases, and idioms
dispela hia ('this-fellow here') this one here
gutpela moa ('good-fellow more') very good
Haus i bikpela ('House he big-fellow') The house is large./It's a big house.
meri ('Mary, marry') woman, girl, wife; female; feminine
holim meri ('Hold him marry') to have sexual intercourse
Kanu i ran ('Canoe he runs') The canoe speeds.
manki little boy
mankimeri ('monkey-marry') boys and girls; children
manmeri ('man-marry') men and women
Mi no manki bilong yu ('Me no monkey belong you') I am not your boy/servant/slave.
Paia i kukim haus olgeta ('Fire he cook-him house altogether') The fire burnt down the house.
namba wan taim the first time
Solwara i stret olgeta ('Salt water he straight altogether') The ocean is calm.

Examples taken from Francis Mihalic, *The Jacaranda Dictionary and Grammar of Melanesian Pidgin*, Australia and Papua-New Guinea: The Jacaranda Press 1971.

Panel 1.2 A German classic re-expressed in kinds of English

In 1986, the German Anglicist Manfred Görlach published (with Helmut
Buske Verlag, Hamburg) an unusual volume of poetry called *Wilhelm Busch,
Max and Moritz, in English dialects and creoles.* Below are the opening eight
to ten lines of ten versions of Busch's tale (in High German, Standard
English, Scots, Northumberland dialect, Northern Ireland dialect,
Shetlandic, Jamaican Creole/Patwa, Sierra Leone Krio, Kamtok, and Tok
Pisin). Five other versions included in the original volume but
unrepresented here are Anglo-Saxon, Middle English, Middle Scots, and
Glasgow and Aberdeenshire Scots. This *tour de force* by Görlach and his
team of eminent writers is a unique showcase for markedly different kinds
of English. It should be noted however that, although the texts are parallel,
they are re-interpretations of Busch and not direct translations: that is, they
are works of the spirit rather than the letter.

(1) High German: Busch's 'Max und Moritz'
Ach, was muß man oft von bösen
Kindern hören oder lesen!!
Wie zum Beispiel hier von diesen,
Welche Max und Moritz hiessen;
Die, anstatt durch weise Lehren
Sich zum Guten zu bekehren
Oftmals noch darüber lachten
Und sich heimlich lustig machten.

(2) Standard English: Elly Miller's 'Mac and Murray'
Think how frequently one reads
of some youngsters' wicked deeds.
Take for instance Mac and Murray
who caused pain and harm and worry;
who instead of being good,
doing everything they should,
mocked at kindness, laughed at virtue,
only practised what might hurt you.

(3) Scots: J. K. Annand's 'Dod and Davie'

What for maun we thole wee laddies	maun *must*	thole *suffer*
when they are sic awfu baddies!	sic *such*	
For ensample let me save ye		
frae a pair like Dod and Davie,	frae *from*	
wha insteid o tryin harder		
to be guid lads, get nae farder;	guid *good*	farder *farther*
slee wee deils, they smirk and snicker,	slee *sly*	deils *devils*
lauchin gars their badness siccar.	lauchin *laughing*	gars *makes*
		siccar *sure*

(4) Shetlandic: Derick Herning's 'Jarm an Jeemsie'

Nooadays der mony boys
taen till fir der weekit ploys!   taen *taken*   weekit *wicked*
Laek dis twa here, be me feth,
Jarm an Jeemsie, oolets baith.   oolet *brat*
Döin weel an lear dey haetit,   lear *learning* (cf. lore)
idders' wirds dey nivver leetit,   idders *others*   leetit *heeded*
bit dey skirl an laach laek donkeys,   skirl *shriek*   laach *laugh*
smeeg, whin telt at dey ir monkeys.   smeeg *smirk*   at *that*

(5) Northumberland: Roland Bibby's 'Meyk an Moas'

Ee, sic tyales – nee ward uv a lee!   ward *word*   lee *lie*
Tyales o baiorns thit's wickid, hwee,   baiorns *children*
kennin bettor than thor daas,   kennin *knowing*   daas *dads*
mock at hyamely wisdim's saas,   hyamely *homely*   saas *saws*
swaapin monny a wink an gaiorn.   monny *many*   gaiorn
                                                                          grimace

Mischif's aal thi ivvor laiorn.   ivvor *ever*   laiorn *learn*
Sic a paior waas Meyk an Moas,   sic *such*
aarly weaned as mankeynd's foas.   aarly *early*   foas *foes*

(6) Northern Ireland: Loreto Todd's and A. N. Seymour's 'Mack and Maurice'

We've heard tell or seen it writ
o weeans that nivir diz their bit,   weeans *children* ('wee ones')
                                                 diz *does*

lek these baygles Mack and Maurice   baygles *ill-mannered kids*
see their thrahin in these stories.   thrahin *wicked behaviour*
Far from thryin to mik their sowl   mik their sowl *be spiritual*
                                                 ('make their soul')

wʌdn't do what they was towl;   towl *told*
wʌdn't lissen till their betthers –
what kin you expect from ketthers?   *ketthers* badly adjusted people

(7) Jamaican Creole (Patwa): Jean D'Costa's 'Max an Marris'

Lissen now, some pickney bad: pickney *child(ren)*
                                                 (cf. piccaninny)

Two bway rude so tell dem mad!   bway *boys*
All me talk a suo-so truut: suo-so *so-so = only*
Max an Marris in dem yout   dem *their*
neva stody, troble teacha,
neva pay no mine to preacha.
Dem so fiesty in dem ways   fiesty *impudent*
fi-dem mout should wash wid Jeyes.   Jeyes *a brand of disinfectant*
Coke-nut saafa dan dem head   saafa dan *softer than*
School mean notten to de dread.   notten to de dread *nothing to*
                                                 Rastamen (wearing their hair in
                                                 dreadlocks)

(8) Sierra Leone Krio: Freddy Jones's 'Maks ɛn Mɔris'

A, wi kin rid plɛnti tin
ɔ yɛri bɔt bad pikin!

    yɛri *hear*
    pikin *child(ren)*

Luk lɛk Maks ɛn Mɔris so
we, fɔ mek dɛn tink ɔ sho
se dɛm nɔ kɔmɔt na waf,

    kɔmɔt na waf
    come from the wharf
    (= ill-mannered, like

nɔ bisin, bɔt kin jɛs laf
ɛn mek jok bɔt aw dɛm tan
to dɛm sɛf sɛf gud gud wan.

    longshoremen)
    tan = *are*
    dɛm sɛf sɛf *themselves*

(9) Cameroon Pidgin (Kamtok): Loreto Todd's 'Tar an Tava'

A! Di tori dɛm di tɔk
fɔ pikin wei du bad wɔk.
Jɔs laik dis tu Tar an Tava
wei soso sabi fain palava.

    tori *story*
    pikin *child(ren)*

    sabi fain palava *know how*
    to find palaver (= know
    how to make mischief)

Dɛm nɛva trai fɔ lisɛn wɛl
fɔ gud ting wei man di tɛl.
No, dɛm sabi laf an plei
hambak pipul ɛni dei,
soso trɔng-hɛd fɔ dɛm skul,

    hambak pipul *annoy people*
    soso trɔng-hɛd
    so stubborn (strong-headed)

dis pikim dɛm laik fɔ ful.

(10) Papua-New Guinea Tok Pisin: Don Laycock's version 'Max na Moritz'

Pasin bilong manki i olsem:

    pasin *behaviour*
    manki *boy*
    olsem *like this*

long olkain trik i no ken sem.
Ol i hambak, ol i kranki.

    olkain *every ('all kind')*
    hambak *annoy*
    kranki *wrong*

Nau mi stori long tupela manki,
Max na Moritz, ol i kolim.

    ol i kolim *everybody calls*
    them

Tupela i no save holim
gutpela tingting bilong ol tisa;

    holim *to hold, handle*
    gutpela *good*
    tingting *thought*
    tisa *teacher*

tupela i save lap long misa,
tok bilas long meriman,
hambak nabaut long evriwan.

    lap *laugh*
    tok bilas *insult*

Panel 1.3 Decorative English in East Asia

A sampling of occurrences of English for Ornamental Purposes in four East Asian countries, as provided by Brock ('The Good Feeling of Fine: English for Ornamental Purposes', *English Today* 26, April 1991) and Dougill ('English as a decorative language', *English Today* 12, October 1987):

○ Japan
on a shopping bag Foppery Let's go out looking smartened up (Dougill)
on a T-shirt Let's sport violent all day long (Dougill)
the slogan of a telephone company My tasty time (Dougill)
on the cover of a photo album The wind has shifted to the south-east. I am exposing myself comfortably to it (Dougill)
on stationery I always feel there is something wonderful at the top of the upward slope and I will surely meet a stunning he standing there down up to the slope (Brock)

○ Hong Kong
on a blazer
Champs
Boys Love Big Sun Shine
Green Grass
Little Girls Scream
They are named
Champs (Brock)

○ Korea
in a notebook My boastful hot apple tea (Brock)

○ Indonesia
on a ruler
The breeze touching their cheeks
They just remember remote from place
When they sees quietly the level. (Brock)

Panel 1.4 Japan: A selection of words borrowed from English

A selection of English-derived expressions drawn from: Tazuko Ajiro Monane, *Japanese Made Easy* (Rutland, Vermont and Tokyo: Tuttle, 1979/1991); Kumiko Makihara, 'Troubling Tales of Seku Hara', *Time Magazine*, 8 January 1990; Gillian S. Kay, 'Gairaigo', in McArthur (ed.), *The Oxford Companion to the English Language*, 1992, pp. 427–8; Nicholas D. Kristof, 'Japan's Favorite Import from America: English', *The New York Times International*, 21 February 1995. All such borrowings follow Japanese syllabic structure, as written in katakana characters.

(1) Full word forms
aisukurimu ice cream
appuru pai apple pie
chimu team
erebeta elevator

erekutoronikkusu electronics
hanbaga hamburger
kohii coffee
kurisumasu Christmas
miruku milk

purutoniumu plutonium
rabureta love letter
ridashippu leadership
remonedo lemonade
sukotchi uisukii Scotch whisky
takushi taxi
tishatsu T-shirt

(2) Abbreviated word forms
apato apartment building
engejiringu engagement ring
hamu sando ham sandwich
masukomi mass communication
pato expert
seku hara sexual harassment
sekusu pato sex expert
terebi television
wapuro word processor

(3) Word forms with 'made in Japan' meanings and uses
bakkumira ('back mirror') rear-view mirror

bodi-kon garu ('body-conscious girl') young woman wearing tight clothes
konpanion female guide or hostess
manshon high-class apartment block
moningusabisu ('morning service') set breakfast
poke beru ('pocket bell') beeper/bleeper
pureigado ('play guide') ticket agency
raifurain ('lifeline') utility like electricity or gas
shiruba hauzingu ('silver housing') accommodation for the elderly
shiruba maketo ('silver market') the elderly as consumers
sumato ('smart') slim

Panel 1.5 Bahasa Malaysia: a selection of words borrowed from English

In recent years, the Dewan Bahasa dan Pustaka (Ministry of Education) in Kuala Lumpur has engaged through its Bahagian Peristilahan (Terminology Division) in the systematic adaptation of English words, especially technical terms, into Bahasa Malaysia, the national language. The following items, drawn from Carmel Heah Lee Hsia, *The Influence of English on the Lexical Expansion of Bahasa Malaysia*, published by the Dewan in 1989, conform to her classification and are not necessarily all officially converted words, many having existed for some time prior to the government decision to import English words.

(1) Individual words
cek cheque/check
derebar driver
gazet gazette
inci inch
injin engine
kabin cabin
kafling cuff-link

koboi cowboy
lesen licence
lokap lock-up
loyar lawyer
mekap make-up
mesin machine
opis office
pikap pick-up

prikik free kick
resit receipt
saman summons
sekeru screw
sepiar sphere
setesen station
wayar wire

(2) Truncated loanwords
(fitting a common disyllabic
pattern among Malay words)
gabnor/gamnor governor
gomen government
lamnet lemonade
kamsen commission
opsir officer
orkes orchestra
prinsip principle
simpatik sympathetic

(3) Standard compound
constructions (Malay reversing
the English order)
bom atom atom bomb
lif hidraulik hydraulic lift
musik pop pop music
orkestra simfoni symphony
    orchestra
status sosial social status

(4) Loanblend compounds
(Malay with English)
bantuan moral moral support
bom waktu time bomb

jet pejuang fighter jet
krisis perlembagaan
    constitutional crisis
nilai kalorifik calorific value
sebutan standard standard
    pronunciation
tenaga solar solar energy

(5) Tautological compounds
(Malay and English-derived
word together, probably
helping to nativize the
foreignism)
alat instrument instrument
baju weskot waistcoat (AmE vest)
kasut but boots
mangkuk bol bowl
pagar rel rail(ing)
roti biskut biscuit

(6) Loanblend derivatives
○ *English-derived affix and Malay
base*
anti-pencemaran anti-pollution
pro-kerajaan pro-government
sub-golongan sub-group
○ *Malay affix and English-derived
base*
berdigniti dignified
berdiplomasi diplomatic
keharmonian harmony
kestabilan stability
pemuzik musician
pengeksport exporter

2   A universal resource

Bilingual within a language? – *The scale and scope of English*

For good or ill, at the end of the second millennium AD and the fifth full
millennium since recorded history began, English is unique. No language
has ever before been put to so many uses so massively by so many people
in so many places – on every continent and in every sea; in the air and in
space; in thought, speech, and writing; in print on paper and screen; in
sound on tape and film; by radio, television, and telephone; and via electronic networks and multimedia. It is also used as mother tongue or other
tongue – fluently, adequately, or haltingly; constantly, intermittently, or
seldom; happily, unhappily, or ambivalently – by over a billion people.
Perhaps a fifth of the human race. François Chevillet, Professor of English
at Université Stendhal in Grenoble, France, has described the situation as
follows:

> Depuis le milieu du XIXe siècle, le rôle de l'anglais n'a fait que croître.
> Le déclin de l'empire britannique n'a pas entraîné le recul de la langue
> (cf. le sort du français), bien au contraire. L'anglais n'est pas une *langue
> internationale*, à l'instar de l'espagnol ou du russe, mais c'est une *langue*

mondiale, en raison de la puissance économique et culturelle du monde anglo-saxon (États-Unis) et du rôle croissant des médias.

(*Histoire de la langue anglaise*, Paris: Presses universitaires de France, 1994, p. 118.)

[My translation: Since the middle of the nineteenth century, the role of English has done nothing but grow. The decline of the British Empire has not entailed a corresponding decline in the language (compare the fate of French) – quite the contrary. English is not an *international language*, after the fashion of Spanish or Russian, but a *world language*, a consequence of the economic and cultural strength of the Anglo-Saxon world (the United States) and the increasing role of the media.]

By calling Spanish, Russian, and in effect French *international languages* while giving the title *world language* only to English, Chevillet sets it apart not only from other currently prominent languages but from all languages ever. Such comments by a noted French observer are particularly compelling because in his own homeland resistance to the 'Anglo-Saxon' (or *anglo-américain*) juggernaut has been particularly fierce.

In another study, Chevillet points not only to the inordinate spread of English in recent times but also to the linked facts that, as the language has expanded, it has become more varied, and some commentators have suggested it might therefore break up into mutually unintelligible forms, much as once happened to Latin. (See chapter 8.) Chevillet takes a more equable and less apocalyptic view, but even so he challenges received opinion regarding 'International Standard English', the variety so widely used (and, he would argue, abused) for business, tourism, and the like. Chevillet notes in this regard:

Ce genre de «standardisation» semblerait être en passe de se généraliser. Il rendra vraisemblablement de grands services au XXIe siècle. Mais il ne sera jamais satisfaisant pour le poète, le romancier, car il est inapte à rendre les sentiments et l'expérience humaine dans toute leur complexité. C'est pourquoi tout anglophone – qu'il soit américain, anglais, jamaïquain ou indien – se verra bientôt dans l'obligation de devenir bilingue: d'une part, il continuera à peaufiner un anglais riche, spécifique et idiosyncratique afin d'affirmer son identité, et d'autre part il lui faudra maîtriser un anglais mondial lui permettant de communiquer à l'échelle planétaire.

(*Les variétés de l'anglais*, Paris: Nathan, 1991, p. 221.)

[My translation: This kind of 'standardization' would appear to be spreading. It will be of truly great use in the twenty-first century. But it will never be enough for the poet or the novelist, because it is not equipped to express human experience in all its complexity. That is why every speaker of English – whether American, English, Jamaican, or Indian – will soon need to be bilingual: on the one hand, to continue refining a rich, particular and personal English so as to affirm their own identities, on the other to master a world English that lets them communicate on a planetary level.]

Traditionally, most people have regarded languages as ethnic and com-municative monoliths, regardless of any regional or other differences within them: Basques speak Basque and Navajos Navajo, Arabs use Arabic from Morocco to Yemen, and the French speak French, which they mani-festly perceive as *their* language despite the fact that many Belgians, Canadians, Senegalese, Swiss, Tunisians, and others use it in their own ways, increasingly without seeing themselves as secondary. Matters are seldom as clear-cut as with Basque and Navajo. Kinds of Arabic spoken as far apart as Morocco and Yemen are highly differentiated and by no means always mutually intelligible, while many citizens of France have lan-guages other than French as *their* mother tongues, whether indigenous (as with Basque, Breton, Corsican, and Occitan) or immigrant (as with Arabic and various West African tongues). (See chapter 9.)

Yet by and large we still tend to think 'to each nation its language', although it has often in fact been 'to each nation its languages' (witness Canada, India, and Singapore) and not uncommonly 'to each language its nations' (witness Arabic, French, and Spanish). In addition, some languages can be so close to each other geographically, ethnically, and/or linguistically that it is hard to be sure whether – despite the names given them and the way people feel and think about them – they *really* are all that different in world terms. Danish, Norwegian, and Swedish are cases in point, despite all kinds of variations and delicate issues among the three and within each one. By and large their speakers intercommunicate, some more easily, some with greater difficulty, as a consequence of which the question arises: Do Danes, Norwegians, and Swedes speak and write different Scandinavian languages or different varieties of one Scandinavian language? Indeed, paradoxically, they may well do both at the same time, the 'right' answer to the question depending on one's emphasis at any given moment.

There is something comparable to the Scandinavian situation in Chevillet's idea of bilingualism within world English. Although such an approach is greatly at odds with traditional English Studies, he is by no means alone in expressing it, and it was discussed longer ago than one might suppose. Thus, the British scholar C. L. Wrenn, a pioneer observer of English as a world language, observed nearly fifty years ago:

> One effect of universal schooling is the weakening of regional dialect and
> the growth of 'modified' standard English in imitation of teachers and
> through their efforts after producing the 'received standard'. Many
> children now shew a sort of 'bilingualism', speaking one form of English
> at home and another at school.

(*The English Language*, London: Methuen, 1949, p. 199)

In more recent times, Edmund Weiner, co-editor of *The Oxford English Dictionary* (2nd edn), 1989, has made a similar point as regards the word-store of the language, commenting a little earlier than Chevillet:

> The English vocabulary is now federated rather than centralized. No one person's English is all English, but each English speaker is to some extent 'multilingual' within English.
>
> ('The Federation of English', in Christopher Ricks and Leonard Michaels (eds.), *The State of the Language*, London: Faber and Faber, 1990, p. 501)

In addition, some commentators have for some decades been using the term *bidialectal* with regard to the majority of Scots, who since the union of England and Scotland in 1707 have had two distinct (though related and mixed) forms at their disposal: the King's Scots and the King's English. (See chapters 1 and 6.) Overwhelmingly, however, and certainly until the Second World War, the English language at large was treated for most purposes (despite a strong awareness of variety and multiplicity) as if it were – or ought to be – a single thing, a standpoint naturally encouraged by the use of a single comprehensive name, although some might talk informally about 'Scots' or 'Yorkshire' or 'American' as if distinct. This was the usual state of affairs both for the public at large (which generally continues to take this view), and for language scholars (more and more of whom appear to be dissatisfied with the once-comfortable and 'obvious' unitary approach). (See chapter 3.)

An imperial consensus: *The heyday of British institutions*

When the first of the two *Shorter Oxford* definitions at the head of this chapter was printed in the 1930s, English was widely regarded, in a serious but ill-defined way, as the property of England or, more expansively, of the United Kingdom (and perhaps Ireland). Communities using English elsewhere – a number of them since at least the seventeenth century – consequently saw themselves, comfortably or uncomfortably, as linguistic offspring of a 'Mother Country' whose monarch, upper classes, and cultural institutions served as the exemplars and unofficial arbiters of linguistic as well as social good taste. Although there was no Royal English Academy to match the Académie française in Paris or the Real Academia in Madrid, there was nonetheless a sociocultural consensus, embodied or expressed for large parts of this century by, among others, three institutions and four more or less institutionalized individuals:

○ **Oxford University Press**
Primarily in terms of dictionaries and usage books, such as *The Concise Oxford Dictionary* (1911), edited by the Fowler brothers, Henry and George, and the magisterial *Oxford English Dictionary*, edited by Sir James Murray and his colleagues (1928).

○ **The Fowler brothers**
Primarily for their views on usage, especially as expressed in *The King's*

English (1906) and the *Dictionary of Modern English Usage* (1926), both published by Oxford and still in print, the former unrevised, the latter revised by Sir Ernest Gowers in 1965 and Robert W. Burchfield in 1997.

○ **The phonetician Daniel Jones**
Primarily for the 'right' accent (first called *Public School Pronunciation* or *PSP*, renamed in the 1920s *Received Pronunciation* or *RP*), and pre-eminently through his *English Pronouncing Dictionary*, published by Dent (London: 1917), never out of circulation since, and significantly revised by A. C. Gimson (from 1964), Susan Ramsaran (1988), and Peter Roach and James Hartman (1997: Cambridge University Press).

○ **The British Broadcasting Corporation**
Founded in London (1922): transmitting at home through various services and abroad through its World Service (in English and other languages), its English-language announcers becoming known worldwide for their 'BBC accents' (Jonesian RP) and use of 'BBC English'.

○ **The British Council**
Founded in London (1934): principally through its cultural programmes and the promotion of British English, especially overseas.

○ **The civil servant Sir Ernest Gowers**
For advice to bureaucrats and others on clear writing, especially in *The Complete Plain Words*, Her Majesty's Stationery Office (London: 1954), and also as a reviser of Fowler's *Modern English Usage*.

This cumulative 'imperial' consensus held up well until the 1970s, despite at least the following six destabilizing factors: (1) the self-evident importance of the United States, a development which became undeniable during and especially after the Second World War; (2) widespread social discontent in Britain between the World Wars; (3) crises in Africa and elsewhere since at least the Boer War, at the turn of the century; (4) the independence of India and Pakistan in 1947, followed by most of the other Asian and African imperial territories in the next two decades; (5) the impact of Marxism in vast areas where Russian and Mandarin have long been the primary languages; (6) the growth of a Western European economic-cum-political bloc which, by the 1970s, Britain could no longer safely ignore, and indeed finally had to join, with on-going misgivings.

However, sixty years after the first *Shorter Oxford* definition of *English* (as shown above), when the *New Shorter Oxford English Dictionary* appeared in 1993, the imperial and immediately post-imperial consensus had become history – even though for many older people worldwide it still held more or less true, and even though the institutions and publications just listed exist, in altered but still recognizable forms. Paradoxically (as Chevillet hints), a major reason for the vanishing away of consensus was the sheer success of English in and beyond the erstwhile Empire, as is also implied by the list of key ('white') English-using countries in the *NSOED*: Britain, Ireland, Australia, New Zealand, the US, and Canada. The language was used in the same places in 1933, but at that time no one at Oxford or anywhere else felt the need to say so. In the 1990s, however, it would be sociopolitically incorrect to leave the main members of a post-imperial English-speaking world unlisted – although other significant but ethnically, culturally, and linguistically complex territories (such as India, Ghana, Nigeria, Pakistan, the Philippines, Singapore, and South Africa) could be safely covered by 'and many other countries'.

In point of fact, however, and long before the 1930s, the survival of English had ceased to depend on any one English-speaking territory, whether the UK in terms of its tradition and empire, the US in terms of its size and population, or even the 'white' countries as a whole, in terms of their British-derived heritages. The language was already an international resource, although few people were thinking in terms of such resources at that time. But the language and the societies where it is used have moved on, with the result that Chevillet in the 1990s can unsentimentally identify English as not just *international* but *universal* – not the property of any particular group or groups and therefore the property of anyone on earth with any kind of stake in it.

Indeed, so many globally significant matters have been managed for so long wholly or largely in English that millions of people who do not (yet) use it – and (perhaps hope they) never will – have a stake in it all the same, because it is the major language for which movies are dubbed or subtitled, the key language of air traffic control, sea-borne travel, and electronic communication, and the primary working language of the United Nations (among many other things). Yet because of its history and uses, English remains at one and the same time an emollient which makes diplomatic, commercial, and other contacts easier for everybody everywhere and an irritant which distresses those who are afraid for the vigour, autonomy, purity, and even survival of other languages – including in many instances their own. This may have been true to some degree with other 'world languages' in the past, such as Latin in the Roman Empire or Arabic since the emergence of Islam, but the situation today for English far exceeds anything that happened in the past – as Chevillet and others have made clear. (See also chapter 9.)

Europe's diaspora languages: *Portuguese, Spanish, French, and English*

From the late fifteenth century onward, Portuguese navigators sailed progressively further down the west coast of Africa and into the Indian Ocean, outflanking the Muslim lands of North Africa and West Asia. Following this success, the Spanish (led by an Italian) sought to reach South and East Asia from yet another direction that was beyond the reach of Islam – westward across the Atlantic, where they found by accident a whole new world. With these and other voyages the two Iberian nations set in train a diaspora of European traders, soldiers, settlers, bureaucrats, goods, religions, and languages to every corner of the world. Eight West European languages in course of time became both the standards and the lingua francas of empire: Danish, Dutch, English, French, German, Italian, Portuguese, and Spanish (all coincidentally members of the Indo-European language family).

The mercantile, military, religious, political, social, and cultural competition among so many empire-builders was fierce, and out of this mêlée four of the eight languages – English, French, Spanish, and Portuguese – have become significant forms of communication in no fewer than 183 out of 232 internationally recognized territories (78 per cent: see panel 2.1). English is routinely used in 112 of these locations, French in 54, Spanish in 27, and Portuguese in 12. In several instances, two of the four languages are used in the same territory, usually English and another, such as English and French in Cameroon, and Spanish and English in Puerto Rico. The remaining territories – of uncertain number, depending on what one considers a territory for this purpose – have not traditionally been closely associated with any of these tongues, but are currently, without exception, opening up in varying degrees to English, so that the statistical gap continues to widen between English and the other four.

Danish, Dutch, German, and Italian are not so widely used or as internationally influential as they once were, but hundreds of millions of people far from Europe use the English, French, Spanish, and Portuguese languages with as much ease as the British, French, Spanish, and Portuguese do. Indeed, more people speak three of these languages beyond Europe than within Europe (English, Spanish, and Portuguese), a fact with serious implications for their centres of gravity. It used to be beyond dispute that all four had those centres in Europe, to which everyone, at home and abroad, might look for confirmation and comfort (if they so wished). Nowadays, however, there are no such metropolitan centres, regardless of any lip service or tokens of apparent fealty that may still be paid to London, Madrid, Lisbon, and Paris. If France continues to be seen as the home of the 'best' French it is probably because there is no massive Francophone community elsewhere comparable to the US for English, Brazil for Portuguese, and Mexico and Argentina for Spanish. Quebec, the heartland of North American French, with a French-speaking population of some five million, is not demographically strong enough to serve as a separate centre of linguistic gravity.

Yet political, sociocultural, and psychological quirks and tensions may still arise between what are taken to be central and peripheral communities. Thus, in recent years in Britain, the language-teaching company Linguaphone has sold materials for the study of French, Spanish, and other languages, listing their various learning packages in magazine advertisements that invite readers to mark their language of choice on a coupon which they can then despatch to the company. All but two of the languages so listed are unexceptional, the exceptions being 'English' and 'American English'.

Linguaphone apparently wanted to respond to an interest among non-native-speaking people in the UK in English as used on the other side of the Atlantic. To do this, the company chose to list the two varieties as (if they were) distinct languages – probably because that was the only way they listed their products. Linguaphone chose, however, not to call the home variety 'British English', but left it unmarked, the implication being – intentional or not – that British is so obviously primary that it does not need further identification. In addition, the contrast between 'English' and '*American* English' implies that the British variety is more comprehensive and therefore more widely applicable than the American variety – despite the fact that American English is used by well over half the world's native speakers of English and utterly dominates such key areas as information technology and the media worldwide.

A comparable though less stark bias towards the English of the UK occurs in the introduction to Godfrey Howard's *The Good English Guide: English Usage in the 1990s* (London: Macmillan, 1993), where he writes:

> *The Good English Guide* is about British English, but American English and other varieties of English come into it many times, because there is an ever-increasing overlap. Nor is this cause for dismay. Immigrant influences, bouncing back at the language in ceaseless bombardment, have kept English on its toes as the most lively and adaptable language the world has ever known. And linguistic history shows that English has an instinctive genius, absorbing or rejecting changes without losing its cadence and poetry.

Here, although British English is at first explicitly identified, delimited, then contrasted with American English, Howard shifts within two sentences into implying (perhaps without intending to do so) that American English 'and other varieties' are 'immigrant influences' on 'the language', in much the same way as Hindi. (See also chapter 9.) Linguaphone and Howard demonstrate that even sophisticated organizations and individuals can perpetuate the assumption (usually implicitly and without much if any reflection) that the place from which a language has spread will always be its centre of gravity – if not indeed its only true location.

This survey indicates that English has not become the most significant language in the world in a vacuum. Rather, eight living Indo-European languages were propelled into global roles during much the same period

38 THE ENGLISH LANGUAGES

in a single West European exploring and colonizing diaspora. Among them, English – for reasons broadly linked with British industrialization, colonization, educational developments at home and overseas, and commercial, naval and military success – eventually became the predominant medium. But English was never alone at the top. French was in the eighteenth and nineteenth centuries the world's primary language of diplomacy and *avant-garde* culture, and in geopolitical terms Spanish currently holds a formidable second position whose heartland is not Europe but the Americas. In addition, a number of other languages (European and non-European, including non-Indo-European) have powerfully influenced communication and culture in large areas, notably Arabic, the Hindi-Urdu complex, Mandarin/Putonghua in and around China, Malay (in its Malaysian, Indonesian, and Bruneian forms), Swahili, Tamil, Turkish (extending to the Turkic family of languages in Central Asia), and Russian, with its vast impact in Eastern Europe and Northern Asia.

The roles and status of English: *De facto* and *de jure* uses

It has become difficult to travel anywhere in the world without finding English in daily use, especially in large cities. It dominates international popular culture, notably through pop music transmitted by radio and by terrestrial and satellite television, as well as in undubbed US movies and TV shows. English is prominent in the everyday public life of many countries where it is not a primary language but has acquired a secondary and often supranational function – such as bilingual road signs in Greece and trilingual road signs in Israel (Hebrew, Arabic, and English). There is also a cachet attached to its liberal contemporary use on shopfronts in the world's major cities, in the naming of businesses and products, and in advertisements. English is the lingua franca of airports and major hotels, of civil aviation and the shipping lanes. It is the leading language of science, medicine, technology, and academic publication – and its US variety utterly dominates computer hardware, software, networking, email, and the vast creative chaos of cyberspace.

Most of what takes place in English around the world is unregulated and haphazard, part of people's day-to-day actions and needs and of the social forces that operate on them. But the language is also tightly regulated in various ways, much more indeed than many might suppose when we consider that there has never been an Academy or any major legislative intervention on behalf of good usage in any English-speaking territory.

This is the case even though English is not the declared official language of either the United Kingdom or the United States. In both countries, it is the sole usual language of government, administration, education, and so forth, but this is a *de facto*, not a *de jure*, state of affairs. English has no statutory role in either country at the national level, probably because no one ever supposed it necessary – although there is currently a campaign in the US to amend the constitution in order to make English the *de jure* official language at the federal level. This 'English Only' movement has had considerable success at the level of state legislation and, at the time of writing, legislation for the constitutional recognition of English has made some headway in Congress. There has never been anything comparable in the UK to the US federal/state dichotomy, with the possible exception of Welsh (unseated as the administrative language of Wales in the mid-sixteenth century), which has however never had official parity with English. There is no indication of an 'English Only' campaign emerging in the UK at the present time, because there is no presumed threat to the role of the language from any minority comparable to the large Hispanic community in the US.

Generally speaking, English is given explicit legal status only when a government feels the need or is required by its citizens to establish it unequivocally as a medium of government in general or of administration, law, and/or education in particular. Such status tends to be common in territories where it might be surprising to outsiders that English has any publicly reinforced role at all. Although the Americans and the British have not (yet) felt the need for a legally established English, many territories have felt such a need, and have acted on it. Panel 2.2 lists 113 territories in which English, especially in its standard form, is significant, and indicates its status and major role(s) in each of them, to the best of my knowledge at the time of writing (such matters not always being easy to establish unequivocally). Such roles vary from place to place, including within long-established nation-states. Indeed, the variety is so great that eight categories relating to the status of English can be identified at the present time:

1 *English as a* <u>de facto</u> *official language, the standard variety co-occurring with other varieties and other languages*
Examples:
(1) In the UK, Standard British English co-exists and mixes with regional dialects in England, Scotland, Wales, and Northern Ireland, with creoles from the Caribbean and elsewhere, and with two categories of other language: indigenous (Welsh in Wales, Gaelic in Scotland, and marginally Cornish in Cornwall) and immigrant (Bengali, Hindi, Punjabi, Cantonese, etc., especially in large urban areas). (For Scots, see chapter 6.)
(2) In the US, Standard American English co-exists and mixes with regional dialects, with several English-based creoles (such as Gullah), with creole-linked dialects (such as varieties of African-American English), and with two categories of other language: indigenous

(Aleut, Hawaiian, Iroquois, Navajo, etc.), and settler-cum-immigrant (German, Italian, Spanish, etc.). English was at the time of writing the *de facto* official language of 27 states of the Union and the *de jure* official language of 23. (For details, see panel 2.2.) There is currently political pressure to amend the constitution so as to make English the *de jure* official language of the entire nation.

2 *English as a de jure official language, the standard variety co-occurring with other varieties and sometimes with indigenous or immigrant languages*

Examples:
(1) In the Anglophone Caribbean generally, official usage contrasts with English-based creoles, the latter generally the majority usage, as in Jamaica and Barbados.
(2) In Belize (on the Central American mainland), such usage contrasts with an English-based creole, several varieties of Spanish, and several Amerindian languages.
(3) In Guyana, it contrasts with English-based Creolese, the immigrant languages Bhojpuri, Hindi, and Urdu, and several Amerindian languages.
(4) In Trinidad and Tobago, it contrasts with at least an English-based creole and the immigrant languages French, Spanish, Bhojpuri, and Hindi.
(5) In Saint Lucia, it contrasts with the French-based creole called Kweyol.

3 *A de jure official language, despite never having been indigenous or a settler language, co-occurring with other languages and perhaps with a pidgin or creole*

Examples:
(1) In Nigeria, English is official because as a colonial and postcolonial second language it has been ethnically neutral, generally accessible, and acceptable *faute de mieux* to the many distinct regional communities, the foremost of whose languages are Hausa, Igbo, and Yoruba.
(2) Similar situations prevail in many Anglophone African countries, such as Ghana and Sierra Leone. English-based pidgins-cum-creoles are typical of West Africa as a whole, but not in East and Southern African countries.

4 *A de jure national co-official language, often in diverse sociolinguistic contexts*

Examples:
(1) In Canada, English is co-official with French, the other major settler language. There are many indigenous languages, such as Cree and Inuktitut, and settler-cum-immigrant languages such as Cantonese, Punjabi, Scottish Gaelic, and Ukrainian.

(2) In Cameroon, English is co-official with French, there is a widespread English-based pidgin-cum-creole, Kamtok, also known as Cameroonian Pidgin (English), and there are many indigenous languages.

(3) In Botswana, English is co-official with Setswana, the majority indigenous language.

(4) In Singapore, English is co-official with Malay, Mandarin, and Tamil, but is the sole language of administration and the primary language of education.

(5) In South Africa, English is co-official with ten other languages: Afrikaans (until recently its sole official partner), and the indigenous languages Ndebele, Pedi, Northern Sotho, Southern Sotho, Swati, Tsonga, Venda, Xhosa, and Zulu. Although English is the most widely used official language, it is a minority language in the country as a whole.

5 A non-official language, but with a distinctive secondary de jure status

Examples:

(1) In Kenya, Swahili is the official national language and English the second national language.

(2) In Bangladesh, Bengali is the official language and English the statutory language of higher education.

(3) In Malaysia, Bahasa Malaysia (Malay) is the official language and English is the compulsory second language of education.

6 Not official or with special legal status, but nonetheless significant

Examples:

(1) In Denmark, Norway, Sweden, and the Netherlands, English is the second language, which everyone learns and many use for personal and professional purposes at home and abroad.

(2) In Israel, Hebrew and Arabic are the official languages, and English, Russian, and Yiddish, among others, are widely used in the home, business, the media, and professional life. Hebrew, Arabic, and English appear on official road signs.

7 An official language at several levels and for various purposes

Example:

Uniquely, in India, English has three *de jure* roles:

(1) As the associate official language, with Hindi as the official language.

(2) As a national language along with Hindi, Bengali, Gujerati, etc., because like them it is the official language of a state of the Union: in fact, uniquely, of four separate states.

(3) As the official language in eight Union Territories, all directly controlled from New Delhi. (For details, see panel 2.2.)

8 An official language for international purposes

Examples:

(1) In the United Nations, English is one of six official working languages,

the others being Arabic, French, Mandarin, Russian, and Spanish. Of these, it is the most widely used, and in official documents follows British conventions.

(2) In the European Union, English is with French one of two official working languages, and one of eleven official languages: Danish, Dutch, English, Finnish, French, German, Greek, Italian, Portuguese, Spanish, and Swedish. It is increasingly used as a high-level EU lingua franca, and in official documents follows British conventions.

These categories, along with the information in panel 2.2, illustrate the diversity of the 113 listed territories which currently use English on a widespead, sustained basis. However, to describe the official status and other roles of English in such localities is not enough. Scholars interested in the global condition of English have also in recent decades taken into account its situation wherever it is learned and used.

A tripartite model: *ENL, ESL, EFL*

Although there is nothing simple about the nature and growth of English around the world in the later twentieth century, one relatively straightforward and economical set of categories has been widely used by linguists and language teachers: a tripartite model described as follows in 1970 by Barbara M. H. Strang, Professor of English Language and General Linguistics at the University of Newcastle upon Tyne in England:

> At the present time, English is spoken by perhaps 350 to 400m people who have it as their mother tongue. These people are scattered over the earth, in far-ranging communities of divergent status, history, cultural traditions and local affinities. I shall call them A-speakers, because they are the principal kind we think of in trying to choose a variety of English as a basis for description. The principal communities of A-speakers are those of the UK, the USA, Canada, Australia, New Zealand and South Africa. There are many millions more for whom English may not be quite the mother tongue, but who learnt it in early childhood, and who lived in communities in which English has a special status (whether or not as an official national language) as a, or the, language for advanced academic work and for participation in the affairs of men at the international, and possibly even the national level. These are the B-speakers, found extensively in Asia (especially India) and Africa (especially the former colonial territories). Then there are those throughout the world for whom English is a foreign language, its study required, often as the first foreign language, as part of their country's educational curriculum, though the language has no official, or even traditional, standing in that country. These are the C-speakers.

> (*A History of English*, London: Methuen, 1970, pp. 17–18)

Strang was not alone at the time in organizing the world's users of English into three such groups. An influential variant of her classification was published two years later by Randolph Quirk and Sidney Greenbaum (of University College London), Geoffrey Leech (of the University of Lancaster, England), and Jan Svartvik (of the University of Lund, Sweden), the editors of the leading reference grammar of the period. They put the matter as follows, without using Strang's letter categories and providing a lower estimate of the world's population of native English-speakers:

> English is the world's most widely used language. It is useful to distinguish three primary categories of use: as a *native* language, as a *second* language, and as a *foreign* language. English is spoken as a native language by nearly three hundred million people.

(*A Grammar of Contemporary English*, Harlow: Longman, 1972, p. 3)

This tripartite model has been widely adopted by English-language professionals, in the course of whose work the categories have become systematized as *English as a Native Language* (*ENL*), *English as a Second Language* (*ESL*), and *English as a Foreign Language* (*EFL*). For convenience, commentators often refer to relevant localities as ENL, ESL, and EFL *countries*, but here I use the term *territories* because it permits the inclusion of localities which, though not independent, are linguistically significant, such as Gibraltar (an internally self-governing British colony) and Puerto Rico (a 'commonwealth' in association with the United States). (See panels 2.2 and 2.3.) The abbreviations *ESL* and *EFL* are common currency in the worldwide English-teaching industry, but *ENL* is little used there or among teachers of English as a native language, who do not appear to have felt the need for a label. The model, however, is widely understood and used, whatever labels may have been applied to its elements, and has proved useful. But at least six provisos need to be taken into account when working with it:

1 ENL variation

English varies markedly from one ENL territory to another, and often from one region to another within heavily populated countries such as the US and UK, a state of affairs which, as travellers know well, can lead to problems of intelligibility. In the UK, for example, there are significant differences of accent, grammar, and vocabulary between Anglophone visitors to London and many of the local people (speakers of Cockney and near-Cockney), as well as in Scotland, where many people routinely mix Scots and English. In the US, there are significant differences between many speakers of African-American (or Black) English and what is sometimes called 'mainstream English'. (See chapter 9: Ebonics.) It is therefore risky to classify a territory as ENL and leave it at that, the ENLhood of a place being no guarantee whatever of

unhampered communication in English. There are also noticeable variations in Standard English in many territories, most especially the US,
the UK, and Australia.

2 *The distribution of pidgins and creoles*
English-based pidgins and creoles do not fit the tripartite model well,
but run inconveniently across the three categories. Thus, they are
found in ENL settings in the Caribbean and along the Atlantic coast of
the Southern US, in ESL settings in West Africa, in both ENL and ESL
settings in Australasia-Oceania, and in the otherwise EFL settings of
Togo and Fernando Po in Africa and Nicaragua, Panama, and Surinam
in the Americas. In addition, the tripartite classification does not
address either of the following two situations which involve creoles (as
already mentioned in chapter 1):

○ *The distinctness of creoles*
The massive presence in the Anglophone Caribbean of creoles so distinct
from both the standard language and traditional dialects that some
scholars consider that they are not English at all but are either distinct
languages or varieties of a single region-wide distinct language (an
English-based Creole) linked in various complex ways with creoles
based on Dutch, Portuguese, Spanish, and French. (See also chapter 7.)

○ *Creoles official alongside Standard English*
The special circumstances of Papua New Guinea, the Solomon Islands,
and Vanuatu, where indigenous languages are used alongside both
Standard English and related and highly distinct English-based creoles:
Tok Pisin in PNG, Pijin in the Solomons, and Bislama in Vanuatu.
Standard English is co-official with all three.

3 *ENL speakers in ESL/EFL territories*
Significant groups of native speakers of English have traditionally been
present in certain ESL territories (for example, the Anglo-Indian community in the Indian subcontinent and the British expatriate community in Hong Kong) and also in EFL territories (for example, the now
largely assimilated Anglo-Argentine community in South America,
British residents on the Mediterranean coast of Spain, and a small number of bilingual British families which are prominent in the port-wine
industry in the Douro Valley of Portugal).

4 *ESL/EFL speakers in ENL territories*
There are significant numbers of non-native speakers of English in ENL
territories, often as a result of more or less recent immigration (for
example, ESL speakers in the US with Spanish as their mother tongue)
but also in long-established enclaves where individuals may not use
much English (for example, in the US the Amish, a German-speaking

community in Pennsylvania, and the indigenous Navajo people in the South-West).

5 Code-mixing and hybridization

Although the three categories cover the co-existence of English with other languages (as touched on in chapter 1 and listed in panel 2.2), they do not take into consideration the influence of English on such languages, the influence of those languages on English, and any code-mixing and code-switching which occurs among them: for example, in Wales (English with Welsh, sometimes informally called 'Wenglish'); in Cameroon and Canada (English with French, nicknamed 'Camfranglais' in the first and both 'Frenglish' and *franglais* in the second); in Texas (English with Spanish, variously referred to casually as 'Spanglish', 'Tex-Mex', and 'Border Lingo'), and in the Philippines (English with Tagalog, nicknamed 'Mix-Mix', and either 'Taglish' or 'Engalog', depending on the dominant direction of the mixing). (See chapters 1 and 9.)

6 Native-speakers and foreign learners

Although the divisions in the tripartite model are valid, they tend to obscure – and divert attention from – the more basic, longstanding binary division in most people's minds between 'native speakers' and 'foreign learners'. The contrast here is between a group defined by *birthright* (widely taken to be a primary qualifying condition) and one defined by *acquisition* (usually perceived as a consequence of education, and almost always taken to be secondary to birthright). In traditional terms, a 'native' user is by definition prior (and implicitly superior) to a 'foreign' user, no matter how inept the native or adept the foreigner. However, in a world where English has become Chevillet's *langue mondiale*, unreflecting chauvinism at the heart of things is likely to be increasingly disputed. It is already challenged from time to time by competent but frustrated ESL and EFL users who know well that they have a richer command of the standard language than many born to English.

The tripartite model fits fairly comfortably within the traditional monolithic view of English, because it asserts that, although three distinct groups of people use it, there is only one language, and it is implicitly the property of the ENL group (or a majority within that group). Such an assumption, however, although it serves the ends of worldwide English-language teaching well enough, does not fit comfortably with the above provisos and the other points discussed. The questions that arise as a result are hardly trivial:

○ *Mutual intelligibility*
Using a traditional unitary model, how can we convincingly account for variation in ENL territories so extensive and profound that the result can be mutual unintelligibility?

○ *The distribution of pidgins and creoles*
Using such a model, how do we deal practically and theoretically with the distribution of pidgins and creoles across both the world and the three categories? How can the same kinds of usage (which some call varieties of English and others call distinct languages) be classified under ENL in one instance, ESL in another, and EFL in a third? Or does the model effectively ignore them as minor and irrelevant inconveniences?

○ *Hybridization*
What must visitors to some apparently Anglophone territories do when they find that local people at all social levels unreflectingly blend Standard English with dialects, creoles, nativized varieties, and/or other languages, with the result that it can be difficult or even impossible for visiting Anglophones to understand them when they are talking to each other?

○ *English a de jure official language where it is least used*
How can one square 'ethnic' ENL territories in which the language is only *de facto* official with 'non-ethnic' ESL territories where it is *de jure* official but (because it is not conventionally indigenous) few have it as a mother tongue? In addition, what should visitors conclude when some people in those territories use a dialect, creole, nativized variety, or hybrid unlike anything with which they themselves were raised or schooled, yet nonetheless call it English?

○ *International mobility*
How do people come to terms practically as well as academically with the current – and increasing – mobility of all speakers of English (ENL, ESL, or EFL), with the result that no matter where they are they cannot predict the accent, grammar, vocabulary, rhythm, idioms, or level of internationally manageable fluency of the next English-speaking stranger they encounter – face to face or on radio, television, or the telephone?

Such questions put considerable pressure on the conventional view that English is – or should be – a unity despite its vast diversity. Since at least the 1970s, Anglicists have been thinking about such matters, and the next chapter outlines how they have in the process been steadily moving away from the old monolithic model of this versatile and volatile 'language'.

Panel 2.1 The international distribution of English, French, Spanish, and Portuguese

Note: In the territories listed, the various languages are significant for one or more reasons. In some they have official status; in others they do not.

Europe
1 *English* Belgium, the Channel Islands, Cyprus, Denmark, England (UK), the Faroe Islands, Gibraltar, the Irish Republic, the Isle of Man, Malta, the Netherlands, Northern Ireland (UK), Norway, Scotland (UK), Sweden, Switzerland, Wales (UK). *17 territories (including the 4 parts of the UK) – 3 shared with French, 1 with Spanish.*

2 *French* Andorra, Belgium, the Channel Islands, France, Italy, Luxembourg, Monaco, Switzerland. *8 territories, 3 shared with English, 1 with Spanish.*

3 *Spanish* Andorra, the Balearic Islands, Gibraltar, Spain. *4 territories, 1 shared with English, 1 with French.*

4 *Portuguese* the Azores, Portugal. *2 territories.*

Africa
1 *French* Algeria, Benin, Burkina Faso, Burundi, Cameroon, the Central African Republic, Chad, the Comoros Islands, Congo, Djibouti, Egypt, Gabon, Guinea, the Ivory Coast, Madagascar, Mali, Mauritania, Morocco, Niger, Rwanda, Senegal, Togo, Tunisia, Zaire. *24 territories, 3 shared with English.*

2 *English* Botswana, Cameroon, Egypt, Ethiopia, Gambia, Ghana, Kenya, Lesotho, Liberia, Malawi, Namibia, Nigeria, Rwanda, Sierra Leone, Somalia, South Africa, Sudan, Swaziland, Tanzania, Uganda, Zambia, Zimbabwe. *22 territories, 3 shared with French.*

3 *Portuguese* Angola, Cape Verde, Guinea-Bissau, Madeira, Mozambique, Sao Tomé and Principe. *6 territories.*

4 *Spanish* the Canary Islands, Equatorial Guinea. *2 territories.*

The Americas (including the Caribbean)
1 *English* Anguilla, Antigua and Barbuda, Argentina, the Bahamas, Barbados, Belize, Bermuda, Canada, the Cayman Islands, Costa Rica, Dominica, Grenada, Guyana, Honduras, Jamaica, Montserrat, the Netherlands Antilles, Nicaragua, Panama, Puerto Rico, Saint Christopher and Nevis, Saint Lucia, Saint Vincent and the Grenadines, Surinam, Trinidad and Tobago, the Turks and Caicos Islands, the United States, the Virgin Islands (US), the Virgin Islands (British). *29 territories, 3 shared with French, 8 with Spanish.*

2 *Spanish* Argentina, Belize, Bolivia, Chile, Colombia, Costa Rica, Cuba, the Dominican Republic, Ecuador, El Salvador, Guatemala, Honduras, Mexico, Nicaragua, Panama, Paraguay, Peru, Puerto Rico, the United States, Uruguay, Venezuela. *21 territories, 8 shared with English.*

3 *French* Canada, French Guiana, Guadeloupe, Haiti, Martinique, Saint Lucia, Saint Pierre et Miquelon, Trinidad and Tobago. *8 territories, 3 shared with English.*

4 *Portuguese* Brazil. *1 territory*

Asia

1 *English* Bahrain, Bangladesh, Bhutan, Brunei, Burma/Myanmar, Hong Kong, India, Israel, Jordan, Kuwait, Malaysia, Lebanon, Nepal, Oman, Pakistan, the Philippines, Qatar, Singapore, Sri Lanka, the United Arab Emirates. *20 territories, 1 shared with French, 1 with Spanish.*

2 *French* Cambodia, Iran, Laos, Lebanon, Pondicherry, Syria, Vietnam. *7 territories, 1 shared with English.*

3 *Portuguese* Macau, Goa, East Timor. *3 territories.*

4 *Spanish* the Philippines. *1 territory, shared with English*

Australasia/Pacific Ocean

1 *English* Australia, Belau, the Cook Islands, the Federated States of Micronesia (FSM), Fiji, Hawaii, Kiribati, the Marshall Islands, Nauru, New Zealand, the Northern Marianas, Papua New Guinea, the Solomon Islands, Tonga, Tuvalu, Vanuatu, American Samoa, Western Samoa. *18 territories, 1 shared with French.*

2 *French* French Polynesia, New Caledonia, Vanuatu, the Wallis and Futuna Islands. *4 territories, 1 shared with English.*

Indian Ocean

1 *English* British Indian Ocean Territory (BIOT), the Maldives, Mauritius, the Seychelles. *4 territories, 2 shared with French.*

2 *French* Mauritius, Réunion, the Seychelles. *3 territories, 2 shared with English.*

South Atlantic Ocean

English Ascension (Island), the Falkland Islands, Saint Helena, Tristan da Cunha. *4 territories.*

SUBTOTALS English *112 territories,* **French** *54,* **Spanish** *27,* **Portuguese** *12*

TOTAL *183 territories (discounting overlaps)*

Remaining world territories Afghanistan, Albania, Armenia, Aruba, Austria, Azerbaijan, Belarus, Bosnia-Herzegovina, Bulgaria, China, Croatia, the Czech Republic, Estonia, Finland, Georgia, Germany, Greece, Greenland, Hungary, Iceland, Indonesia, Iraq, Japan, Kazakhstan, Kirghizia, Korea (North), Korea (South), Latvia, Libya, Liechtenstein, Lithuania, Macedonia, Moldavia, Mongolia, Poland, Romania, Russia, San Marino, Saudi Arabia, Slovakia, Slovenia, Taiwan, Tajikistan, Thailand, Turkey, Turkmenistan, Ukraine, Uzbekistan, the Vatican City, Yemen, Yugoslavia. *52 territories*
GRAND TOTAL *232 territories in all (discounting overlaps)*

Panel 2.2 The worldwide status and roles of English

Europe

1 *Belgium* with French, a working language of the European Union, in Brussels (Dutch/Flemish, French, and German official; also immigrant languages)
2 *The Channel Islands* *de facto* official (also French)
3 *Cyprus* lingua franca (Greek and Turkish official)
4 *Denmark* 'first' second language (Danish official)
5 *England (UK)* *de facto* official (also immigrant creoles and other languages)
6 *The Faroe Islands* third language (Faroese and Danish co-official)
7 *Gibraltar* official (also Spanish)
8 *Irish Republic* co-official with Irish Gaelic
9 *Isle of Man* *de facto* official
10 *Malta* co-official with Maltese (a form of Arabic)
11 *Netherlands* 'first' second language (Dutch official)
12 *Northern Ireland (UK)* *de facto* official (also Ulster Scots and immigrant languages)
13 *Norway* 'first' second language (Norwegian official)
14 *Scotland (UK)* *de facto* official (also Gaelic and Scots, and immigrant languages)
15 *Sweden* 'first' second language (Swedish official)
16 *Switzerland* lingua franca (French, German, Italian, and Romansch official)
17 *Wales* *de facto* official (also Welsh, and immigrant languages)

Africa

1 *Botswana* co-official with Setswana, the majority language
2 *Cameroon* co-official with French (also Kamtok, an English pidgin-cum-creole, and local languages)
3 *Gambia* official (also Aku or Gambian Creole English, and local languages)
4 *Ghana* official (also Ghanaian Pidgin English, and local languages)
5 *Egypt* lingua franca (Arabic official, and French also a lingua franca)
6 *Ethiopia* lingua franca (Amharic official; also local languages)
7 *Kenya* official second language (Swahili official; also local languages)
8 *Lesotho* co-official with Sesotho, the majority language
9 *Liberia* official (also Liberian Creole English; also local languages)
10 *Malawi* co-official with Chichewa (also local languages)
11 *Namibia* official (formerly co-official with Afrikaans) (also local languages; Afrikaans and some German used)
12 *Nigeria* official (also Nigerian Pidgin English, creolized in towns; also local languages, foremost among them Hausa, Igbo, and Yoruba)
13 *Rwanda* co-official with French and Rwanda
14 *Sierra Leone* official (also Krio, an English creole, and local languages)
15 *Somalia* lingua franca (Somali official)

16 *South Africa* co-official with Afrikaans and nine indigenous languages:
    Ndebele, Pedi, Northern Sotho, Southern Sotho, Swati, Tsonga, Venda,
    Xhosa, and Zulu (before 1995 co-official with Afrikaans alone); also
    other local languages
17 *Sudan* lingua franca (Arabic official; also local languages)
18 *Swaziland* co-official with Siswati, the majority language
19 *Tanzania* co-official with Swahili (also local languages)
20 *Uganda* official (also local languages)
21 *Zambia* official (also local languages)
22 *Zimbabwe* official (also local languages)

The Americas (including the Caribbean)
 1 *Anguilla* <u>de facto</u> official (also a creole)
 2 *Antigua and Barbuda* official (also a creole)
 3 *Argentina* home language of the Anglo-Argentine community (Spanish
    official; also Italian and Guarani)
 4 *Bahamas* official (also a creole)
 5 *Barbados* official (also a creole)
 6 *Belize* official (also a creole)
 7 *Bermuda* <u>de facto</u> official
 8 *Canada* co-official with French (also settler-cum-immigrant and
    indigenous languages)
 9 *Cayman Islands* official (also a creole)
10 *Costa Rica* lingua franca (Spanish official; also an English creole)
11 *Dominica* official (also a creole)
12 *Grenada* official (also a creole)
13 *Guyana* official (also a creole)
14 *Honduras* home language on the Bay Islands (Spanish official)
15 *Jamaica* official (also the creole variously known as Jamaican Creole,
    Patwa, and Nation Language)
16 *Montserrat* <u>de facto</u> official (also a creole)
17 *Nicaragua* Miskito Creole (on the Caribbean coast; Spanish official)
18 *Panama* lingua franca, especially in the Canal Zone, and a creole
    (Spanish official)
19 *Puerto Rico* co-official with Spanish
20 *Saint Christopher and Nevis* official (also a creole)
21 *Saint Lucia* official (also a French creole known as Kweyol)
22 *Saint Vincent and the Grenadines* official (also a creole)
23 *Surinam* lingua franca and three creoles (Dutch official)
24 *Trinidad and Tobago* official (also a creole, and French)
25 *Turks and Caicos Islands* official (also a creole)
26 *US Virgin Islands* <u>de facto</u> official (also a creole)
27 *British Virgin Islands* <u>de facto</u> official (also a creole)
28 *United States* <u>de facto</u> official at federal level; <u>de jure</u> official in 23
    states: Alabama (1990), Arizona (1988), Arkansas (1987), California
    (1986), Colorado (1988), Florida (1988), Georgia (1986), Hawaii
    (co-official with Hawaiian, 1978), Illinois (1969), Indiana (1984),
    Kentucky (1984), Louisiana (1912), Mississippi (1987), Montana

(1995), Nebraska (1920), New Hampshire (1995), North Carolina (1987), North Dakota (1987), South Carolina (1987), South Dakota (1995), Tennessee (1984), Virginia (1950), Wyoming (1996) (also several creoles, many indigenous languages, and a range of settler/immigrant languages)

Asia

1 *Bahrain* lingua franca (Arabic official; various immigrant languages)
2 *Bangladesh* recognised for higher education and law (Bengali official; also local languages)
3 *Bhutan* lingua franca (Dzongkha official)
4 *Brunei* co-official with Malay
5 *Burma/Myanmar* lingua franca (Burmese official; also local languages)
6 *Hong Kong* co-official with Cantonese
7 *India* (1) associate official language (Hindi official); (2) national language, with Hindi, Bengali, Gujerati, Marathi, Tamil, etc., because state language of: Manipur; Meghalaya; Nagaland; and Tripura; (3) official language of eight Union territories: the Andaman and Nicobar Islands; Arunachal Pradesh; Chandigarh; Dadra and Nagar Haveli; Delhi; Lakshwadip; Mizoram; and Pondicherry
8 *Israel* lingua franca and additional language (Hebrew and Arabic official)
9 *Jordan* lingua franca (Arabic official)
10 *Kuwait* lingua franca and second language in education (Arabic official)
11 *Lebanon* lingua franca (Arabic and French official)
12 *Malaysia* compulsory second language in education (Bahasa Malaysia [Malay] official; also local languages)
13 *Nepal* lingua franca (Nepali official; also local languages)
14 *Oman* lingua franca (Arabic official)
15 *Pakistan* co-official with Urdu (also local languages)
16 *Philippines* co-official with Filipino/Tagalog (also local languages)
17 *Qatar* lingua franca (Arabic official)
18 *Singapore* co-official with Mandarin Chinese, Malay, and Tamil (also other languages)
19 *Sri Lanka* often used in government (Sinhala and Tamil co-official)
20 *United Arab Emirates* lingua franca (Arabic official)

Australasia/Pacific Ocean

1 *Australia* official (also creoles, and Aboriginal and immigrant languages)
2 *Belau* second language (Belauan official)
3 *Cook Islands* official (also local languages)
4 *Federated States of Micronesia (FSM)* official (also local languages)
5 *Fiji* co-official with Fijian/Bauan (also local and immigrant Indian languages)
6 *Hawaii* (a state of the US) co-official with Hawaiian
7 *Kiribati* co-official with Kiribati/Gilbertese

8   *Marshall Islands* _de facto_ official
9   *Nauru* lingua franca (Nauruan official)
10 *New Zealand* official; co-official with Maori in courts of law (also other Polynesian languages)
11 *Northern Marianas* _de facto_ official
12 *Papua New Guinea* co-official with the English-based creole Tok Pisin and the local creole Hiri Motu (also local languages)
13 *Solomon Islands* co-official with Pijin/Solomon Islands Pidgin (also local languages)
14 *Tonga* co-official with Tongan
15 *Tuvalu* co-official with Tuvaluan
16 *Vanuatu* co-official with French and the English-based creole Bislama (also local languages)
17 *American Samoa* _de facto_ official (also Samoan)
18 *Western Samoa* co-official with Samoan

Indian Ocean
1   *British Indian Ocean Territory (BIOT)* _de facto_ official
2   *Maldives* lingua franca (Maldivian/Divehi official)
3   *Mauritius* official (also French; also the French-based creole Morisiê; also Hindi, Urdu, and Hakka Chinese)
4   *Seychelles* co-official with French and the French-based creole Seychellois

South Atlantic Ocean
1   *Ascension (Island)* _de facto_ official
2   *Falkland Islands* _de facto_ official
3   *Saint Helena* _de facto_ official
4   *Tristan da Cunha* _de facto_ official

TOTAL 113 territories

Panel 2.3 ENL, ESL, and EFL territories

A The ENL territories

The great majority of people in these territories have English as their first and, in very many cases, their only language. The category can be subdivided into two groups – without major competition, and co-existing with one or more other major languages:

A1 without major competition

Anguilla, Antigua and Barbuda, Ascension (Island), Australia, Bahamas, Barbados, Bermuda, British Indian Ocean Territory (BIOT), the Cayman Islands, Dominica, England (UK), the Falkland Islands, Grenada, Guyana, Hawaii, Liberia, Jamaica, the Irish Republic, the Isle of Man, Montserrat, New Zealand, Northern Ireland (UK), Saint Christopher and Nevis, Saint Helena, Saint Lucia, Saint Vincent and the Grenadines, Scotland (UK), the Turks and Caicos Islands, Trinidad and Tobago, Tristan da Cunha, the United States [but see next paragraph], the Virgin Islands (US), the Virgin Islands (British). *30 territories.*

A2 with one or more other major languages

Belize (also Spanish), Canada (also French), the Channel Islands (also French), Gibraltar (also Spanish), South Africa (also Afrikaans, Xhosa, Zulu, and other major local languages), Wales (UK: also Welsh). (It can be argued that the US belongs in this group, with Spanish as its demographic second language.) *6 territories.*

B The ESL territories

Many people in these territories use English for specific purposes, and in some places it has an official, educational, or other role: see panel 2.2. Competence may vary greatly, from a native-like fluency to 'broken English'. The language may be generally accepted, or may to varying degrees be a controversial (and politicized) issue. The territories are:
Bahrain, Bangladesh, Belau, Bhutan, Botswana, Brunei, Cameroon, the Cook Islands, Costa Rica, Egypt, the Federated States of Micronesia (FSM), Fiji, Gambia, Ghana, Hong Kong, India, Israel, Jordan, Kenya, Kiribati, Lebanon, Lesotho, Malaysia, Malawi, the Maldives, Malta, the Marshall Islands, Mauritius, Namibia, Nauru, Nepal, Nigeria, the Northern Marianas, Oman, Panama, Puerto Rico, Pakistan, Papua New Guinea, the Philippines, Qatar, Rwanda, Seychelles, Sierra Leone, Singapore, the Solomon Islands, Sri Lanka, Surinam, Swaziland, Tanzania, Tonga, Tuvalu, Uganda, Vanuatu, American Samoa, Western Samoa, Zambia, Zimbabwe. *57 territories.*

C The EFL territories

Many people in these territories learn English (using a British or American model of the standard language) for occupational reasons, usually as part of their education. Sometimes, acquisition may be more casual, within a family, at a place of work, or even on the street. Competence varies from basic survival to native-like fluency. The category can be subdivided into two groups:

C1 English a virtual second language
Argentina, Belgium, Burma/Myanmar, Denmark, Ethiopia, the Faroe Islands, Honduras, Kuwait, the Netherlands, the Netherlands Antilles, Nicaragua, Norway, Somalia, Sudan, Sweden, Switzerland, the United Arab Emirates. *17 territories.*

C2 English learned as the global lingua franca (the rest of the world)
Afghanistan, Albania, Algeria, Andorra, Angola, Armenia, Aruba, Austria, Azerbaijan, the Azores, the Balearic Islands, Belarus, Benin, Bolivia, Bosnia-Herzegovina, Brazil, Bulgaria, Burkina Faso, Burundi, Cambodia, the Canary Islands, Cape Verde, Central African Republic, Chad, Chile, China, Colombia, the Comoros Islands, Congo, Croatia, Cuba, Cyprus, the Czech Republic, Djibouti, the Dominican Republic, Ecuador, El Salvador, Equatorial Guinea, Estonia, Finland, France, French Guiana, French Polynesia, Gabon, Georgia, Germany, Goa, Greece, Greenland, Guadeloupe, Guatemala, Guinea, Guinea-Bissau, Haiti, Hungary, Iceland, Indonesia, Iran, Iraq, Italy, the Ivory Coast, Japan, Kazakhstan, Kirghizia, Korea (North), Korea (South), Laos, Latvia, Libya, Liechtenstein, Lithuania, Luxembourg, Macau, Macedonia, Madagascar, Madeira, Mali, Martinique, Mauritania, Mexico, Moldavia, Monaco, Mongolia, Morocco, Mozambique, New Caledonia, Niger, Paraguay, Peru, Poland, Pondicherry, Portugal, Réunion, Romania, Russia, Saint Pierre et Miquelon, San Marino, Sao Tomé and Príncipé, Saudi Arabia, Senegal, Slovakia, Slovenia, Spain, Syria, Taiwan, Tajikistan, Thailand, Timor, Togo, Tunisia, Turkey, Turkmenistan, Ukraine, Uruguay, Uzbekistan, the Vatican City, Venezuela, Vietnam, the Wallis and Futuna Islands, Yemen, Yugoslavia, Zaire. *122 territories*

TOTAL *232 territories*

Panel 2.4 A chronology of ENL and ESL territories

The arrangement in five numbered periods shows when English was first used in each territory or when each was formed or settled. Some subterritories, such as US states or Canadian provinces, are included because of their special significance at particular times.

1 Fifth to sixteenth century
What later became England (*c.* AD 450 onward); what later became Scotland (*c.* 600 onward); Ireland (1171 onward, especially during the

Plantations in 1560-1620); Wales (1282 onward, especially on union with England in 1536/1542); Newfoundland (settlement of St John's, 1504, formalized as England's first North American colony, 1583).

2 Seventeenth century
Jamestown, Virginia (1607); Bermuda (1612); Surat (1612: first trading station in India); Plymouth Plantation, Massachusetts (1620); Barbados (1627); Madras (1640); the Bahamas (1647); Jamaica (1655); Saint Helena (1659); Hudson's Bay (1670); Bombay, from Portugal (1674); Calcutta (1690).

3 Eighteenth century
Quebec (1759); the East India Company uniting its territories under Calcutta (1774); Declaration of Independence of the American colonies (1776); Botany Bay penal colony, Australia (1786); Upper and Lower Canada (1791: now Ontario and Quebec); New Zealand (1792).

4 Nineteenth century
Ceylon, Trinidad (1802); Louisiana Purchase (1803); Cape Colony, South Africa (1806, 1814); Sierra Leone (1808); Malta, Mauritius, Saint Lucia, Tobago (1814); Gambia (1816); Singapore (1819); US purchase of Florida from Spain (1819); US settlers in Mexican territory of Texas (1821: independence 1836, US state 1845); Australia at large (1829); British Guiana (1831: now Guyana); Hong Kong (1842: returned to China, 1997); Natal, South Africa (1846); Mexico cedes California, etc., to the US (1848); Bay Islands (1850: ceded to Honduras, 1858); Lagos (1861: now Nigeria); British Honduras (1862: now Belize); British North America officially named Canada, Alaska purchased from Russia by US (1867); Basutoland (1869: now Lesotho); the Gold Coast (1874: now Ghana); South East New Guinea (1884: now Papua); Bechuanaland (1885: now Botswana); Burma (1886); Kenya, Uganda, Zanzibar (1888–94); US annexes Hawaii, Spain cedes Philippines and Puerto Rico to US (1898); Sudan becomes a condominium of Britain and Egypt (1899).

5 Twentieth century
South Africa (1910); Britain and France invade German colony of Kamerun (1914: formally ceded in 1919, now Cameroon); Germans cede Tanganyika and New Guinea (1919); Germans cede German West Africa, administered for the UN by South Africa as South West Africa (1920: now Namibia); British India is partitioned into India and Pakistan (1947); Bangladesh secedes from Pakistan (1971).

[Primary geopolitical sources: Tom McArthur (ed.), *The Oxford Companion to the English Language* (Oxford University Press, 1992), *Philip's World Handbook: Country by Country*, compiled by Richard Widdows *et al.* (London: Reed Consumer Books, 1993), and John W. Wright (ed.), *The Universal Almanac 1993*, (New York and Kansas City: Universal Press Syndicate).]

3   Cracks in the academic monolith

> **monolith** *mon'o-lith*, *n* a single block of stone forming a pillar or column; anything resembling a monolith in uniformity, massiveness or intractability. – *adj* **monolith'ic** relating to or resembling a monolith; (of a state, an organization, etc) massive, and undifferentiated throughout; intractable for this reason...
>
> (definition, Catherine Schwarz (ed.)
> *The Chambers Dictionary*, Edinburgh: 1993)

An apostolic succession? – *Reviews of the language*

The study of English is an international industry. Tens of thousands of scholars engage in it throughout the world, teaching a student population of millions and producing innumerable books, periodicals, monographs, dissertations, papers, articles, reports, conference proceedings, class notes, course books, newsletters, and Internet contributions. Their total output is more than any one of them can ever hope to digest, and in many cases few will see – or even be informed about – every publication or other document which touches on their areas of special interest. By and large, however, academics and others who are engaged professionally in the study of English know – or at least know about – the pre-eminent publications in their field. Many such publications have appeared throughout this century, at least nine of which have had the same archetypal title, *The English Language*. (For details, see panel 3.1.)

Although these books differ considerably in perspective, aim, content, and style (and have no official link one with another), the deliberate manner in which their authors and publishers have used the same all-encompassing title lends them an institutional quality. The authors as it were proceed in apostolic succession, each charged with producing the latest interim report on the same vast on-going project. Although all report that the object of their study has been diverse from the beginning and has changed over the centuries, their shared title suggests – despite all such diversity and change – that the subject has nonetheless stayed the same. It was English 1,500 years ago when its disunited speakers arrived in

Britain; it was English despite the consequences of the invasions of first the Norse then the Normans; it then remained English despite centuries-long infusions of vocabulary from French, Latin, Greek, and other sources; it was still English after it had spread from the home archipelago to every continent in the world; and it remains English, as its varieties burgeon and its more-or-less standard more-or-less internationalized form becomes the most universal linguistic entity that humankind has ever known.

Many other twentieth-century books, both academic and general, and with a wide range of titles, have also subscribed to the same generally monolithic perspective. (For details, see panel 3.2.) They have had different viewpoints, aims, contents, and styles – some very different indeed, as for example Strang's, whose history runs backwards, and the work by McCrum, Cran, and MacNeil, which was tied in with a TV series. Yet, radical or received, specialized or popular, all the listed works – with two exceptions to which I will return – have taken a commonsense unitary view of their subject: the norm since such books began to be written on the subject in the eighteenth century. Recently, however, attitudes and approaches have been changing, and just over ten years ago the first cracks began to appear in this venerable monolith.

The pressures of pluralism: *The English language and literatures*

In September 1984, a conference about English (and how it can best be taught and learned worldwide) was held in London to mark the fiftieth anniversary of the formation of the British Council. The participants consisted of twenty scholars from the United Kingdom, ten British Council officers concerned with English-language education, and forty-two Anglicists from thirty-eight other countries. The proceedings of the conference were published a year later by Cambridge University Press as *English in the World*, jointly edited by Randolph Quirk of University College London and Henry Widdowson of the Institute of Education, London.

In his foreword to this book, John Burgh, then director-general of the British Council, drew attention (p. viii) to what he regarded as two key issues emerging in both the papers read to the conference and the discussions that they evoked:

○ A general insistence on the plural form 'English literatures' – referring not only to what is produced in countries where English is traditionally the first language, but also in places where it has the status of second language.

○ A fascinating ferment in the development of 'Englishes' (that is, varieties of English) world-wide.

An examination of the conference papers confirms Burgh's observations, but also suggests that there was at the meeting a marked difference of perspective and approach between Randolph Quirk, who opened the discussion with a paper on English in a global context, and several other participants. At the beginning of his paper, Quirk quotes the Elizabethan schoolmaster Richard Mulcaster, writing in 1582, where he observed that English was 'of small reatch, it stretcheth no further than this Iland of ours, naie not there over all'. Quirk then notes that the language probably had about seven million speakers in Mulcaster's time, and adds:

> The contrast with the position of English four hundred years later is extraordinary: now in daily use not by *seven* million people but by seven *hundred* million – and only half of them native speakers of the language. No longer 'of small reatch' but a language – *the* language – on which the sun does not set, whose users never sleep.... so that at this present time, English is more widely spread, and is the chief language of more countries than any other language is or ever has been.

> (*English in the World*, Cambridge University Press, 1985, p. 1)

However, he points out, the enormous global expansion of ENL (English as a native language), ESL (English as a second language), and EFL (English as a foreign language) not only imposes serious strains on the standard language, but has encouraged a fierce debate about whether one or more than one standard form exists or is even desirable. He observes:

> Small wonder that there should have been in recent years fresh talk of the diaspora of English into several mutually incomprehensible languages. The fate of Latin after the fall of the Roman Empire presents us with such distinct languages today as French, Spanish, Romanian, and Italian. With the growth of national separatism in the English-speaking countries, linguistically endorsed not least by the active encouragement of the anti-standard ethos I have just mentioned, many foresee a similar fissiparous future for English. A year or so ago, much prominence was given to the belief expressed by R. W. Burchfield that in a century from now the languages of Britain and America would be as different as French is from Italian.

> (*English in the World*, p. 3)

English could, in this view, suffer the same fate as Latin at the dissolution of the Western Roman Empire. (See also chapter 8.) However, Quirk emphasizes as a counterbalance the existence and value of – and the need to support – the standard variety of English that (with some variation between the usage of at least the United Kingdom and the United States) is currently available to all. While acknowledging diversity within the language, he draws attention at the close of his presentation to the success of this international standard:

> The English language works pretty well in its global context today: certainly the globe has at present no plausible substitute. But let me

underline my main point by giving four examples of English working best in the global context. They are the BBC World Service of London; All India Radio of Delhi; the *Straits Times* of Singapore; and the *Japan Times* of Tokyo. They represent oral and printed media, and they represent ENL, ESL, and EFL countries. And there are several outstanding features in common to these and to the scores of analogous examples that might have been selected. They all use a form of English that is both understood and respected in every corner of the globe where any knowledge of any variety of English exists. They adhere to forms of English familiarly produced by only a minority of English speakers in any of the four countries concerned. And – mere accent alone apart – they observe as uniform a standard as that manifest in any language on earth.

(*English in the World*, p. 6)

None of the other participants disputed the picture that Quirk drew, but in their papers some indicated that they saw things from a different perspective. For example, the second speaker, Braj B. Kachru, of the University of Illinois at Urbana-Champaign (and ultimately from India), also considers English in a global context, but focuses on totality and variety rather than on standard usage. Kachru proposes a variant of the ENL/ESL/EFL model in which the ENL countries constitute an 'inner circle' of English, the ESL countries an 'outer circle', and the EFL countries an 'expanding circle', making up when taken together a vast and varied community of what he calls *world Englishes*. The inner-circle Englishes he sees as 'norm-providing varieties' (especially through the standard forms of British and American English), those in the outer circle are 'norm-developing varieties', and those in the expanding circle are 'norm-dependent varieties'. In such a model, it would appear that, although the existence of and need for norms are recognized, any international standard or standards are likely to be – or to become – much less homogeneous than Quirk's description suggests.

Colin MacCabe of Strathclyde University, in his paper concerning English literature in a global context, commented on an old issue located not far in global terms from the heartland of Standard British English:

Can Scottish literature be understood in terms of a set of national themes and obsessions? Or is it more important to consider it in relation to the problems posed by a standard literary language, defined from the seventeenth century onwards by a Southern English dialect? We are perhaps more honest when we talk of literatures and languages than when we talk of political institutions.

(*English in the World*, p. 38)

And Keith Jones of the British Council universalized this point when he noted:

The main feature of the global context of English literature seems to me to be a healthy pluralism – a plurality of literatures in Englishes, a

plurality of critical and interpretative procedures, a plurality of
connections perceived and propagated between literature and society and
literature and language, a plurality of teaching purposes and procedures,
a plurality of readerships and audiences.

(English in the World, p. 50)

Such a range of linguistic and social pluralism can, however, prove dis-
turbing, as Quirk suggested when he discussed the apparent disintegration of Latin. Ramón López-Ortega of the Universidad de Extremadura in
Spain sounded a comparable warning to Quirk's on a possible collapse of
worldwide English through sheer overload:

It is evident that these literatures spring from different cultural settings,
having in common the important fact that they are written in English, in
one or another of its social or geographical varieties... [One wonders,
however,] whether the varieties of English in some of the literatures
referred to are not in danger of deviating from the commonly intelligible
norms so markedly as to become unrecognizable... The above
considerations raise an important question concerning the new status of
English as international literary currency: will English assimilate the
enormous cultural flux of these new literatures, and so increase its
metaphoric and expressive potential? Or, on the contrary, will it be
overwhelmed by this powerful stream, and prove unable to integrate the
new literary voices from these distant and distinct cultures?

(English in the World, pp. 64–5)

However, in the roundup at the end of the conference, John Sinclair of
Birmingham University observed:

Although it was news to no one, it was important for Conference to be
told, gently but firmly, that English was no longer the exclusive province
of the native speaker... The English language was much too valuable
around the world for it to remain in the control of one special group;
the native speakers had, it would appear, exported their language only
too successfully. Whereas a previous Conference might have worried
about the range of models available among native speakers, this
Conference accepted a much more pluralistic view, more readily perhaps
on the literary side than on the purely linguistic.

(English in the World, p. 248)

Willingness to agree about plurality in literature was radical enough in
1984, and it is hard to imagine a comparable conference on English a
decade earlier going so far so comfortably. As a consequence of the
broadly prevailing view at this conference, the full title of the proceedings
runs: 'English in the World: Teaching and learning *the language and literatures*' (my italics). While it was clearly a significant development, with
hindsight one can see that this blend of singular and plural was an uneasy
compromise. It pointed – hesitantly, almost reluctantly – towards a more
radical symmetry, in which the various autonomous 'literatures' would

relate not to one language but a group of 'languages' so close-knit that they might well have already existed for some time without their differences being adequately registered – perhaps because their distinctness (and often mutual unintelligibility) could not be fully acknowledged until they were shepherded into the international limelight through a literary rather than a linguistic door.

An affirmation of pluralism: *The Englishes*

At the time of the British Council conference, Braj Kachru was discussing with the British publisher Pergamon the re-launch of a journal called *World Language English*. The plan was to turn what had been a periodical for EFL teachers (whose pedagogical centre of gravity was at that time the usage, or at least the aspiration, of middle-class south-eastern England) into a scholarly review with no such centre of gravity anywhere. The outcome in 1985 was in effect an entirely new publication: *World Englishes: The Journal of English as an International and Intranational Language*, jointly edited by Kachru in Illinois and Larry E. Smith of the East–West Center, Honolulu, Hawaii. Since then, *WE* has been a vehicle for the discussion, both general and specific, of varieties of English worldwide, and has in the process firmly underlined the neologism *Englishes* in linguistic and educational circles. The journal's editorial stance is that all 'world Englishes' (native and non-native) belong equally to all who use them and merit serious and consistent study both individually and collectively.

Although this use of the expression *Englishes* is new, its form is not. In the seventeenth century, the expression *an English* meant both a sentence to be translated from English into a foreign language and the equivalent in English of a foreign word (as in 'The first column contains some Englishes': from W. Walker's *Dictionary of English Particles*,1679, cited in the *OED*). However, such a use faded long ago and the new use, of which the first citations date from the 1970s, appears to be *sui generis*. The first new use known to me is from a historical study already touched on; the others appear in the titles as well as pages of three later articles:

○ 1970
  'You will hear, perhaps, the English of your family, localised or non-localised; of shopkeepers and bus-conductors, probably localised; if you are a student, you will hear lecturers using different Englishes, probably at least one of them having a foreign accent.' Barbara Strang, in *A History of English*, London: Methuen, p. 19.

○ 1977
  Title: 'The new Englishes and old models', Braj B. Kachru, *English Language Forum* 15:3.

○ **1980**
   Title: 'The new Englishes and old lexicons', Braj B. Kachru, in Ladislav
   Zgusta (ed.), *Theory and Method in Lexicography*, Columbia, S.C.:
   Hornbeam.

○ **1982**
   Title: 'World English and the world's Englishes', Peter Strevens, in
   Journal of the Royal Society of Arts 120.

In the early 1980s, the new usage appeared in the markedly similar
titles of three books, one published in the US, the others in the UK:

○ **1982**
   New Englishes, ed. John Pride, Rowley, Mass.: Newbury House.

○ **1984**
   The New Englishes, John Platt, Heidi Weber, and Mian Lian Ho, London:
   Routledge and Kegan Paul.

○ **1984**
   Modern Englishes: Pidgins and Creoles, Loreto Todd, Oxford: Basil
   Blackwell.

These citations and items from the British Council conference indicate
that while Strang's early use is imprecise, it sets the stage for the well-
defined pluralist view associated notably with Kachru, which had
emerged strongly by the mid-1980s. Since then, the form has appeared in
many publications, seminars, lectures, debates, and conversations worldwide, including in three prominent works of the 1990s: *The Oxford
Companion to the English Language* (1992), where it has an entry, *The New
Shorter Oxford Dictionary* (1993), where it is cited at *English*, and *The
Cambridge Encyclopedia of the English Language* (1995), where it occurs,
for example, in the phrase 'Regional Standard Englishes' (p. 113).
Singular uses occur, but are rarer, as for example in the following:

○ **1984**

   As long as we try to retain an International English for international
   communication we should welcome the diversity and creativeness of
   the New Englishes.

                          (John Platt, 'Growth of the New Englishes', *EFL Gazette*,
                                                          London, September)

○ **1985**

   Countering those who pointed... to the existence of a world English,
   Burchfield argued that such indications overlooked one vital fact.

                                        (McCrum *et al.*, *The Story of English*,
                                    London: Faber and BBC Publications, p. 308)

o **1991**

> There must... be provision for each English to have a distinctive lexical set that will express local cultural content.
>
> (Gerry Abbott, 'English across cultures', *English Today* 28, October)

o **1994**

> [G]iven the extralinguistic situation, the types of innovation in a particular New English are, to a limited extent, predictable.
>
> ('The origins and development of emigrant Englishes', Manfred Görlach, given at the Second Rasmus Rask Colloquium, Odense, 3–4 Nov, p. 6 of typescript)

o **1995**

> We can have an English for speakers of each foreign language. The English pronunciation is generally predictable from a knowledge of the sounds of the foreign language, e.g. Germanized English.
>
> (Warren Shibles, 'Received Pronunciation and *Realphonetik*', *World Englishes*, 14:3, p. 358)

This countable usage appears to have its origin in two converging practices:

(1) As a cover term for such expressions as *American English, British English, Canadian English, Indian English, Nigerian English, Singapore English*, etc. Robert W. Burchfield uses the term in this way in 1985:

> The rest of this chapter will be devoted to the main changes that have affected the home variety of English – British English – since 1776. Some of them are shared by Englishes abroad: others are not.
>
> (*The English Language*, Oxford University Press, p. 38)

(2) As an elliptical shorthand for the phrases *varieties of English* and *English varieties*, usages which have been increasingly common in recent years because they avoid the often negative and emotive connotations of *dialects of English* and *English dialects*. Peter Strevens points to this in his paper 'English as an International Language' in 1992:

> Today the trend in referring to different forms and varieties is to accept differentiation within English and even to employ a new plural, 'Englishes'.
>
> (*The Other Tongue*, 2nd edn, ed. Braj B. Kachru, University of Illinois Press, p. 28)

However, the new usage is more striking and radical than any of the expressions it covers or replaces. The forms *an English* and *Englishes* imply actual or potential autonomy: the many varieties may not – yet? – all be sociopolitically equal, but nevertheless cats may look at a king. The

British-cum-American-cum-international standard of the language may be dominant and enormously valuable, as Quirk asserts, but it is not – even from this fresh perspective – the only legitimate English in the world: let it be *primus inter pares* by all means, the users of the expression seem to be saying, but not – or no longer – the yardstick or set of yardsticks by which all other forms are to be measured under all possible circumstances. Kachru has put it as follows:

> English has 'multiple identities' in its international and intranational functions... We must recognize the linguistic, cultural and pragmatic implications of various types of pluralism: That pluralism has now become an integral part of the English language and literatures written in English in various parts of the non-Western world. The traditional presuppositions and ethnocentric approaches need reevaluation. In the international contexts, English represents a repertoire of cultures, not a monolithic culture.
>
> ('Teaching world Englishes', *Indian Journal of Applied Linguistics* 15:1, 1989, pp. 86 and 92–3)

Traditionalists concerned about safeguarding the language – the linguistic right wing, as it were – are not likely to have much sympathy with this point of view or favour a solecism that is itself living proof of slipping standards: *'Englishes' indeed!* But the linguistic centre and left have been less alarmed; they have responded positively to the concept of plurality or shown no strong feelings either way. As has happened often enough in the past, a generation may shortly grow up wondering what all the fuss was about, finding *an English* and *Englishes* no more contentious than *a wine* and *wines*. Certainly, there now appears to be no escape from the new countability. Thus, Robert Burchfield uses the plural freely in the introduction to Volume 5 of *The Cambridge History of the English Language: English in Britain and Overseas: Origins and Development* (1994), of which he is editor, noting (p. 5) that:

> The volume spans five main areas: 1 dialects of England; 2 English in the originally Celtic-speaking lands, Scotland, Wales and Ireland; 3 the 'settler Englishes' of Australia, New Zealand and South Africa; 4 creole Englishes of the Caribbean; 5 the Englishes (largely non-native) of South Asia (i.e. the subcontinent that was all once called India).

It has taken the emergence of a particular sociocultural climate to bring such expressions as *English literatures* and *the Englishes* to the fore. The Second World War set in train the breakup of the British Empire and ushered the United States in as the world's leading English-using nation. But, even so, it has taken decades for the various cats – including the large American cat – to look at the old British king as confidently as they might wish. Indeed, residual cat-and-king problems are likely to continue into the next century. It is unlikely that the proconsuls of Empire would, in their heyday, have had much patience with 'English literatures' and 'Englishes' but in a postcolonial, postmodernist age Anglophone communities throughout the world have become free to assert their autonomy, especially when writers from such communities win world-class awards, and established scholars make assertions on their behalf at major conferences and in cutting-edge publications.

An assertion of pluralism: *The English languages*

I have already mentioned *The Story of English*, the book and TV series jointly created by Robert McCrum, a British writer and publisher (the editorial director at the time of Faber and Faber), William Cran, a British television producer (who had worked in the UK, Canada, and the US), and Robert MacNeil, a Canadian broadcaster and writer working in the US (notably as presenter and executive editor of the MacNeil–Lehrer Newshour, PBS). Both series and book appeared in 1986, which means that the ideas animating them had been circulating for some years beforehand. In the introduction to the book, the writers note (p. 11):

> We have tried to tell the whole story. Some academic studies tend to dwell on the catalogued literary past rather than on the messier, teeming present, on Chaucer and Noah Webster at the expense of Caribbean creole or space-speak. Until recently, the focus of scholarship has been on the Anglo-American story, and while giving proper weight to this main narrative, we have also explored some of the newer subplots of the language, in places like China, Singapore, Holland and West Africa. A more accurate title for this book might have been *The English Languages*, an idea to which we shall return in the final chapter.

The assertion of multiplicity in language is made as plainly here as it was made for literature at the British Council conference. However, the phrase *the English languages* appears only once in the book, there was never any likelihood that it would be the title of either the TV series or the book, and the idea with which the writers close in the last chapter is less radical. The title of that chapter is in fact *The New Englishes,* and on pp. 366–7 (in the notes section) are mentioned both Loreto Todd's *Modern Englishes* and *The New Englishes* of Platt, Weber, and Ho ('whose title we gratefully acknowledge'). This closing chapter is as multiform as the conference speakers Kachru, MacCabe, and Sinclair might have wished, opening in London as ancient hub of Empire, then discussing the imperial diaspora and moving in succession to Jamaican dub poetry and Creole, British Black English, Krio in Sierra Leone, Indian English, and finally Singlish, the vernacular of Singapore.

The radical phrase re-appears, however, in a UK newspaper interview connected with the book and the TV series, in which Nicholas Shakespeare quotes McCrum as saying:

> Seven years ago I was reading V. S. Naipaul's *A Bend in the River*. Suddenly it struck me that there I was, in New York, reading a book about disappearing Africans by a Trinidadian of Indian extraction. I thought I would like to read something on the history of English languages but there was nothing. Everything concerned the history of English in England.

(The Times, London, 13 September 1986)

In 1984, I became founding editor of the quarterly *English Today: The international review of the English language* (launched by Cambridge University Press in January 1985), and in 1986 began work on *The Oxford Companion to the English Language*. I had been thinking for some time about the issues touched on above and had become intrigued by the idea of a multiple perspective on English. I therefore published in *English Today* some of my own thoughts, to which I attached the following lead-in:

> In recent years there have been suggestions that English could break up into mutually unintelligible languages, much as Latin once did. Could such a break-up occur, or are we in need of a new appreciation of the nature of World English?

('The English Languages?', in English Today 11,
Cambridge University Press, July 1987)

Arguments about the Latin analogy occupy most of the article, and I will return to them in chapter 8. Here it is enough to quote one paragraph which chimes with the observations of the pluralists at the British Council conference:

> At the present time, various other 'Englishes' [than the traditionally dominant British and American varieties in their standard forms] are developing such institutions as their own dictionaries and grammars, powerful markers of autonomy. Some, like Canadian and Australian English, share in the common text-linked tradition of the standard; others, like Tok Pisin in Papua New Guinea and Krio in Sierra Leone are bafflingly far removed from the standard language, and are most patently distinct languages.

In the same year I contributed the tenth and closing chapter to the revised edition of Bolton and Crystal's *The English Language* (the tenth and final volume in the Sphere History of Literature: see panel 3.1). This chapter deals with the present-day role of English in the world and with its prospects in the immediate future, and has the title 'The English language or the English languages?' Just as, at the London conference, no one went openly beyond the phrases *the Englishes* and *the English literatures,* so three years later, first in the article then in the chapter, I adorned the risqué new phrase with the fig-leaf of a question mark.

Also in 1987, the phrase appeared in Michael Baber's British school workbook *GCSE English* (that is, English for the General Certificate of Secondary Education, in England and Wales). The first section of his contents list runs:

1 The English language – What's yours called?
How many English languages are there?
Is this your problem?
Regional accents and dialects.
Slang, catch phrases and colloquial expressions.
Idioms.
Written and spoken English – basic differences.

The most notable development, however, occurred at the end of the decade, when in 1989 Robert Clark of the School of English and American Studies at the University of East Anglia, in Norwich, proposed to the Council of University English (the organization that represents university teaching of especially English literature in Britain) that:

European integration implied the need for a pan-European body which could represent the interests of the [university English] profession to Brussels, help support national associations where the need arose, and generally aid in the development of English studies throughout Europe. Such a body would also encourage English teachers in Britain to see English studies as part of the study of European culture.

(UEA Annual Report 1990–1991, p. 19)

As a consequence of the School's initiative, a conference took place at Norwich in September 1991, at which the European Society for the Study of English (ESSE) was formed. The initiating conference was attended by six hundred and thirty European Anglicists, and the society which they approved claimed by 1994 to represent around five thousand five hundred university teachers of English in Europe at large. The wording of the leaflet which announced the inaugural conference and gave the reason for ESSE's existence indicates that, although the society's name treats English as unitary, multiplicity co-exists with it: 'The European Society for the study of English has been founded to encourage European understandings of English languages, literatures and cultures.' In little more than a decade, then, a revolution took place in the world of English Studies, both literary and linguistic, a revolution which has however had a long gestation period. (For additional citations, see panel 3.3.) But beyond this significant but limited academic world the shift in perspective has hardly been noticed, and even within that world it is not yet banner headlines. It is nonetheless clear, however, that many Anglicists had already moved on from a cautious pluralism in the early 1980s to an increasingly confident assertion of multiplicity and distinctiveness by the close of that decade.

Panel 3.1 The *English Language* tradition in publishing

1912: UK
Logan Pearsall Smith, Oxford University Press
A concise history by an American living in England, intended for the British public, and without an explanatory introduction: reprinted 17 times 1917–42, with a reset but unrevised edition in 1948: 36 years in all. Such a work could not now run for even ten years without being revised.

1928: UK
Ernest Weekley, London: Ernest Benn
A concise history of the language intended for the British public, without an explanatory introduction.

1949: UK
C. L. Wrenn, London: Methuen
A historical work for the British public, in eight parts with an introduction and such themes as 'Vocabulary', 'Spelling and Pronunciation', and 'Individuals and the Making of Modern English'.

1963: US
W. Nelson Francis, New York: W. W. Norton
Subtitled 'An Introduction' and intended for students and an American-cum-international public: 'presents sufficient fact and theory about the language to serve as a background to literary study' (preface). Also a UK edition.

1966/69: UK
W. F. Bolton (ed.), Cambridge University Press
A specialist two-volume collection of chronologically-ordered essays, with an American editor, the second co-edited with the British linguist **David Crystal**. The introduction notes: 'The twenty essays in this book illustrate both the internal and the external history of literary English since the end of the fifteenth century.'

1975: UK
W. F. Bolton and David Crystal (eds.), London: Sphere
Tenth volume in the *History of Literature* series, revised edition 1987: aimed at a readership primarily interested in English literature. There are ten essays contributed by specialists.

1985: UK
Robert W. Burchfield, Oxford University Press
A New Zealand-born author, who notes in the introduction: 'This book is offered to the new generation at schools and universities, and to people in other walks of life, who wish to acquire a knowledge of the pedigree and credentials of their own language.'

1988: UK
David Crystal, Harmondsworth: Penguin
For the general reader. From chapter 13: 'Two main themes can be traced through the earlier chapters in this book: the regional and the social diversification of the English language. English has never been a totally homogeneous language, but its history is primarily the story of the way it has become increasingly heterogeneous.'

1993: UK
Charles Barber, Cambridge University Press
Subtitled *A Historical Introduction*, for students and general readers worldwide. Preface: 'This is a book about the history of the English language, from its remote Indo-European origins down to the present day. It is a complete revision and rewriting of an early work, *The Story of Language*, published in 1964.'

Panel 3.2 Some other twentieth-century works on the English language

The list below covers a range of works on English that deal with areas discussed in this study. It excludes dictionaries, works devoted mainly or entirely to grammar and/or style and usage, and academic journals. Titles that suggest diversity and multiplicity are asterisked (*).

1904: UK
Henry Bradley, *The Making of English*, London: Macmillan.

1905: UK
Otto Jespersen, *Growth and Structure of the English Language*, Oxford: Blackwell.

1914: UK
Henry Cecil Wyld, *A Short History of English*, London: Murray.

1919: US
Henry L. Mencken, *The American Language*, New York: Alfred A. Knopf.

1935: US
Albert C. Baugh, *A History of the English Language*, 1st edn, New York: Appleton-Century; 2nd edn, Appleton-Century-Crofts, 1957; 3rd edn, New York: Prentice-Hall, 1978; 4th edn, Prentice-Hall, 1993 (with imprints by Routledge in the UK). Thomas Cable became co-editor with the third edition.

1945: Australia
Sidney J. Baker, *The Australian Language*, Sydney: Currawong Press.

1950: UK
Simeon Potter, *Our Language*, London: Pelican.

1962: UK
Randolph Quirk, *The Use of English*, London: Longman (2nd edn, 1968).

1970: UK
Barbara M. H. Strang, *A History of English*, London: Methuen.

1971: UK
Juanita V. Williamson and Virginia
M. Burke, *A Various Language:
Perspective on American Dialects,*
New York: Holt, Rinehart and
Winston.

1976: UK
Charles Barber, *Early Modern
English,* Oxford: Blackwell.

1980: UK
Leonard Michaels and
Christopher Ricks (eds.), *The State
of the Language,* University of
California Press in association with
the English-Speaking Union, San
Francisco Branch.

1982a: UK
Peter Trudgill and Jean Hannah
(eds.), *International English: A
Guide to Varieties of Standard
English,* London: Edward Arnold
(2nd edn, 1985, 3rd edn, 1994).

1982b: US
Richard W. Bailey and Manfred
Görlach (eds.), *English as a World
Language,* Ann Arbor: University of
Michigan Press (reprinted for world
circulation, Cambridge University
Press, 1984).

1982c: US
Whitney F. Bolton, *A Living
Language: The History and Structure
of English,* New York: Random
House.

1983a: US
Robert Claiborne, *Our Marvelous
Native Tongue: The Life and Times of
the English Language,* New York:
Times Books.

1983b: UK
Dick Leith, *A Social History of
English,* London: Routledge (2nd
edn, 1997).

1983c: India
Braj B. Kachru, *The Indianization
of English: The English Language in
India,* Delhi: Oxford University
Press.

1985a: UK
Randolph Quirk and H. G.
Widdowson (eds.), *English in the
World: Teaching and Learning the
Language and Literatures,*
Cambridge University Press.

1985b: UK
Sidney Greenbaum, *The English
Language Today,* Oxford: Pergamon.

1986a: UK
Robert McCrum, William Cran,
and Robert MacNeil, *The Story of
English,* London: Faber and the BBC.

1986b: UK
Braj B. Kachru, *The Alchemy of
English,* Oxford: Pergamon.

1987: UK
Roger Lass, *The Shape of English:
Structure and History,* London:
Dent.

1989: US
C. M. Willward, *A Biography of the
English Language,* New York: Holt,
Rinehart and Winston.

1990a: UK
Jenny Cheshire (ed.), *English
Around the World: Sociolinguistic
Perspectives,* Cambridge University
Press.

1990b: UK
Bill Bryson, *Mother Tongue: The
English Language,* London: Hamish
Hamilton (author US).

1990c: UK
Christopher Ricks and Leonard
Michaels (eds), *The State of the*

Language: 1990 Edition, University of California Press (and in the UK, London: Faber and Faber).

1991a: US
Richard W. Bailey, *Images of English: A Cultural History of the Language*, Ann Arbor: University of Michigan Press (US), and Cambridge University Press (UK).

1991b: UK
Tony Crowley, *Proper English? – Readings in Language, History and Cultural Identity*, London: Routledge.

1992a: UK
Tom McArthur (ed), *The Oxford Companion to the English Language*, Oxford University Press.

1992b: UK
Richard M. Hogg (general editor), *The Cambridge History of the English Language*, 5 vols., Cambridge University Press (vols. 1 and 2 in 1992, vol. 5 in 1994, others in preparation).

1992c: UK
Stephan Gramley and Kurt-Michael Pätzold, *A Survey of Modern English*, London: Routledge.

1992d: US
J. L. Dillard, *A History of American English,* Harlow: Longman.

1992e: UK
David Burnley, *The History of the English Language: A Source Book,* Harlow: Longman.

1994: UK
Mike Hayhoe and Stephen Parker, (eds.), *Who Owns English?*, Buckingham: Open University.

1995a: UK
David Crystal, *The Cambridge Encyclopedia of the English Language,* Cambridge University Press.

1995b: UK
Jeff Wilkinson, *Introducing Standard English,* Harmondsworth: Penguin.

1996a: UK
Norman F. Blake, *A History of the English Language,* London: Macmillan.

1996b: UK
Jeremy Smith, *An Historical Study of English: Function, Form and Change,* London: Routledge.

1996c: UK
David Graddol, Dick Leith, and Joan Swann (eds.), **English: History, Diversity and Change,* Buckingham: Open University and London: Routledge (first in *The English Language: Past, Present and Future* series).

1996d: UK
Janet Maybin and Neil Mercer (eds.), *Using English: from Conversation to Canon,* Buckingham: Open University and London: Routledge (second in *The English Language: Past, Present and Future* series).

1996e: UK
Neil Mercer and Joan Swann (eds.), **Learning English: Development and Diversity,* Buckingham: Open University and London: Routledge (third in *The English Language: Past, Present and Future* series).

1996f: UK
Sharon Goodman and David Graddol (eds.), **Redesigning English: New Texts, New Identities,*

Buckingham: Open University and London: Routledge (fourth in *The English Language: Past, Present and Future* series).

1997a: UK
Gerry Knowles, *A Cultural History of the English Language*, London: Arnold

1997b: UK
David Crystal, *English: The Global Language*, Cambridge University Press.

1998: UK
Tom McArthur, *The English Languages,* Cambridge University Press.

Panel 3.3 Perceptions of two or more 'English languages', in historical and contemporary terms

The commentators cited below may: (1) imply that there is more than one English language, without necessarily pursuing the matter or being particularly aware of the implication; (2) verge on proposing two or more separate languages; (3) explicitly adopt a plural approach.

1858: UK
Richard Chenevix-Trench:
> As soon as a standard language has been formed, which in England was the case after the Reformation, the lexicographer is bound to deal with that alone; before that epoch, however, the English language was in reality another name for the sum of a number of local languages.

> *(A Proposal for the Publication of a New English Dictionary by the Philological Society, London)*

1906: UK
H. W. and F. G. Fowler:
> Americanisms are foreign words, and should be so treated. To say this is not to insult the American language... [The expression *I guess* is shared by both Americans and Chaucer but] though it is good old English, it is not good new English. If we use the phrase..., we have it not from Chaucer, but from the Yankees, and with their, not his, exact shade of meaning. It must be recognized that they and we, in parting some hundreds of years ago, started on slightly divergent roads in language long before we did so in politics.

> *(The King's English,* Oxford University Press, p. 33)

1912: UK
Logan Pearsall Smith:
> We find at first a purely Germanic race, a group of related tribes, speaking dialects of what was substantially the same language – the language which is the parent of our present English speech. This Anglo-Saxon or (as it is now preferably called) 'Old English' language belonged to the great Teutonic family of speech.

> *(The English Language,* Oxford University Press, p. 2)

1928: US
Robert L. Ramsay:

I think much may be said in favor of beginning [a historical review] with Modern English and proceeding backward. It is perfectly true that a student who has already studied Old and Middle English will be better prepared to understand the problems of Modern English; but it is also true that a student who has first gained some insight into the nature of a living language will be more ready to realize that Old and Middle English were once living too.

> (from the minority report by Professor Ramsay (University of Missouri), appended to the report of a committee of nine linguistic scholars submitted to the National Council of Teachers of English)

1965: UK
David Abercrombie

First let me make clear what I mean by Standard English. This phrase is used in a variety of senses. I shall use it, as many other people do, to mean that kind of English which is the official language of the entire English-speaking world, and is also the language of all educated English-speaking people. What I mean by Standard English has nothing to do with the way people pronounce: Standard English is a language, not an accent.

> ('R.P. & local accent', in *Studies in Phonetics and Linguistics,* Oxford University Press, p. 10)

1966: UK
Simeon Potter:

Like [Walter] Scott, however, [Thomas Carlyle] brought such Scottish words into English as *feckless, lilt* (with the meaning of 'cadence'), and *outcome,* and made them current.

> (*Our Language,* rev. edn, London: Penguin, p. 81)

1979: US
Charles Gilman:

'Cameroonian Pidgin English, a neo-African language'

> (title of a paper in Ian F. Hancock (ed.), *Readings in Creole Studies,* Ghent: Story-Scientia)

1983: UK
Randolph Quirk:

India is estimated to have over eighteen million people using English as a necessary part of their daily working lives. This means that India vies with Canada as the country with the greatest number of English speakers after the USA and the UK... 'Indian English', a cover term for the varieties and range of English uses in the subcontinent, is thus a vitally significant language, one that commands a great deal of interest, and one whose serious study is impeded by dauntingly severe complexities, both linguistic and sociological.

> (Foreword to Braj B. Kachru, *The Indianization of English,* Delhi: Oxford University Press)

1985a: UK
Robert Burchfield:
The political results of the dispersal of English speakers abroad are well
known. So too are the linguistic results although these are not so easily
measured or classified. There are no constitutional processes leading to
declarations of linguistic independence as there are in politics. No flags
are run up as signs or symbols of linguistic sovereignty. There are no
governor-generals of language, and no linguistic Boston Tea Parties.
Languages break free without ceremony.

(*The English Language,* Oxford University Press, p. 160)

1985b: UK
Adam Mars-Jones:
[The book] *The New Englishes* aims to give these languages [such as
Nigerian and Singaporean English] a dignity and status; it makes a
good case.

(from the review 'Standard Englishes', *The Sunday Times,*
London, 17 February)

1986: Germany
Manfred Görlach:
Although Krio, Cameroon Pidgin and Tok Pisin must be classified as
distinct languages, and not dialects of English, the case of Jamaican
Creole makes it clear that decreolization can lead to a point where it is
appropriate to categorize such a language as a 'dialect' of English again.

(Introduction to *Wilhelm Busch, Max and Moritz in English Dialects
and Creoles,* Hamburg: Helmut Buske Verlag, p. 26)

1988: UK
David Crystal:
Maybe one day, it is said, English will be transformed into a family of
new languages – just as happened to Latin, less than 2,000 years ago...
Some people think that the process has already begun. The history of
language shows us that any such development would be entirely
natural, and it could easily happen to English.

In present-day English, word order is relatively fixed. The reason why
the order in Old English could vary so much is that the relationships
between the parts of the sentence were signalled by other means. Old
English was an *inflected* language.

(*The English Language,* Harmondsworth: Penguin, pp. 11 and 151)

1989: UK
Robert Burchfield:
The earliest recorded version of our ancestral tongue [Old English] is
now virtually a foreign language. To acquire a working knowledge of its
rules and procedures, native English speakers need to regard it as if it
were as unEnglish as, say, modern Flemish or Swedish or German.

(*Unlocking the English Language*, London: Faber and Faber, p. 23)

1990a: UK
Randolph Quirk and Gabriele Stein:
The 600 years separating us from Chaucer give us some difficulty in
reading *The Canterbury Tales*, and the further 500 separating him from
King Alfred who died in 899 force us to cross a threshold where we seem
to confront a different language – and (in the view of many)
appropriately designated with a different name, 'Anglo-Saxon'.

(*English In Use*, Harlow: Longman, p. 28)

1990b: UK
Sidney Greenbaum:
On the basis of comprehensive descriptions, linguists [in countries
where English is a second language] should promote variants [of the
local standard varieties] that have international currency... There are of
course some variants among the national standard languages of mother-
tongue countries, but it would be a pity to add unnecessarily to their
number from the emerging standard languages.

('Whose English?', in Ricks and Michaels (eds.),
The State of the Language, London: Faber and Faber)

1990c: Singapore
Anne Pakir:
The fact remains that in Singapore the degree of mastery over the
language called Standard English is more often than not correlated with
the number of years spent in formal schooling.

('Education and Invisible Language Planning: The Case of English
in Singapore', in Thiru Kandiah and John Kwan-Terry (eds.),
English and Language Planning: A Southeast Asian Contribution,
Singapore: Times Academic Press)

1992a: UK
Anthony Burgess:
It has been difficult for many inhabitants of a class-ridden country like
England to see virtue in Standard English or even accept that it is
possible to learn it, as one learns any foreign language... We like to clear
an English dialect of the charge of being a foreign language by pointing
to elements in it that seem foreign only because they are archaic.

(*A Mouthful of Air: Language and Languages, Especially English*,
London: Hutchinson, pp. 4 and 145)

1992b: UK
David Burnley:
The overall structure of the book sustains the consensus view of the
development of the language through successive historical periods
towards the goal of present-day standard English. Thus, apart from one
letter from King James VI of Scotland, Scottish texts have not been
included, since they are considered to belong to a distinct and
specialised development.

(preface of *The History of the English Language: A Source Book*,
Harlow: Longman, p. x)

1992c: UK
Stephan Gramley & Kurt-Michael Pätzold:

[In the Caribbean] English is truly a minority language, for the vast majority of people in the anglophone countries are speakers not of StE [Standard English], but of English creoles... the major languages on most of the anglophone islands... The term *English creole* refers to a vernacular form which is strongly related to English in the area of lexis, since the English creoles share a major portion of their vocabulary with StE. Syntactically, however, they diverge so strongly that it is not unjustified to regard them as separate languages rather than dialects of English.

(*A Survey of Modern English*, London: Routledge, p. 384)

1993: UK
Robert Clark and Piero Boitani (eds.):

The Inaugural Conference of the European Society for the study of English was held at the University of East Anglia, Norwich on 4–8 September 1991. It was the culmination of two years' planning by European scholars committed to the study of the many cultures, languages and literatures denominated by the word 'English' around the world.

(Introduction to *English Studies in Transition: Papers from the ESSE Inaugural Conference*, London: Routledge)

1994a: UK
Laurie Bauer:

Students who are not native speakers of English, but foreign learners, are usually presented with modern English as a homogeneous entity. This homogeneity is inevitably a fiction. Moreover, it is usually a *conservative* fiction, showing the particular standard English as it was some thirty years ago or more... It is one of my aims in this book to shatter the illusion of homogeneity.

(*Watching English Change: An Intoduction to the Study of Linguistic Change in Standard Englishes in the Twentieth Century*, Harlow: Longman, p. 10)

1994b: US
Alan S. Kaye:

The major theme of the book is the 'false sense of mutual intelligibility' (p. 2) which has been created by English's becoming the number one international language in use. In essence, what this boils down to is that one can make a case for English being not one but many languages.

(review of Ofelia García and Ricardo Otheguy (eds.), *English Across Cultures: Cultures Across English* (Berlin: Mouton de Gruyter, 1989), in the *Canadian Journal of Linguistics*, 39:2, p. 161)

1994c: US
John A. Holm:

Creole English in the West Indies can be considered a single language, historically related to – but distinct from – both English (a parent language) and the creoles of Suriname (sister languages rather than dialects, if only because there is so little mutual comprehension).

> ('English in the Caribbean', in Robert W. Burchfield (ed.), *The Cambridge History of the English Language,* Vol. V, *English in Britain and Overseas (Origins and Development)*)

1994d: South Africa
Peter Titlestad:

In Ndebele's words, 'South African English must be open to the possibility of becoming a new language.'

> (review of Neville Alexander's *Language Policy and National Unity in South Africa/Azania* (Cape Town: Buchu Books, 1989), in *English World Wide*, 15:1, p. 168)

1995a: UK
Jeff Wilkinson:

The growth of the East Midlands dialect [of English] as a national language led to its increasing codification and prescription, particularly in the seventeenth and eighteenth centuries, in grammar books and usage manuals. The dialect of one part of the country thus became the national, standard written language for the whole country.

> (*Introducing Standard English*, Harmondsworth: Penguin, p.4)

1995b: US
Ronald Shibles:

If most countries set RP with given specific IPA paradigms as the standard [for pronunciation in the teaching of English as a foreign language], it is a strong argument for its continuance. But there still remains a problem as to whether AP or RP should be used. Both are world-class languages. RP drives on the left, making for linguistic collisions with AP, which drives on the right.

> ('Received Pronunciation and *Realphonetik*', *World Englishes*, 14:3, p. 368)

1995c: Germany
Manfred Görlach:

Languages like Scots and Jamaican Creole are, by contrast, eminently appropriate for such shifts of style.

> ('Max and Moritz in Scots', in Görlach, *More Englishes: New Studies in Varieties of English, 1988–1994*, Amsterdam and Philadelphia: John Benjamins, p. 239)

1996: UK
Christopher Zann:

Like most young Papuans lucky enough to get an education, [Peter Pundia, a student] speaks three languages: his local dialect, English, and Pidgin.

> ('Leaving the stone age by degrees', *Guardian Weekly*, London, 1 September 1996)

4   Models of English

> **model**... **14 a :** a description, a collection of
> statistical data, or an analogy used to help
> visualize often in a simplified way something
> that cannot be directly observed (as an atom)
> **b :** a theoretical projection in detail of a possi-
> ble system of human relationships (as in eco-
> nomics, politics, or psychology)...
>
> (definition, Philip Babcock Gove (ed.), *Webster's*
> *Third New International Dictionary*,
> Springfield, Mass., 1966)

Describing a 'language': *Two truisms and three models*

The first truism is that the day-to-day language acts of users of English
worldwide – thought, spoken, written, typed, printed, broadcast, taped,
telephoned, faxed, and emailed – are so vast and varied that no person,
group, or system could ever catch and catalogue them all. Even the most
extensive, subtle, and flexible computer corpus currently imaginable
could not encompass all the registers and usages of Standard English,
leave alone the rest. No language has ever been easy to describe and catalogue, but the relatively modest scale of most of the world's languages has
allowed – and still allows in many cases – a sense of comprehensiveness in
relation to any grammars, dictionaries, and other works associated with
them. But the scale of present-day English does not permit any such comfortable illusion.

The second truism is that since total knowledge of the subject is impossible, our efforts to describe, prescribe for, and teach English – however
extensive, elegant, and influential they may be – are incomplete, indirect
and, in the last analysis, fictive. As a consequence of insight and effort there
has often been an impressive match (as far as we can tell) between scholarly models and the system likely to underlie the ungraspable whole, resulting in many eminently practical achievements. But all the models ever
made are exercises of the imagination, not embodiments of God's truth.

In addition, and paradoxically, each new descriptive and explanatory
framework adds to the complexity of what there is to study, and may in
due course become an object of investigation in its own right, part of

received tradition. What is more, such a framework may serve to underpin and validate the methodology and content of English teaching in particular places for particular purposes at particular times. When this kind of thing happens (notably with French from the seventeenth century onward, after the creation of the Académie française), such a model may be elevated by teachers and others to the status of *the* model: the only possible way of representing and teaching the language, to be amended only modestly and under carefully regulated conditions. When this happens, a model – however valuable – can become an impediment rather than an aid to knowledge.

Such an elevation of description for prescriptive purposes has led people in various times and places to label as 'uncouth', 'barbarous', 'corrupt', or 'deviant', etc., any usage which fails to fit the model – however much and however widely that usage may be employed. This kind of elevation happened within upper- and middle-class English in the London area in the eighteenth century, by analogy partly with the perceived glories of classical (Augustan) Latin, and partly with courtly and literary French, the most prestigious form of language in Europe at that time. As a result, a tradition of 'refined' usage grew up, based pre-eminently on: the style of such 'Augustan' writers as John Dryden and Alexander Pope; the nature and content of Samuel Johnson's dictionary of 1755; the precepts of Robert Lowth's grammar of 1762; and a group of dictionary-writing 'orthoepists', such as John Walker, who claimed to know how to pronounce the language properly. This neo-Classical tradition became for the next two centuries the dominant paradigm for the analysis, discussion, teaching, and use of what began at about that time to be called 'Standard English'. (See chapters 5 and 8 for further discussion.)

The rapid decline of this venerable and potent tradition over the last few decades is currently highlighted by a ferment of debate in various Anglophone countries about how the language should be taught and what the term 'Standard English' has meant, means, might mean, might be made to mean, or should most categorically mean. Few people taking part in such discussions think explicitly of this inherited tradition – or any possible replacements for it – as a 'model' of language, but in essence the argument is about models: about how one pictures what is going on.

Whenever anyone (academic or otherwise) describes a language or an aspect of a language, a model of some kind comes into play, because no one can directly lay a language out for public inspection. Any such model may be explicit or implicit, may be precise or vague, may be called a model or given no label at all, while those involved in the process may be conscious that they are using a model or not at all conscious of doing so. More or less inevitably, when so much is implicit, the metaphorical nature of the model(s) involved tends to be unclear or pass unnoticed, and the possibility that bits of several models may be at work (often fitting uneasily together) is usually not considered. Currently, for example, many teachers of English have for several decades been employing elements of the traditional unitary, prescriptivist model of Standard English alongside elements of a more recent multiple, descriptivist model, sometimes more aware of what they have been doing, sometimes less so – and seldom having an easy time.

Up to this point I have been contrasting a venerable unitary model – 'English' – with two innovative pluralist models – 'the Englishes' and 'the English languages'. This approach may have been taken to imply that, as I see it, no one seriously contemplated the diverse immensity of English (or any comparable language, such as French or Arabic) before about 1975. In fact the opposite is true. While generally adhering to the concept of one language flowing through time and across space, scholars have for decades, if not centuries, been aware of variety. To help them manage this variety, they have developed a set of models and submodels founded on a range of metaphors, such as time, family, and life. Indeed, these models and submodels have been so useful and successful that, as I suggested above, they have become part of the background scenery of English and other languages, and have often therefore been taken for granted as the natural apparatus of description: God's truth once again.

English through time: *Chronological model-making*

Philologists in the late eighteenth and the nineteenth century were primarily concerned with the history of languages and their elements, and especially how those languages and elements change, especially as evidenced in texts. As a result, they needed frameworks within which to discuss and assess such change adequately. For English and various other languages they favoured the division of their subject into time-phases, primarily three in number, each with boundary dates. The names, dates, and identifying aspects usually assigned to the three fundamental phases of English have been the following (see also panel 4.1.):

○ **Old English (duration c.650 years)**
Generally agreed to have begun c.AD 500, when the language had become established by at least the Angles, Saxons, and Jutes in many areas of southern Britain (a region which had formerly been a Roman colony). The phase ended c.1150, the approximate point at which the linguistic effects of the Norman Conquest of 1066 began to be felt in what had till then been the Anglo-Saxon-cum-Danish kingdom of England.

○ **Middle English (duration c.300–350 years)**
Generally agreed to have begun c.1150 and variously regarded as having ended in c.1450, c.1475, or c.1500, all three dates belonging to

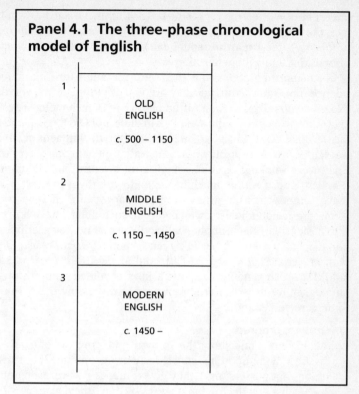

Panel 4.1 The three-phase chronological model of English

1

OLD
ENGLISH

c. 500 – 1150

2

MIDDLE
ENGLISH

c. 1150 – 1450

3

MODERN
ENGLISH

c. 1450 –

the period when printing by movable type was spreading throughout Western Europe.

○ Modern English (formerly also called New English: duration *c.*535 years)

Generally agreed to have begun *c.*1450–1500 and, by and large, to be continuing at the present time. In this period, the language has gone from being the vernacular of virtually the whole of England, the Lowlands of Scotland, and small groups in Wales and Ireland to serving in the late twentieth century as the primary international medium for much of the human race.

Analogical symbolism lies at the heart of all models, even if it is not always overtly discussed. Thus, for most people, the diagram in panel 4.1 implies – crudely – that English is a box within which three smaller boxes are sequentially nested. An invisible arrow of time indicates how 'the language' has passed (upwards or downwards) from box to box to box, or how one language state becomes another and then a third, all linked but different, and retaining the same general name and nature. Other metaphors may also be suggested by the framing of the diagram (for example, the rungs of a ladder) but, whatever the symbolism used (explicitly or implicitly), the tripartite model can be interpreted in two ways: a more monolithic and a more pluralist way.

Such representations and their interpretations are matters of convenience, not God's truth, yet they are well removed from everyday reality. No one who talked to King Alfred about the Danish menace ever thought, 'He and I are speaking the West Saxon dialect of Old English and the Danes are speaking Old Norse.' No one labouring in the kitchens of a Plantagenet prince or sweating it out in an Australian penal colony considered that they were thinking, arguing, singing, or swearing in Middle or Modern English. And if a time machine had allowed them to meet, none would have understood the others in speech or writing (if they could read). Comparative philologists, well aware of such points, have however found the basic tripartite chronological model useful in the description of many languages: *Old French, Middle French,* and *Modern French*; *Old, Middle,* and *Modern Persian*; *Old, Middle,* and *Modern Russian*, and so forth. In addition, such timelines receive a kind of added value through certain analogical terms which are often used in discussing them, but deserve a little care and caution:

○ Growth, progress
When people talk about the 'growth' and 'progress' of a language, they are bestowing upon it – consciously or unconsciously – attributes that it does not possess: first, they give it life, as if it were a plant or animal (a 'vitalist' model of language), second, they give it forward and upward momentum (a 'teleological' or 'excelsior' model of language). Perhaps, on some occasions, something called 'growth and progress' – or 'decay and decline' – is identified in terms of specific sociocultural institutions and trends, but such metaphors are rhetorical devices, at best indirect images, at worst ideology-based falsifications of what may be happening in a language.

○ Change, evolution, degeneration
When people talk about 'change' and 'evolution' in a language, they may well be seeking objective ways of describing what happens. However, although *change* is a relatively value-free term, *evolution* has for over a century carried with it the weight of Darwinism and needs to be used and interpreted with care. If one wishes to adopt a Darwinian model of language, one should be aware of it and say so and, among other things, consider what the implications of natural selection ('survival of the fittest') may be for such a phenomenon. Such care is even more important if one wishes to assert that a language is less worthy today than it was at some point in its past, having 'degenerated' or 'decayed' rather than 'evolved' and 'progressed'.

○ **Drift**

When scholars talk about 'drift' in a language, they may have decided to replace the teleological and Darwinian implications in such terms as 'grow' and 'evolve' with a sense of undirected or less directed change, yet even here the metaphor of physical motion remains, helping to portray languages as entities capable of moving through time – however aimlessly – rather than as phenomena on which the process of time 'operates' as a consequence of human activity.

In addition, and curiously, in a conventional chronological model of language, as above, the word 'Old' represents not 'age' but a 'youth' which occurred long ago, while 'Modern' represents a maturity and up-to-date-ness that – for many traditionally minded people – is neither fresh nor exciting, but fraught with degeneracy, decay, and decline. For better or worse, there is no shortage of paradox when analogies and images of model-making play too powerful a role, and yet it is hard to discuss language without bringing in metaphor. The only safeguard may be to make such matters as conscious as possible, and decide (as it were) where we stand in relation to the images we employ so freely.

The approach shown in panel 4.1 can be called a *container model*, because in it English has been closed off from all other languages, and certain aspects of English have been closed off from one another and from comparable aspects or stages of other languages – despite the haziness of the dates when, for example, Old English ends and Middle English takes over. In addition, it is implied that French too has its boxes-cum-ladders, as have German, Dutch, Italian, Spanish, Portuguese, and so forth, that there are (at least for the purposes of initial discussion) no serious overlaps or indeterminate boundaries among the boxes, and that any such subtleties do not need to be covered because the levels of description involved are introductory and should not be taken too seriously.

As a result, linguists often use such models in a provisional way, re-formulating or abandoning them as they move to more demanding analytical levels. But even so the same linguists have tended to return to such models when in need of general accounts of the language, and accept them (especially because they have acquired the sanctity of tradition) as in some important foundational sense 'true'. In other words, although *Middle English* is a fuzzy concept, Chaucer did indeed write in it, *not* in Old English or Modern English – and *we* know this even if *he* didn't. It is possible to think like this because, despite the arbitrariness and limitations of the chronological model (which have long been obvious), scholars have generally found the box, ladder, or phase model useful. Some time ago, however, it proved necessary to divide the three phases into subphases based on an additional contrast of 'Early' and 'Late(r)', so that one could have for example an *Early Old English* and a *Late Middle English*. In terms of the third phase, for which the distinction is most commonly used, the dichotomy is:

○ Early Modern English (duration c.210–250 years)
Generally agreed to have begun c.1450–1500 and regarded as having ended either in 1660, the year of the Restoration of the Monarchy in England, or c.1700, a convenient point during the Augustan Age.

○ (Later) Modern English (duration c.355–395 years to date)
Generally agreed to have begun c.1660–1700 and to be continuing at the present time.

The result has been a four-phase variant which has dominated (?conditioned) the thinking of historians of English for many years, and continues to be a handy framework for the more panoramic books (see panel 4.2). Because this is the most common variant, I will call it 'the standard chronological model', noting however that some scholars have added a fifth phase at the beginning, to create a five-in-one model which is becoming more common:

○ Pre-Old English (duration unknown)
Covering the period before c.500, and including: (1) The early decades of direct Anglo-Saxon settlement in Britain; (2) An earlier period in which minor Germanic settlements appear to have been permitted in Britain in Roman times; (3) The indefinite period on the European mainland when West Germanic speech was fairly uniform across a wide area, but Angle, Saxon, and other dialectal differences were emerging.

However, in all such versions of the chronological model there is a cardinal difference between the earlier Englishes (whatever their nature and number) and the last English: the phases from *Old English* to *Early Modern English* are finite and finished (whatever scholars may consider their durations to have been), and *Pre-Old English* is also finished, though its duration and beginnings are uncertain, but *Modern English* is open-ended, because – at least until recently – modernity has been regarded as on-going.

This most recent phase is however proving to be as negotiable, divisible, and incremental as the others, new sections being added in new editions of established histories of English so as to be able to report on fresh developments and viewpoints. Although such sections have not usually been given a new name, they imply that since the end of the Second World War 'Modern English', as traditionally conceived and dated, has been superseded by a new, rather messy phase. More or less informally, at least the six following names have been given to that new phase between the 1940s and 1990s. They are:

○ Present-day English
The British scholar C. L. Wrenn, in *The English Language*, London: Methuen 1949, p. 23, presciently observed: 'It might... in view of the con-

Panel 4.2 The four-phase variant of the chronological model

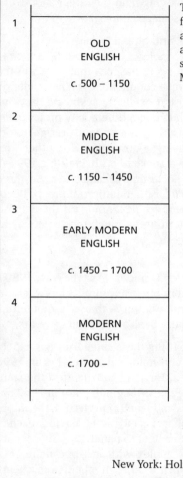

1

OLD
ENGLISH

c. 500 – 1150

2

MIDDLE
ENGLISH

c. 1150 – 1450

3

EARLY MODERN
ENGLISH

c. 1450 – 1700

4

MODERN
ENGLISH

c. 1700 –

This variant is currently the standard form of the model. One version (using another analogy, implying still earlier and later phases, and offering a different set of dates) appears in a work by C. M. Millward in 1989. The description runs:

Although linguistic change is a slow but unceasing process, like a slow-motion movie, so to speak, it is impracticable to try to describe the changes in this way. Instead, we must present them as a series of still photographs, noting what has changed in the interval between one photograph and the next... The history of the English language is normally presented in four such still photographs – Old English, Middle English, Early Modern English, and Present-Day English. We will retain these traditional divisions, but also glance at the prehistory of English and speculate to some extent about English in the future... Old English (OE) is that stage of the language used between A.D. 450 and A.D. 1100. The period from 1100 to 1500 is Middle English (ME), the period between 1500 and 1800 is Early Modern English (EMnE), and the period since 1800 is Present-Day English (PDE).

(*A Biography of the English Language*, New York: Holt, Rinehart and Winston, 1989, p. 13)

siderable changes which seem to be taking place in English to-day, be a good thing to separate current usage from what history tells us about the language, and to speak of the tongue of our own generation as "Present-day" English.' (See also note to panel 4.2.)

○ Contemporary English (compare *le français contemporain*)
A term occurring in the titles of Randolph Quirk, Sidney Greenbaum, Geoffrey Leech, and Jan Svartvik's *A Grammar of Contemporary English*

(Harlow: Longman, 1972), Paul Procter's *Longman Dictionary of Contemporary English* (Harlow, 1978), and my own *Longman Lexicon of Contemporary English* (Harlow, 1981). 'Contemporary' has had in recent decades a fresher, more positive ring than the rather shop-worn 'modern', and may well have helped sell such books.

○ **World English, international English, and global English**
Terms that focus on geography and geopolitics rather than on time: the current outcome of the Western European diaspora that began in the sixteenth century. (See chapter 2.) Some commentators have evidently favoured *world/World English* because it explicitly acknowledges – or asserts – the planetary reach of the language; others may prefer *international/International English* because it is not so total(itarian) in its implication of (pre)dominance, leaving elbow room for other languages. The word *global* began to be associated with *English* c.1996–7 because of the buzzword status of *global* and *globalization*. All three terms *world, international,* and *global* rather indiscriminately begin with upper and lower case letters, perhaps depending on the dispositions of their writers at the time of writing, in much the same way as 'standard English' and 'Standard English'.

○ **World Englishes**
A term in use (as we have seen in chapter 3) since at least the early 1980s, combining both geopolitics and plurality, but in its plurality less total and final – and perhaps therefore less intimidating – than the monolithic *World English* (a term about which I have been ambivalent for years).

To the best of my knowledge, no one using these categories has explicitly integrated them into the standard chronological model, but in 1996 David Graddol of the Open University in England restructured the standard model to allow for a 'Late Modern English' beginning not in 1660 but 1950. However, whatever the categories and label(s) preferred, the implication is clear: the number of boxable phases is indefinite, having reached six here and seven in Graddol's work. (See note to panel 4.3.) Six or more time phases are a lot for a language complex with just one name, but English is not alone in accumulating such a large number, Greek being commonly represented as passing through six phases between the fourteenth century BC and the present day: *Mycenaean, Archaic, Classical, Hellenistic, Byzantine (Romaic),* and *Modern.*

The recurrence of one name, such as *Greek* or *English,* throughout such models privileges continuity over change and asserts an on-going unity that is not normally proposed for a cognate language complex which emerged in Italy three thousand years ago. Scholars refer to the earliest known stages of this complex as 'Italic dialects' (within the Indo-European language family), after which comes a dialect-cum-language called Latin,

Panel 4.3 The six-phase variant of the chronological model

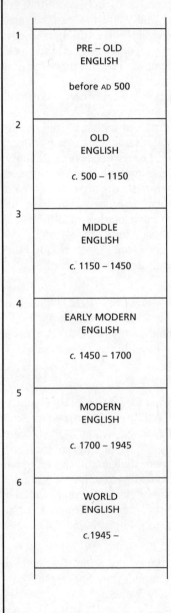

1	PRE – OLD ENGLISH before AD 500
2	OLD ENGLISH c. 500 – 1150
3	MIDDLE ENGLISH c. 1150 – 1450
4	EARLY MODERN ENGLISH c. 1450 – 1700
5	MODERN ENGLISH c. 1700 – 1945
6	WORLD ENGLISH c.1945 –

In 1996, in *English: History, Diversity and Change* (London: Routledge and Buckingham: Open University), David Graddol, Dick Leith, and Joan Swann present a variant called 'the seven ages of English': *Pre-English* (to *c.*AD 450), *Early Old English* (*c.*450–*c.*850), *Later Old English* (c.850–1100), *Middle English* (*c.*1100–1450), *Early Modern English* (*c.*1450–1750), *Modern English* (*c.*1750–1950), and *Late Modern English* (*c.*1950–). Graddol has also formulated a 'postmodern or globalized model of English as an international *lingua franca*', relating particularly to 'services and "knowledge-intensive industries"'.

This seven-phase model also appears in David Graddol, *The Future of English? – A guide to forecasting the popularity of the English language in the 21st century*, London: The British Council, 1997, p.7.

which later begets Italian (whose own dialects co-occur with a Tuscan-based standard). Yet the whole of this complex has essentially the same continuum structure as Greek and English. But a key reason for Latin and Italian not having the same name is the spread of Latin beyond Italy, giving rise to further complexes such as French and Spanish. It can, however, be argued that Italian bears a greater resemblance to Latin than Modern Greek does to Classical Greek *and than contemporary English does to Old English/Anglo-Saxon*. Names, it would appear, can obscure connections as well as reveal them.

Observers focusing on *dis*continuity can, however, reconceive box models created for any language complex as a succession of shifts from one entity to another rather than as successive phases within a single entity, and it is also possible (and useful) to view the same construct from both positions – continuity and discontinuity – as one's needs and emphases may require. Indeed, some commentators *have* created discontinuity models of the English language complex, to stress the distinctness of two or more phases, but these have been minority positions that have not attracted much discussion. Below are two such models of a 'bilingual' nature, the first a single-line model like those above, the second (on a small scale) the kind of branching model commonly used, among other things, for the Indo-European language family as a whole:

o **Anglo-Saxon and English**
   Some scholars, most notably Henry Sweet (1845–1912), have preferred *Anglo-Saxon* to *Old English*, as in *Sweet's Anglo-Saxon Primer* (Oxford University Press, 1882), to emphasize the fact that speakers of 'Modern English' cannot understand 'Old English' any more than speakers of Italian can understand Latin.

o **Scots and English**
   Traditionally, scholars of Scots have divided the history of their subject into three (or four) phases: *Old English* (or *Anglo-Saxon*); *Older Scots* (usually divided into *Early Scots* and *Middle Scots*); and *Modern Scots*. (See panel 4.4.) In the general unitary model of English (however many the boxes), Scots is simply a northern dialect and therefore has no explicit place, but in the Scotticists' model English and Scots are distinct but related offspring of the same 'parent', implying that instead of only one Germanic language, English, the island of Britain has had three (all with written forms): Anglo-Saxon, English, and Scots. (See also chapters 1 and 6.)

To my knowledge, no one has ever questioned the right of scholars of Scots to create for their own purposes any model they find useful – not even one which separates Scots off completely from English.

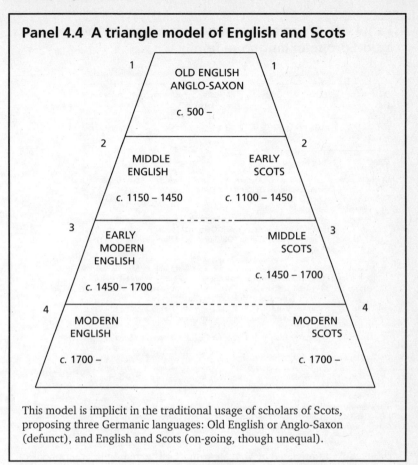

Panel 4.4 A triangle model of English and Scots

This model is implicit in the traditional usage of scholars of Scots, proposing three Germanic languages: Old English or Anglo-Saxon (defunct), and English and Scots (on-going, though unequal).

Language as a living thing: *Biological model-making*

Chronological models of English have long made use of two metaphors taken from living things. The first, which dates from Classical times, presents language as a plant (usually a tree) with roots, stems, and branches – but without leaves, blossoms, or fruit. The second, which derives from the taxonomies of the Swedish biologist Carolus Linnaeus in the eighteenth century and the evolutionary theories of the British biologists Charles Darwin and Alfred Russell Wallace in the nineteenth, presents languages as members of families with mothers, sisters, and daughters – but no fathers, brothers, and sons. (Ernest Weekley in *The English Language* in 1906 (p. 13) *did* write that 'Anglo-Saxon may thus be described as the brother of Dutch and Frisian and the half-brother of the

Panel 4.5 An inverted branching model of the Indo-European language family

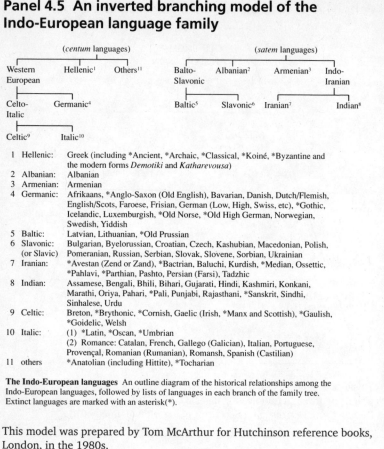

The Indo-European languages An outline diagram of the historical relationships among the Indo-European languages, followed by lists of languages in each branch of the family tree. Extinct languages are marked with an asterisk(*).

This model was prepared by Tom McArthur for Hutchinson reference books, London, in the 1980s.

Scandinavian languages', but such maleness is rare.) The plant and family images – both redolent of fertility and growth – come together when language families are laid out in trees almost identical to those used for genealogies and biological phyla.

Such language trees are additionally peculiar in that (1) they do not grow upwards from the soil of the past but spread their branches either downwards (as in panel 4.5) or sideways (as in panel 4.6), and (2) the roots and stems of word-formation have nothing directly to do with them. No one, however, appears to have had much trouble with such conceptual and presentational oddities, and few people appear to wonder how such models got to be the way they are. Like so many other things, such models

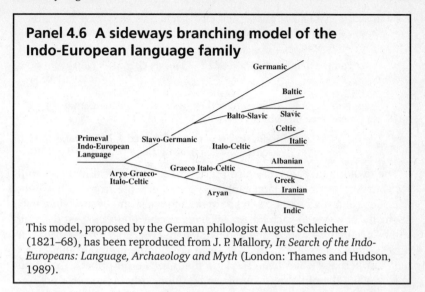

Panel 4.6 A sideways branching model of the Indo-European language family

This model, proposed by the German philologist August Schleicher (1821–68), has been reproduced from J. P. Mallory, *In Search of the Indo-Europeans: Language, Archaeology and Myth* (London: Thames and Hudson, 1989).

and metaphors are simply presented and accepted, like the hands on the face of a clock.

In such a *biological model*, English is one of the progeny of a hypothesized and more or less reconstructed 'mother' called West Germanic, whose 'grandmother' was the hypothesized and somewhat reconstructed prehistoric language known as Proto-Indo-European. In each generation of the Indo-European language family, every virgin-born daughter has a boxed-off purity which bears little relation to the hurly-burly of everyday language in army camps, border settlements, migrant communities, seaports, and other age-old meeting places. In the preparation and discussion of such biological models, little provision is made for further generations: the grandmothers and mothers have reproduced, but the current daughters – despite centuries of 'life' (often as long as the presumed 'lives' of the older languages) – have not proved fertile. Or, to take the metaphor a little further, if the daughters *have* become mothers, none of their births have been officially registered. Occasionally, however, the metaphor can be tweaked by a linguist with a point to make. Below, for example, are three uses of the female imagery, the first conventional (and now very dated in sociopolitical terms), the second making a controversial point within the traditional framework, and the third radically extending it:

○   Here, again, we must not suppose that English is derived from German, or even from Dutch, but we assume that all three are developed... from the same ancestor, which we call Primitive Germanic, and which was a daughter of Primitive Aryan.

(Henry Cecil Wyld, *The Growth of English*, London: John Murray, 1907, p. 190)

○   It is true that English has become almost a half-sister to these 'Romance
     languages', as they are called, and a large part of its vocabulary is derived
     from Latin sources.

          (Logan Pearsall Smith, *The English Language*, Oxford University Press,
                                                                        1912, p. 1)

○   Pidgins and creoles are no longer the unwanted stepdaughter languages
     they were once thought to be.

               (Loreto Todd, review of Dell Hymes (ed.), *Pidginization and
                         Creolization of Languages, Lingua* 32 (1973), p. 136)

   The evolutionary imagery also present in the biological model is indirect but just as potent: later language forms emerge from earlier ones,
whose fossil remains can be laid bare in the rock strata of surviving texts.
Logically, however, if such language change occurred in the past it should
still be occurring – and we know of course that this is so. Over recent centuries, therefore, there must have been development among the daughters, but perhaps it has been the kind that needs a bit of backstreet mid-
wifery while the philologists are keeping things tidy in their front rooms.
Logically, in terms of this model and its mother/daughter analogies,
English has in recent centuries also given birth, as have Portuguese,
Spanish, French, and Dutch. Two groups of the daughters of Mother
English come to mind (as discussed in chapters 1 and 2), the first obvious
(in structural terms), the second less so but no less important (in legal and
official terms):

○ **The English-based pidgins and creoles of Africa, Australasia, Oceania,
the Americas, and Asia**
     As we have already seen, there is no shortage either of daughters (and
     potential foreign fathers), as with Krio in Sierra Leone, Kamtok in
     Cameroon, Tok Pisin in Papua New Guinea, Pijin in the Solomon
     Islands, Bislama in Vanuatu, Hawaii Creole, Patwa in Jamaica, Creolese
     in Guyana, Gullah in Georgia, and Ndjuka, Saramaccan, and Sranan in
     Surinam.

○ **The territorially labelled Englishes**
     These include the varieties used in Australia, Canada, England, Ghana,
     India, Ireland, Jamaica, Kenya, Malawi, New Zealand, Nigeria, the
     Philippines, Scotland, Singapore, South Africa, Uganda, Tanzania, the
     United States, Wales, Zambia, and Zimbabwe. I have used alphabetical
     order here as a neutralizing device, which helps avoid at least six
     prickly issues which emerge when any other kind of ordering is
     attempted: (1) Whether there is a pecking order of world English (as
     touched on in chapter 1); (2) Whether the UK (not listed as such) or the
     US should have pride of place at the head of any such pecking order;
     (3) Whether England should have pride of place over all other English-

using territories, including those in the rest of the UK – even a part of
England over other parts; (4) What might distinguish so-called 'white'
from 'black' Englishes; (5) Who the native and non-native users of
English are; (6) Which regional varieties of English already have viable
standard forms, which may be moving towards them, and which do not
have them at all.

Just as it is impossible to be clear-cut about how and when Common
Germanic became ('gave birth to') West Germanic, West Germanic became
Old English, Old English became Middle English, and Middle English became
Modern English, so one cannot be clear-cut about how and when the territorially labelled Englishes of Africa, the Americas, Asia, and Australasia/
Oceania became – or could become – self-validating systems with their own
newspapers, radio and television services, and increasingly dictionaries,
grammars, histories, style guides, and school books focusing on their own
needs, a state of affairs which is equally true for the English-based creoles.

Danish, Norwegian, and Swedish have long been recognized as distinct
but more or less mutually intelligible national languages that are at one and
the same time varieties of Common Scandinavian (mainland North
Germanic): that is, they are by and large accepted as national varieties of a
non-institutionalized supranational language and national languages in
their own right, attended by all the sociocultural institutions of nation-
states, including written and printed forms. In the same way, it has become
possible – although it is currently unusual – to think of the subcomplexes of
American, Australian, British, Canadian, Indian, Nigerian, and Singapore
English (among others) as national varieties of a common English and
national languages in their own right – as for example in the statement
'English is one of the four official languages of Singapore': It is not British
or American English that is one of these four official languages, nor yet
International English (whatever that may be), but Singapore English in its
standard(izing) form, which however has close sociohistorical links with
British English on the one hand and Malaysian English on the other. In a
serious though paradoxical sense, Singapore English as a totality is at one
and the same time a variety of International English and an official
language, and this is true regardless of whether people in Singapore believe
their model to be British English with an RP accent. There is in fact very little British English with an RP accent in Singapore.

The social shapes of language: *Geopolitical model-making*

In the last two decades of the twentieth century, four models have radically departed from tradition by focusing neither on chronology nor biology but on the geopolitics of English. They are all pluralist constructs

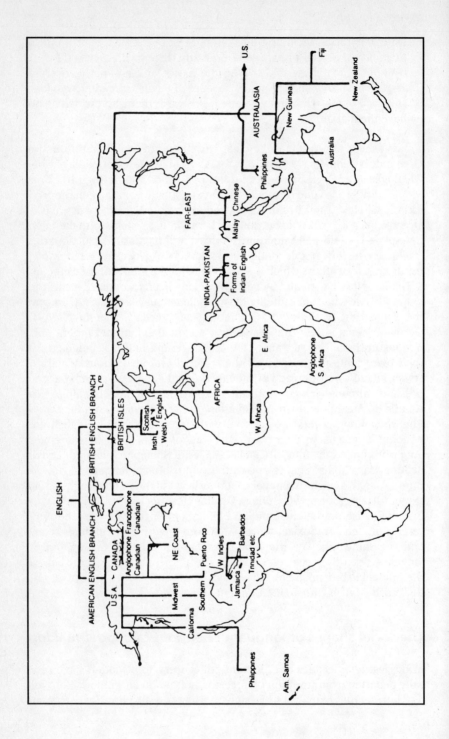

ENGLISH

AMERICAN ENGLISH BRANCH

BRITISH ENGLISH BRANCH

BRITISH ISLES

Scottish / English
Insh / Welsh

U.S.A ~ CANADA

Anglophone Francophone
Canadian Canadian

California
Southern
Midwest
NE Coast
Puerto Rico
W Indies

Jamaica
Barbados
Trinidad etc.

Philippines

Am. Samoa

AFRICA

W Africa
E Africa
Anglophone
S Africa

INDIA-PAKISTAN

Forms of
Indian English

FAR-EAST

Malay Chinese

AUSTRALASIA

U.S.

Philippines

New Guinea

Fiji

New Zealand

Australia

Panel 4.7 Peter Strevens's world map of English

The model on p. 94 imposes a branching diagram on a Mercator projection
of the world. It was first published in 1980 in *Teaching English as an
International Language*, Oxford: Pergamon Press, and reprinted in 1992 in
the paper 'English as an International Language: Directions in the 1990s', in
Braj B. Kachru (ed.), *The Other Tongue*, 2nd edn (University of Illinois
Press), and as part of the article 'Models of English' by Tom McArthur in
English Today 32, October 1992. John Algeo proposed similar branches and
sub-branches in 'A meditation on the varieties of English', *English Today* 27,
July 1991, but in list form. Separate adaptations of the Strevens model have
appeared on the cover of *English Today* to complement the Algeo article and
in David Crystal, *The Cambridge Encyclopedia of the English Language*
(Cambridge University Press, 1995, p. 107) and *English: The Global
Language* (Cambridge University Press, 1997, p. 62). The Crystal adaptation
appears on the following page.

---

whose creators have sought to make sense of the present-day diversity
within the English language complex, in the process freely using such
terms as *Englishes, New Englishes,* and *World Englishes.* The models are:

○ Strevens: A map-and-branch model (1980)
  Formulated by the British applied linguist Peter Strevens, this approach
  employs a map of the world on which is superimposed an inverted-tree
  diagram resembling the branching models of Indo-European. The
  Strevens approach has both synchronic and diachronic implications, its
  taxonomy recalling Darwin while its cartography points to the current
  global situation. Strevens divides English into a *British English Branch*
  and an *American English Branch*, making them first equal in the pecking order and, in effect, the mothers of the rest, British having daughters in Africa, the Caribbean, South Asia, and Australasia, and
  American in the Caribbean and Asia. (See panel 4.7.)

○ McArthur: A circle of World English (1987)
  My own formulation: a wheel with a hub, spokes, and rim. The hub is
  called *World Standard English,* within an encircling band of regional
  varieties, such as the standard and other forms *of African English,
  American English, Canadian English* and *Irish English.* Beyond these, but
  linked to them by spokes marking off eight regions of the world, is a
  crowded (even riotous) fringe of subvarieties such as *Aboriginal
  English, Black English Vernacular, Gullah, Jamaican Nation Language,
  Krio, Singapore English, and Ulster Scots.* (See panel 4.8.)

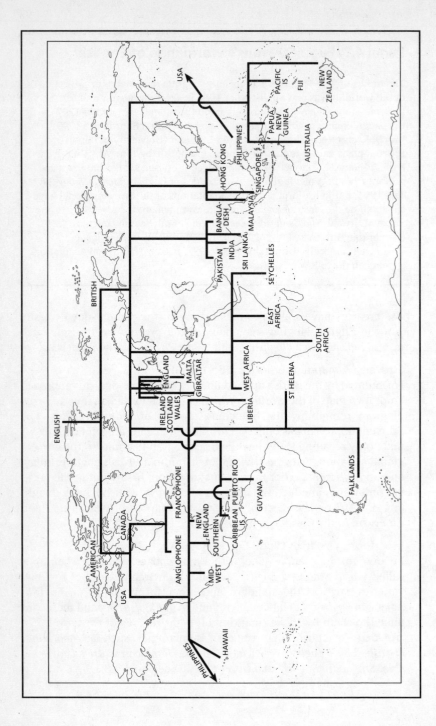

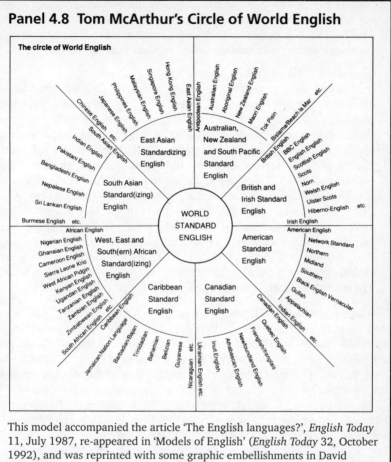

Panel 4.8 Tom McArthur's Circle of World English

The circle of World English

This model accompanied the article 'The English languages?', *English Today* 11, July 1987, re-appeared in 'Models of English' (*English Today* 32, October 1992), and was reprinted with some graphic embellishments in David Crystal, *The Cambridge Encyclopedia of the English Language* (Cambridge University Press, 1995, p. 111).

○ **Kachru: Three concentric circles of English (1988)**

Formulated by the Indian-American linguist Braj B. Kachru, this model is not, despite its name, circular or concentric, but in its best-known form is a set of three contiguous ovals rising one above the other out of smaller unlabelled ovals belonging presumably to the past. The first and lowest labelled oval is *the Inner Circle*, containing the US, the UK, Canada, Australia, and New Zealand, the world's primary native-speaking communities (that is, in effect, the major ENL territories). The second and larger oval, *the Outer Circle*, contains post-colonial English-using countries, such as Bangladesh, Kenya, the Philippines, and

Zambia (ESL). The third and largest oval, in the earliest forms called *the Extending Circle*, later *the Expanding Circle*, holds the rest of the world (EFL). Population statistics are provided for the countries within each oval, adding a demographic dimension. (See panel 4.9.)

○ Görlach: A circle of International English (1988/90)

Formulated by the German Anglicist Manfred Görlach, this wheel model displays 'the status of varieties of English and related languages world-wide'. The hub is *International English* (not explicitly presented as standard), surrounded by a range of 'regional standards' such as *African Englishes, Antipodean English, British English, United States English*, these in turn enclosed by 'subregional semi-standards' such as *Australian English, Irish English, Jamaican English, Scottish English*, and *Southern US English*. Beyond lie such forms as *Aboriginal English, Black English Vernacular* and *Yorkshire*. Again, eight world regions are marked off by spokes, and beyond the rim (outside English proper) are pidgins, creoles, 'mixes', and 'related languages', such as *Anglo-Romani, Krio, Saramaccan, Scots*, and *Tok Pisin*. Within Görlach's circle are Englishes while beyond it are distinct yet related languages whose 'Englishness' as such is rejected. (See panel 4.10.)

I have proposed in this chapter that three kinds of model have been used to describe English: on the one hand, *chronological models* and *biological models* (products mainly of nineteenth-century diachronic scholarship) and, on the other, *geopolitical models* (products mainly of twentieth-century synchronic scholarship). The chronological models tend to depict language change as implicitly a sequence of boxes or rungs, while the biological models tend to depict it explicitly through tree diagrams and an imagery of femaleness and fertility. Only one of the late twentieth-century models (by Strevens) retains something of this genetic directionality, by imposing a tree diagram on a map of the world; the others have circle patterns. All are fictive and figurative, the phenomena they seek to represent having nothing to do with ladders, trees, women, fertility, families, maps, or circles. The models do, however, demonstrate the power of metaphor as both a valid and valuable illustrative device and a way of moulding (and also limiting, usually unintentionally) our capacity to discuss the phenomena so modelled.

I wrote earlier in this chapter that 'Common Germanic became West Germanic, West Germanic became Old English, Old English became Middle English, and Middle English became Modern English', and in its turn Modern English is now conceived as a vast composite of territorially-labelled Englishes and English-based creoles (elements of each category often running into the other). Scholars have generally not spent much time on the status of 'Common Germanic' and 'West Germanic' (the latter term also being applied to the current subset of Germanic languages that includes English). The resulting indeterminacy may be because the entities in question existed long ago, have left few direct traces (so that much of what we think we know about them is hypothetical and reconstructed), and may not in any case have been regarded as proper languages by the scholars in question. That is, Common Germanic and West Germanic in their day were utterly unstandardized: the rough-and-ready stuff of pre-literate (?illiterate), pre-civilized (?uncivilized) peoples. And apart from a limited scribal tradition, Old and Middle English were also diverse. English only became English for psychologically real present-day purposes when it began to be printed and standardized on paper and spoken 'elegantly' in educated circles. Scholars, belonging to those circles, were inevitably influenced by them; like many others, they preferred a single stable English to a mass of slippery, barbarous Englishes, and for many 'the story of English' (and indeed language) from the dawn of history till their own time was the story of how this admirable stability came into being. (And I am not myself opposed to it, as the nature and style of this book demonstrates.)

Today, however, English has manifestly and extravagantly become many again, diversity reaching even into its standard varieties. The period of a widespread and stable languagehood was brief – if indeed it ever really existed. All the above models – chronological, biological, or geopolitical – share and exhibit the multiplicity of the English language complex rather than its uniformity, but where the earlier models could use imagery such as well-tended evolutionary trees and genteelly fecund women, more recent models are more ragged at the edges, demonstrating just how hard it now is to hold the old centre, as so many rough but colourful beasts slouch towards Jerusalem.

Panel 4.9 Braj Kachru's circle model of World Englishes

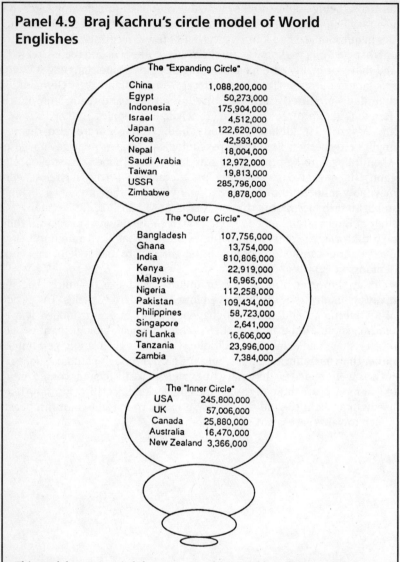

The "Expanding Circle"

China	1,088,200,000
Egypt	50,273,000
Indonesia	175,904,000
Israel	4,512,000
Japan	122,620,000
Korea	42,593,000
Nepal	18,004,000
Saudi Arabia	12,972,000
Taiwan	19,813,000
USSR	285,796,000
Zimbabwe	8,878,000

The "Outer Circle"

Bangladesh	107,756,000
Ghana	13,754,000
India	810,806,000
Kenya	22,919,000
Malaysia	16,965,000
Nigeria	112,258,000
Pakistan	109,434,000
Philippines	58,723,000
Singapore	2,641,000
Sri Lanka	16,606,000
Tanzania	23,996,000
Zambia	7,384,000

The "Inner Circle"

USA	245,800,000
UK	57,006,000
Canada	25,880,000
Australia	16,470,000
New Zealand	3,366,000

This model accompanied the paper 'Teaching World Englishes', in Kachru (ed.), *The Other Tongue* (2nd edn, University of Illinois Press, 1992). It has appeared in various forms in various publications, including *English Today* 16, October 1988, accompanying Kachru's article 'The sacred cows of English', in which the circles are presented in horizontal left-to-right succession, and in David Crystal, *The Cambridge Encyclopedia of the English Language* (Cambridge University Press, 1995, p. 107).

Panel 4.10 Manfred Görlach's circle model of English

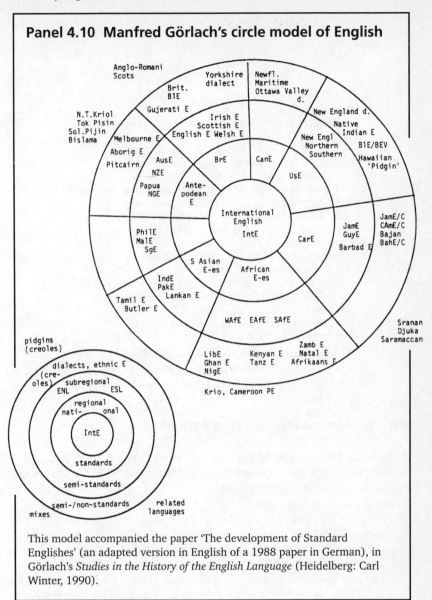

This model accompanied the paper 'The development of Standard
Englishes' (an adapted version in English of a 1988 paper in German), in
Görlach's *Studies in the History of the English Language* (Heidelberg: Carl
Winter, 1990).

5   Standardness

stand.ard (stan'dərd), *n*. **1.** something
considered by an authority or by general con-
sent as a basis of comparison. **2.** an object
regarded as the most common size or form of
its kind. **3.** a rule or principle that is used as a
basis for judgment. **4.** an average or normal
quality, quantity, or level: *The work isn't up to
his usual standard.* **5. standards**, the
morals, ethics, customs, etc., regarded generally or by an individual as acceptable. **6.** the
authorized exemplar of a unit of weight or
measure. **7.** a certain commodity in or by
which a basic monetary unit is stated: *gold
standard....* **12.** a flag indicating the presence
of a sovereign or public official. **13.** a flag or
emblematic figure used as a rallying point for
an army, fleet, etc....

(definition, *Random House Webster's College
Dictionary*, New York: 1991)

Flags and measures: *The king's standard*

In the year 1138, the English and the Scots met in battle at Cowton Moor
in Yorkshire. In the normal course of events, language had little impact on
war between these ancient enemies and war had little impact on
language, but the victory of the English at Cowton was an exception. Their
rallying point was unusual: a cluster of flags on a ship's mast mounted on
a carriage. When the contemporary observer Richard of Hexham later
wrote about this strange device, he quoted a couplet which called it a
'standard', because 'it was there that valour took its stand'. Both the device
and the name were so novel – and proved so effective – that the
encounter came to be called, not the Battle of Cowton, in the usual way of
things, but the Battle of the Standard.

Richard of Hexham has provided *The Oxford English Dictionary* with its
earliest citation of *standard*, in the process letting us know that in the
twelfth century the word was associated with Germanic *stand* ('be upright
in one place') and not Latin *extendere* ('to stretch out'), which the *OED*

gives as its proper source. But associating a battle flag with a place where soldiers 'stand hard' in the face of their enemies made eminent sense in the twelfth century. In immediate terms, *standard* was the Middle English version of Old French *estandard* and Medieval Latin *standardus*, but just as the ultimate link between *standard* and *extendere* was not self-evident to Hexham, so his association of *standard* and *stand* is not self-evident now. We do not see *stand* at work inside *standard* in the same way as *use* inside *useful* or *help* inside *helpless*, because *-ard* is not now a productive word element like *-ful* and *-less*.

In the years after Cowton, the battle flag of England came to be known as *the king's standard*, a phrase that by the fifteenth century had extended to more peaceful matters such as weights and measures guaranteed by the monarch himself. With this extension, *standard* was used attributively, a stage in its long evolution into an adjective as well as a noun: the *standard pound* and the *standard yard* were royal assets, to be kept where loyal subjects could check less secure weights and measures against them:

> The sayd Burgese schall haffe yᵉ standard... the qwhyche measures schuld agre with the kynges standard

> (ordinance, *c.*1450 *[OED]*).

This derivative non-military sense underlies such later usages as *an original standard* (one from which others derive and to which final appeal can be made), *a gold standard* (in which gold is a reservoir of value against which other forms of currency can be checked), *a standard atmosphere* (a unit of air pressure), and the *standard gauge* of a railway. In addition, the features 'uprightness, firmness, and centrality' (which are among the earliest attributes of *standard*) apply to such later referents as an upright pole used as a support, a tall candlestick, a fruit tree trained to grow upright, a principle of honesty and decorum, and a level of excellence or quality. In addition, many expressions of a technical and industrial nature contain *standard* used attributively, as in the following list (the first-citation dates in the *OED* providing the probable time of initial use):

a standard foot	measures	*c.*1650
standard silver	metals	*c.*1690
standard value	economics	*c.*1700
a standard pint	liquids	*c.*1825
a standard cell	electricity	*c.*1870
a standard candle	a unit of light	*c.*1880
a standard error	in statistics	*c.*1895
a standard cable	in telephony	*c.*1900

In the early eighteenth century *standard* began to be associated with literature and language, as for example where Henry Fulton (1709) wrote that 'Among the Romans, Horace is the Standard of Lyric, and Virgil of Epic Poetry', Anthony Ashley Cooper (1711) noted that the Greeks 'brought their beautiful and comprehensive Language to a just Standard', and Jonathan Swift (1712) observed that if English 'were once refined to a certain Standard, perhaps there might be Ways found to fix it forever'. By mid-century the association of *standard* with language was fully established, as illustrated by the English grammarian Joseph Priestley's comment: 'The English and the Scotch, had the kingdoms continued separate, might have been distinct languages, having two different standards of writing.' (For details on these and other such quotations, see panel 5.1.)

At this point, however, we need to ask: What criteria would be used to underpin the standard against which writing, print, and speech might be checked and marked 'good', 'bad', 'right', 'wrong', 'proper', 'improper'? A useful term now existed, but there had to be a tradition of sociolinguistic commentary, comparison, recommendation, cataloguing, and authority to which it could be applied. The above quotations, however, make clear where the tradition lay, Fulton for example referring to the Romans and Ashley Cooper to the Greeks. The classical tradition of Mediterranean Europe had already for centuries provided the insecure nations of the West with models of what a 'high' language should and could be.

High English: *The classical past*

The first primer of a Western language was written by the Greek scholar Dionysius Thrax in the second century BC, not in Europe but in Alexandria in Egypt, and its almost exclusive concern was what he called *he grammatiké tékhne* ('the art of writing', 'the grammatical craft'), the earliest name for the subject now called in English 'grammar'. Speech was not his concern, but the classical view that the spoken word can be judged in terms of the written word had its beginning in his work – a view which was immensely strong in eighteenth-century Britain and still has its advocates throughout the world, for English as for other languages.

The main spoken variety of Greek at the time of Dionysius was *hé koiné diálektos* ('the common language/dialect') spoken widely in the eastern Mediterranean and south-western Asia, and later used as the written language of the Gospels. The *koiné* interested neither such proto-grammarians as Dionysius nor the rhetoricians who, as teachers of oratory and persuasive style, did have a vested interest in speech. Generally, both grammarians and rhetoricians regarded the *koiné* as debased usage, and had instead as their ideal – the first prestigious model for a spoken Western language – the upper-class speech of Attica, the city-state of the Athenians. As a result, orators and compilers of guides to 'the best' Greek were called *Atticists*, and made their living teaching elocution and style to both prosperous but insecure non-Attic Greeks and aspiring Hellenized Asians, Europeans, and North Africans. This basic pattern has been sustained in Western languages ever since, including among the *orthoepists* ('right speakers': that is, elocutionists) of the British Isles in the eighteenth century and in many ESL and EFL settings around the world today, where 'the best' model of English pronunciation – Jonesian RP or 'BBC English' – has been a widely desired commodity for most of this century.

Roman orators and tutors in the first century BC imitated both the Atticists in their speech and style and Dionysius Thrax in matters of writing and grammar, treating the Latin of senatorial Rome as equivalent to Attic Greek. As with the Greeks, *atticismi* were well-turned phrases and refined expressions, which were appreciated – as atticisms – in the self-consciously polished high English of the eighteenth century. With regard to Roman attitudes to good style and usage, embodied for example in Cicero's *De oratore* ('On the public speaker'), the British classicist Roland Mayer has noted:

> [For Cicero] the foundation of good style is pure, clear Latin. Now in this he hardly differed at all from what had been said in an anonymous treatise, composed earlier in the first century [BC], and now entitled *Ad Herennium*. The author of that work... declared that the first requirement was *elegantia* 'correct choice', and that the first prerequisite for achieving this was *Latinitas* (*Ad Herennium* iv.17). This he defined, following a Greek model for pure usage known as *hellenismos*, as simply the avoidance of *solecism* (faulty grammar) and *barbarism* (mistaken word formation).

> ('Metropolitan Latin', in *English Today* 50, April 1997, p. 11)

According to Mayer, Cicero divided Latin into three kinds, in descending order of quality and prestige (a model later adopted by the grammarian and stylist Quintilian). These three were *urbanitas* 'city usage', *rusticitas* 'country usage', and *peregrinitas*, 'foreign usage'. Urbane Latin was spoken and written by the patrician class and others in Rome who shared their values, skills, and upbringing (*not* by ordinary city people); rustic forms were honoured by the patricians because they recalled to the urbane mind the virtues of the early Republic, but were otherwise not quite the thing; and outlandish Latin – although it must be endured throughout the Empire – was to be deplored. Much the same three-fold typology has been notable in the empires of the West generally and the British Empire in particular, whose major period of expansion was the eighteenth century. Quite simply, in London as in Rome, the élite spoke well, the masses by no means so well, and foreigners ('barbarians, babblers') could hardly be expected to get anything right – perhaps indeed shouldn't get it right.

In the Rome-centred Christendom which followed the decline of the Western Empire, Latin as used by the orators and grammarians continued to be the gold against which base vernacular coin could be judged (and variously found wanting). But in the centuries immediately after the fall of the Empire, spoken and written ecclesiastical Latin, while still revered, grew less stylistically influential, the urbane and secular élite declined and disappeared, the clerical community became too large, too linguistically varied, and often too ignorant to sustain the tradition, and influences from the emerging vernaculars and *their* élites were too strong. From the earlier Middle Ages onward, most users of Latin as an international language spoke Italo-Latin, Hispano-Latin, Franco-Latin, and Anglo-Latin with the accents of their mother tongues, and often did not understand one another. The one Renaissance scholar who tried hardest to unify spoken Latin in the sixteenth century was Dutch, Desiderius Erasmus of Rotterdam, who like his present-day compatriots had a serious stake in successful transnational communication.

In 1528, he published his *De recta Latini Graecique sermonis pronuntia- tione* ('On the Correct Pronunciation of Latin and Greek Speech'), which discussed the often mutually unintelligible national accents of Latin that led to confusion, amusement, and often derision at international European gatherings: again, not unlike some encounters today in interna- tional English. Erasmus proposed that pronunciations be based on certain assumptions about how Latin was pronounced in classical times: for example, using 'hard' *c* and *g* in words like *census* and *gens* and insisting on contrasted vowel values, as in the long *o* of *nobilis* and the short *o* of *bonus*. When the Erasmian model of Latin was adopted at Cambridge University by such young radicals as John Cheke and Thomas Smith it met with great resistance, including a university edict in 1542 which forbade this would- be standardizing usage altogether, the penalties including beatings for students and expulsion for masters. According to Stephen Gardiner, the Chancellor who imposed the edict, speakers of Erasmian Latin were unin- telligible to their elders; that is, they did not speak Anglo-Latin.

The Cambridge edict was repealed in 1558, but no internationally agreed pronunciation for 'modern' Latin ever emerged. Instead, use of the language slowly declined and newly confident national vernaculars began to compete to take its place. Foremost among them was French, buttressed in the seventeenth century by a stable monarchy and a unified nation- state. The disunited Italians created the first academy of language in 1582, but Richelieu's Académie française in 1634 gave a boost not only to French as a national and international medium but to the concept of *le bon français* ('good French'), defined as three-fold: speaking like a courtier, writing like 'the best writers' (who in their turn followed the 'best' classi- cal writers), and following the guidance of forty contemporary *académi- ciens* regarded as being in a cultural sense 'immortal'.

In the new Europe, some vernaculars gained and some lost. In France, the northern tongue (in medieval times called *la langue d'oïl*, 'the language of *oïl* [*oui*], because its word for 'yes' came from Latin *ille*, 'that') triumphed over the southern tongue (*la langue d'oc*, 'the language of *oc*', because its word for 'yes' came from Latin *hoc*, 'this'). The Occitan or

Provençal tongue, despite being the language of the troubadours and significant in the Western Mediterranean, dwindled to the status of a *patois* ('rustic speech'), no longer deemed worthy of the name 'language', which properly applied only to the northern tongue, whose urbane and courtly acrolect was singled out as 'good'.

In Britain, the courtly, literary, and Chancery (administrative) level of the East Midland dialect gained a similar ascendancy: first, in England from the fifteenth century; next, in Wales, Scotland, and Ireland from the sixteenth century, then throughout the wider diaspora of English from the seventeenth century. The spoken form of this new 'good English' evolved by the end of the nineteenth century into what Daniel Jones in 1917 called 'Public School Pronunciation', and in 1925 'Received Pronunciation' (RP), and in terms of pronunciation, grammar, and usage into 'Received Standard (English)', Henry Cecil Wyld's term at the same time. Events and processes of this kind, which led in Western Europe to the prominence and spread of the 'high' varieties of particular languages, can be broadly described in terms of the six categories politics, communication, literature, religion, technology, and industrialization:

1 *Politics: the rise of the nation-state*
   Some regions, in which people spoke the same or similar languages, developed a sense of unity which did not extend to politics, as for example speakers of forms of Italian (whose lands were not unified until the nineteenth century). Others developed cultural-cum-political unity much earlier and at much the same time, as for example France and England, whose emergence as kingdoms took place during the later Middle Ages (*c.*1100–1500). By and large, whatever the degree of unity in a territory, 'high' forms of certain languages were fostered in particular cities (often national or regional capitals) and courts (imperial, royal, or ducal), with literary styles that owed much to Latin and to Greek through Latin. Political unification entailed administrative centralization which strengthened the usage of court and capital in, for example, Paris, Madrid, and London (with its scholarly satellites Oxford and Cambridge). In tandem, merchants and professionals in self-governing towns absorbed elements of metropolitan and courtly usage – often despite their own dialect loyalties and their resentment at being disdained as 'provincial'.

2 *Communication: the heritage of Latin*
   Especially during the Renaissance, the 'downward' flow of very high Greco-Latin usages into the higher forms of many vernaculars made them increasingly effective symbols of status and vehicles of learning, conferring on them a Latin-like prestige and even sound. Such acrolects had as a common reservoir the entire Greco-Latin complex, so that those who knew Latin could continue to use its vocabulary, with suitable

adjustments, in their mother tongues, and others could catch up to some degree with the help of what in English have been called 'hard-word dictionaries'. Classicized vernaculars like these probably sounded to the unlearned as incomprehensible and intimidating as Latin itself – much as an Anglo-hybrid may sound to many people in some parts of the world today. In terms of French, a Romance language, the influx of Greco-Latin was a *re-Latinization*, while for English, a Germanic language, it was a more radical and straightforward *Latinization*. Some commentators from the sixteenth century onward have spoken out against this development, favouring a return to 'Saxon English' and/or the use of 'plain English', in which classical adoptions are not too blatant.

3 *Literature: the growth of vernacular genres*
New literatures developed in Italian, Spanish, French, German, English, and other vernaculars which were all indebted to Latin-cum-Greek for their genres, formulas, symbols, allusions, and styles, although some distinctly new forms developed, such as the *sonnet* and the *novel* (whose very name means 'new'). These literatures had the advantage over their classical precursors of being read and discussed, especially after the invention of print, by far more people than had ever encountered Cicero and Virgil in the original. In addition, writers exploited not only the stories, themes, and motifs of the classical and biblical past but also distinctive material that had grown up (originally in oral form) in their own lands, such as *the Matter of Britain* (legends of King Arthur, the Round Table, and the Holy Grail) and *the Matter of France* (legends of Charlemagne and Roland), creating and confirming a distinctive new Western European culture with its own high languages, styles and broadly agreed canons, to match the works of Virgil and the other great ancients.

4 *Religion: the translation of the Bible*
The questioning of the authority of the Pope and the Roman Catholic Church before, during, and after the Reformation served, among other things, to weaken the hold of Latin on Western Christendom. In northern Europe in particular, the idea that the Bible could only be couched in one sacralized language ceased to be acceptable to a new bourgeoisie chafing to read it in their own mother tongue. When scripture was translated directly from Hebrew and Greek – despite institutional resistance and by-passing Latin altogether – the new medium became itself sacralized and privileged like Latin before it. Thus, Luther's translation profoundly affected German and versions of the Bible in English (especially the Authorized Version of King James in 1611) had a vast influence on English. This translation had a great impact not only on language in England but also on Scots, the vernacular in which James I of England had been raised as James VI King of Scots.

5 *Technology: the invention of movable type*
The exploitation of the printing press, beginning in the Rhine valley in the mid-fifteenth century, led to standardized sets of metal type, uniform book formats and page sizes, as well as regular orthographies for the major vernaculars. The operators of the presses gradually acquired more influence over scriptural, literary, legal, administrative, official, and educational usage (both Latin and vernacular) than classical and medieval scribes ever had over their lettering, manuscripts, and codices. As regards English, William Caxton and his successors (though often anxious about their grammatical usage and orthographic conventions) inherited a relatively stable *script standard* used for decades by among others the clerks of the Chancery in London, for writing official documents. They made the conventions of such script more stable still, laying the foundation of what became five centuries later the markedly homogeneous international *print standard* of English. Compared with that standard, Caxton's seminal work now looks archaic and chaotic.

6 *Industrialization: standard processes and products*
The printing press, which antedated the Industrial Revolution by some three hundred years, was nonetheless a prototype of mechanized mass production. The preparation of text, paper, and ink, the processes of printing and binding, and the stacking and delivery of finished books and pamphlets, etc., was facilitated by the increasingly proficient use of fixed shapes and sizes of materials. As a result language came to be regarded as something which – like metal type – might be 'fixed'. By the time the industrial age was worldwide, in the 1890s, the term *standardization* had been coined to describe a wide range of social, cultural, technical, industrial, and linguistic processes. Print-based standardization was indeed regarded as so beneficial that a language 'fixed' in this way has become for many the only real kind of language, and the only kind to be used in schools. People may talk about a standard language as being both spoken and written, but it is hard to conceive of a language in our time as truly having a standard form if it cannot be printed with all the panoply of modern technology.

From the sixteenth century onward, as far as English was concerned, political unification and other developments meant that the populations of the British-Irish archipelago could use some form of English, either on its own or alongside other languages which had become wholly subordinate to it: Gaelic in Scotland, Ireland, and the Isle of Man, Welsh in Wales, Cornish in Cornwall, and French in the Channel Islands. In addition, Scots (formerly the court language of a Scotland unlinked with England, with its own literature and dialects) became part of 'the rest of English', sharing the same fate as Occitan in France.

High English: *The best and the rest*

In 1775, William Perry's *The Royal Standard English Dictionary* was published in Edinburgh. It is impossible to know now whether Perry meant his
title to be read as (The ((Royal)(Standard English)(Dictionary))), how
people today would interpret it, or (The ((Royal Standard)(English
Dictionary))), how someone aware only of the king's standard might
divide it up. Perry, who was a noted lexicographer in his day but is now
hardly remembered, sought (as did most dictionary compilers of the
period) a uniform and unifying vocabulary for all educated British people
wherever they might be – including America. The date of his book –
which contains the earliest use of the phrase *Standard English* known to
me – is sixty-one years earlier than the first citation for the phrase in the
OED, also from Edinburgh and dated 1836. It runs in part:

> Southern or standard English, which in the fourteenth century was
> perhaps best spoken in Kent and Surrey by the body of the inhabitants.

> (*The Quarterly Review*, anonymous, Edinburgh, February.
> [See panel 5.1 for full citation])

The phrase *Standard English* may by that date have been known to
many scholars, journalists, and teachers, but it does not appear to have
been widely used. Richard W. Bailey of the University of Michigan draws
attention to the same citation, quoting in addition from an earlier statement in the same text:

> Within the English pale the matter is sufficiently clear; all agree in calling
> our standard form of speech the English language, and all provincial
> deviations from it – at least all that assume a distinct specific character –
> dialects.

Bailey then observes:

> This characterization encapsulated what was to become modern
> wisdom in defining three varieties of English: *dialects* with 'a distinct
> specific character'; other forms of speech unnamed which lack such
> 'character' and are not standard; and *our* 'standard form of speech' that
> alone merits the name of 'the English language.'

> (Bailey, *Images of English*, Cambridge University Press, 1991, p. 4)

The characterization certainly encapsulates one kind of modern wisdom, which co-exists uneasily with that other, more recent wisdom in
which dialects do not lurk uncouthly beyond the pale but have as much
intrinsic value as the standard – also regarded as a dialect (however elevated and specialized). But it does seem clear that for the unknown writer
in 1836, and many who have agreed with him, the dialects are not English
at all, or *shouldn't* be, a state of affairs which has left them (and their
speakers) in a cultural and linguistic limbo, one solution for which was to

take shelter within the pale as quickly as was educationally and socially possible.

As Bailey indicates, since at least the eighteenth century there has been a tendency to regard the minority usage of upper- and middle-class life, education, publishing, law, administration, and government as more proper, polite, legitimate, and *real* than anything used by other English-speakers, whoever and wherever they might be. This minority has included academic and professional writers about English, whose books – especially if concerned with grammar and teaching – have tended to discuss only the standard (and failures to achieve or sustain it), often without making it explicit that they have limited their range in this way. Such books have also seldom in recent times indicated that the standard is used comfortably only by the minority to which the writer necessarily belongs while the reader may or may not. In the eighteenth century, such authorities as Samuel Johnson made it abundantly clear that they were not concerned with the shaky, shifting, unschooled language of the masses but only with 'good English', on the strict analogy of *le bon français*.

By the mid-twentieth century, the concept of Standard English had become so much a part of established social and education systems that sustaining Johnson's elegant but brutal frankness hardly seemed necessary. Yet well-founded, liberal works which cover only the standard language have still tended to endorse the viewpoint of the anonymous 1836 writer. Thus, one of the most influential British grammatical works in recent years, *A Comprehensive Grammar of the English Language* (Harlow: Longman, 1985), by Randolph Quirk, Sidney Greenbaum, Geoffrey Leech, and Jan Svartvik – 1,779 pages in length – does not (and was not intended to) cover the syntax and morphology of all English, yet it is called neither *A Comprehensive Grammar of the <u>Standard</u> English Language* nor, more simply, *A Comprehensive Grammar of Standard English*, which is what it is (at least for the British variety).

The titles and often the content of such works demonstrate how English has been perceived and discussed by scholars, teachers, and others since the eighteenth century, and it is this 'duplicity' which Bailey highlights in his study – and regrets. Such works have tended to operate two fuzzily incompatible models side by side: one in which 'English' subsumes a standard and a range of dialects, the other in which only Standard English is English, the dialects being manifestly beyond the social and educational pale. In recent years, as I suggested above, a third model has joined the mix: English perceived as a group of dialects, one of which, the 'standard dialect', operates as first among equals. Here, the other dialects are seen as good in themselves, but are only discussable in the standard, which has evolved for just such purposes – the only variety tailored for print. Yet it would be strange indeed if things were otherwise, given the history of language, print, and education. The two older models remain entrenched, while the third seems sustained in the main by scholars and teachers who do not wish to impugn the usage of students and others not raised in upper- and middle-class homes, or in working-class homes with middle-class aspirations. And this, it seems to me, is as true for North America as for the British and Irish islands, Australasia, and elsewhere.

The *OED* provides eleven citations of the attributive or adjectival use of *standard* (as in *standard language*), three for the nineteenth century and eight for the twentieth. (See panel 5.1.) This is a slender list, considering the importance of this sense of the term, and we may be able to draw some conclusions from it. The term appears to have either been rare throughout the century or most remarkably overlooked by the dictionary's citation-finders. As a result, the *OED* editor in question, Henry Bradley – working on the section 'St' from 1914 to 1919 – had to draw first on one of the project's own early papers (cited anonymously, but written by Richard Chenevix Trench, the initiator of the project) then on an article by the chief editor, James Murray, *to provide two of the three citations that cover the entire century*. Even for that part of the twentieth century when Bradley was defining the word there are only three citations, all technical and by trail-blazers. (To check in 1997 for occurrences throughout the nineteenth century, Donald MacQueen of Uppsala University in Sweden and I searched the entire CD-Rom corpus of the *Times* of London for that period and did not find a single use of the phrase *standard English*.) From the above observations (which are suggestive rather than conclusive), it seems likely that the use of both *standard* in linguistic contexts and *standard English* in any context, though begun in the eighteenth century, became significant only in the twentieth. (See panel 5.1, especially the entries '1859' and '1869'.)

An assured standard: *The King's English*

There has long been a close link (implicitly or explicitly) between two expressions widely used for decades: *a standard language* (whose norms and conventions closely relate to those of education, print, officialdom, and high culture) and *a language standard* (a level below which the use of a language should not fall). Both usages, it seems likely, are linked with senses of *standard* which developed during the Industrial Revolution. The attributive use presupposes a regular item available for general use (*standard-issue equipment, a standard insurance policy*), while the nominal usage suggests that certain levels of quality and ability are to be praised (*a high standard*) or deplored (*a low standard*). The phrase *Standard/standard English* could – should? – therefore mean the broad norm available to everyone who goes to school for a sufficient number of years, and whose general level of performance should not then for any reason fall below a certain point.

The phrase has traditionally been widely associated with *the King's/Queen's English*, used originally for the language of the royal court (as for example by Thomas Wilson in *The Arte of Rhetorique*, 1553) and in the heyday of Empire to denote the best possible English. Indeed, *the King's English* and *the Queen's English* may have served so well for so long that they inhibited the use of *Standard English*. In 1906, for example, Oxford University Press published *The King's English*, by Henry W. and Francis G. Fowler, a work which continues in print to this day. No one apparently thought of calling it *Standard English*, although the term was in increasing use at the time. The current edition, the third, has been unrevised since it appeared in 1931, has been available as a paperback since 1973, and still has on its cover the uncompromising subtitle 'The essential guide to written English'.

In the preface to the third edition, Henry, the surviving brother in 1931, expressed joy that the book was still in print after a quarter of a century; one wonders how he would have felt about its unchanged status sixty-something years later. The book has played a considerable part in keeping the phrase *the King's English* alive during a long period in which *the Queen's English* has been appropriate (as in Victoria's time), but at the end of the century both phrases seem anachronistic. In the meantime, among British subjects, some Commonwealth nations, and that majority of Anglophones over whom neither king nor queen holds sway, there is no consensus about the interplay of standard language and language standards. Rather, there appear to be five kinds of response strung out on a sociolinguistic continuum:

1 *The authoritarian response*

   People with a traditionalist, conservative, and broadly prescriptive approach treat the concepts *standard language* and *language standard* as two sides of the same coin. For them, the standard is self-evidently the highest and best form of the language, set culturally and aesthetically above all dialects, pidgins, creoles, and kinds of slang and in-group usage. Indeed, for them it *is* the language, the only form which an educational system can adopt and to which sensible people will aspire.

2 *The libertarian response*

   People with a liberal approach do not usually tie standard language and language standards so tightly together. Although the standard serves important social ends, it is not in their view higher or better than other varieties. Some, aware that the standard derives from a particular dialect, may argue that it is itself a dialect, and for them the phrase *standard dialect* is not an oxymoron. A language standard, on the other hand, relates to how people use language. On the whole, libertarians appear to favour a high standard in Standard English, but are likely to be less critical of those who fall short – especially if they consider that the rules deemed to be broken are old-fashioned and obscure (such as not splitting infinitives).

3 *The egalitarian response*
People with socialist (and anarchist) views tend to regard standard languages and language standards as ideologically and ethically suspect, concepts that have helped a socioeconomic élite control the masses, devalue their usage, and limit their capacity for self-expression. Many would prefer a thousand linguistic flowers to bloom rather than suffer the diktat of a class primarily concerned with protecting its own blossoms. In their own speech, egalitarians may or may not apply norms, but in writing and print they generally do, either by choice or because their publishers and readers expect it of them and their subeditors impose it on them.

4 *The uncertain response*
Many people – not authoritarian, libertarian, egalitarian, or anything else with much consistency – are often uneasy about standard language, language standards, accents, dialects, 'bad English', and the like. Many therefore worry about the relationship between the standard of their schooldays and the variety with which they have grown up. Publishers often have in mind such people – the 'linguistically insecure' – when commissioning, publishing, and promoting dictionaries, grammars, and guides about good English, public speaking, and effective writing, and the market for such aids is buoyant.

5 *The eclectic response*
Some people – many language professionals among them – adopt a stance that one might call 'principled eclecticism': they are authoritarian, libertarian, or egalitarian, etc., depending on need and situation. Because no one can know all the niceties and nuances, especially in a language with a global reach, they would argue that everybody is at times uncertain and insecure, needs help from dictionaries, style guides, usage mentors, etc., and can benefit from guidance in how best to interpret and act on available help. For them, the standard language is an essential, often admirable social artifact, but not necessarily the pillar without which the temple would fall.

For people of all dispositions, however, those aspects of language labelled *dialect, accent, patois, creole, colloquialism, jargon, cant, slang* and *hybrid* lie out beyond the standard. The delineation and definition of these aspects have never been easy, and so it is understandable that most of the people who think about such things set them to one side, as 'the rest'. As a result, Standard English is at the centre or the summit, a location acknowledged even when someone does not wish to lend credence to dismissive and often hostile judgements about dialect and creole speakers, strangers with funny accents, colloquial usage, and the slang of subgroups.

Commentators, both professional and lay, have tended for decades to lump 'the rest of English' together under the headings *nonstandard, substandard,* or *deviant.* Of these, *nonstandard* is usually (but not always) neutral, *substandard* almost invariably pejorative and negative (even when its users deny that it is), while *deviant* has been used in linguistics for decades as if it were a neutral, objective, and inoffensive term, unaffected by such phrases as *deviant behaviour* and *a social deviant.* In my own experience, this term is by no means neutral, objective, or inoffensive; rather, it is the most socially loaded of the three.

Perceptions of Standard English: *Social and geographical criteria*

Because of its long association with schools and learning, Standard English is widely perceived, and often defined, as the speech and writing of 'educated' people – despite the difficulty of deciding what *educated* means and how it is intended. In addition, in Britain, certain social and geographical criteria (all of them influential around the world) have been applied (some for over a century, some from more recent times) to the question of who *really* uses the standard language, and by and large these criteria can be linked with four groups of people similar to those just described (whose equivalents can be found in most other territories where English is significant):

1 *The strong traditionalists*
   For this diminishing UK group, the 'well-educated' and 'well-spoken' belong to the upper and middle classes of south-eastern England and their equivalents elsewhere at home and abroad. Many have attended those private British boarding schools known as 'public schools', and some have been to Oxford, Cambridge, or another of the more prestigious British universities. For this group, *Standard English, the King's/ Queen's English, BBC English,* and *Oxford English* have generally been taken to refer to the same thing: the speech of the well-educated and well-spoken. *Standard English* therefore necessarily includes *Received Pronunciation* (*RP*), the originally upper-class accent so named by Daniel Jones in his *English Pronouncing Dictionary* (Dent, 1925 edition), the name he gave this accent in the first edition (1917) being *Public School Pronunciation* (*PSP*). For some more assertive people in this group, Americans and other non-British Anglophones do not really speak the same language – or speak the same language but not properly. Strong traditionalists in the US have less to say on the 'best' accent

than their UK equivalents, by and large do not associate their standard with a particular region and/or class, may or may not admire upper-class British speech styles, and may or may not accept the precedence of British English – but they can be as vigorous in the defence of 'good' usage and against declining standards as any Brit. (For further material on the use of the term 'Standard' in relation to British and American English, see panel 5.2.)

2 *The mild traditionalists*

For this larger UK group, the 'well-educated' – but not necessarily the 'well-spoken' – are a pan-national rather than a regionally focused community, are generally middle- and upper-class, have been brought up anywhere in the UK (and some other parts of the world), and are not necessarily the products of public schools and/or ancient universities. But whatever their origins and education, the majority have made com-promises between local varieties of English and RP. In Wyldian terms, they use either the Received or the Modified Standard. The influence of the public-school tradition has been so pervasive throughout Britain and Ireland that many traditionalists, strong or mild (and language professionals as well as lay people), have tended to regard RP as 'accentless' speech. In this sense, an *accent* is not a quality of speech possessed by every human being (the view of phoneticians), but a vocal pattern which differs markedly from that of self-evidently 'well-spoken' people (a social judgement).

Many academics, publishers, and language teachers have in recent decades argued that RP is the best pronunciation model *not* because it is élitist and class-related but because it is the only truly non- or supra-regional accent of English in existence. Such people may themselves be from south-eastern England, are less commonly from elsewhere in the UK, are seldom North American, and have the support of many older non-Anglophones trained to teach 'British English'. However, most Britons and many others (ENL, ESL, and EFL) do not have RP accents and are aware that RP is neither non-regional nor supra-regional, and has long been the auditory icon of the middle- and upper-classes of the Home Counties, royalty, the public schools, and the Conservative party. Even so, many British EFL specialists have advocated RP as a model for all the world's English learners regardless of origin, phonological back-ground, and indeed class politics, on the grounds *not* that it is an élite minority accent but that it is simply the best-described and longest-established model – regardless of how and why this came to be so and of the fact that it has for decades been undergoing change in its place of origin.

However, mild traditionalists elsewhere, the US included, often have a considerable respect for the British Received Standard, and have in mind comparable usage in their own territories when they reflect on what 'Standard English' means to them. In the US, the standard includes most if not all avowedly educated regional accents and usage, as well as – for teaching purposes – an accent loosely referred to (amid scholarly controversy) as both *General American* and *Network Standard,* the presumed usage of radio and television newscasters, etc. Elsewhere in the world, for the milder traditionalists the usage of educated people generally relates to the print standard and perhaps the speech of newscasters, and may include accents, as in Australia, New Zealand, and South Africa, sometimes described by phoneticians as *Near-RP.*

3 The progressives

For this UK group, which has grown greatly in numbers in the last quarter century, the 'educated' (generally not classified as either 'well-educated' or 'well-spoken') include a more or less middle-class range throughout the English-speaking world – essentially those who have completed their secondary-school education, may have gone on to college/university, and manage the language competently in their everyday life (however 'competently' may be defined). The upper classes do not usually enter into the discussion (being implicitly included) nor do the public schools, numbers of whose pupils and younger ex-pupils have in recent years adapted their speech and social style 'downwards' towards more demotic London-area norms. These include an accent-cum-style of the early 1980s identified by the phonetician David Rosewarne as 'Estuary English', often broadly described as a compromise between RP and Cockney.

Many non-traditionalists do not have or expect others to have RP or near-RP accents, and by and large dissociate standard from accent. They appear to assume that individuals like themselves, with accents of divers backgrounds, are generally mutually intelligible, or if not can fairly quickly acclimatize to one other. Many academics and ENL teachers belong in this group and may be condemned by strong traditionalists as permissive radicals mischievously willing to put the integrity of the language at risk while asserting that traditionalists are the enemies of rational discussion. The applied linguist Peter Strevens represents the liberal-progressive scholarly point of view in the following passage:

> [The term] 'Standard English' is potentially misleading for at least two reasons. First, in order to be self-explanatory, it really ought to be called 'the grammar and the core vocabulary of educated usage in English'. That would make plain the fact that it is not the whole of English, and above all it is not pronunciation that can be in any way labelled 'Standard', but only one part of English, its grammar and vocabulary.
>
> ('Standards and the Standard Language', *English Today* 2, April 1985, p. 5)

4 *The uncertain*

Many people in the UK and elsewhere are neither traditional nor progressive with regard to language, but move around on a continuum more or less shaped by the views of the above three groups. Such people may sometimes be regional in their judgements, sometimes national, and sometimes – comfortably, indifferently, or grudgingly – cosmopolitan. However, although they do not have a clear-cut sense of who the well-educated (and well-spoken) are, they often have firm views on the *ill*-educated and *ill*-spoken. Some dialects and accents, typically of working-class city dwellers from London to Glasgow to Belfast to New York, etc., are often singled out for special opprobrium. Even so, however, the general (and apparently increasing) view in the 1990s throughout the Anglophone world, appears to be 'live and let live'.

This said, however, it also seems to be true that the farther people move from a region-bound position (pre-eminently in the UK, but also in the US and elsewhere), the more they are willing to accept variation in accent, tone, rhythm, pronunciation, grammar, spelling, punctuation, vocabulary, and even culture. Indeed, when they become less focused on such ancient touchstones as capital city, metropolitan region, nation-state, high social class, and college education, they are often carried willy-nilly towards *multiculturalism* – a term and concept that has for some years been controversial, especially in the US and Australia. Whereas for progressives *multiculturalism* describes a condition which is on the whole inevitable and even desirable, for many traditionalists it can be a fiercely pejorative label for a wide but hazy range of social, cultural, and ethnic developments which they regard as threatening to their way of life and social values.

The discomfort of having one's linguistic security challenged can prompt nostalgia for a lost golden age, when Standard English *really was* standard and language standards *really did* mean something honest, good, true, and broadly measurable. But no matter where one looks for such a time and place it cannot be found. The nature and use of Standard English (whether in terms of accent, enunciation, spelling, grammar, or composition and style) have been contentious for longer than the phrase itself has existed. And in a world where English at large is increasingly perceived as 'Englishes' and even 'English languages', discussions about the nature, usefulness, and intrinsic worth of that crucial entity, the national-cum-international standard language, are likely to become more contentious and emotional still.

Panel 5.1 A selection of eighteenth- to twentieth-century citations for the linguistic use of *standard* and for *Standard English*

There are 44 citations below, 11 of which are the relevant listings in the *OED*, Second Edition, 1989 (and are so indicated). Many scholars, especially in the twentieth century, have sought to describe standard language, and most of the citations are from their works. The longer citations generally indicate how traditional approaches and assumptions have continued alongside, and mixed with, a broadly liberalizing and internationalizing trend, and indicate in particular diverse approaches to defining the phrase *Standard English*.

1709: UK (English), OED citation
Henry Felton
> Among the Romans, Horace is the Standard of Lyric, and Virgil of Epic Poetry.
>
> (*A Dissertation on Reading the Classics, and Forming a Just Style*)

1711: UK (English), OED citation
Anthony Ashley Cooper, 3rd Earl of Shaftesbury
> 'Twas thus they [the Greeks] brought their beautiful and comprehensive Language to a just Standard... The Standard was in the same proportion carry'd into other Arts.
>
> (*Characteristicks of Men, Manners, Opinions, Times*, III, p. 138)

1712: UK (Anglo-Irish)
Jonathan Swift
> But the English Tongue is not arrived to such a Degree of Perfection, as to make us apprehend any Thoughts of its Decay; and if it were once refined to a certain Standard, perhaps there might be Ways found to fix it for ever.
>
> (*A Proposal for Correcting, Improving and Ascertaining the English Tongue*)

1754: UK (English)
Philip Dormer Stanhope (Lord Chesterfield)
> I had long lamented that we had no lawful standard of our language set up, for those to repair to, who might chuse to speak and write it grammatically and correctly... I cannot help thinking it a sort of disgrace to our nation, that hitherto we have had no such standard of our language.
>
> (Letter to *The World*, 28 November)

1762: UK (English)
Joseph Priestley
> The English and the Scotch, had the kingdoms continued separate, might have been distinct languages, having two different standards of writing.
>
> (*Theory of Language and Universal Grammar*, p. 129)

1763: UK (Scottish)
Alexander Donaldson

An Universal Dictionary of the English Language. In which The Terms made use of in Arts and Sciences are defined; The Words explained in their Various Senses; The Accents properly placed, to facilitate the true Pronunciation; The Parts of Speech denoted; and, The Spelling throughout reduced to an uniform and consistent standard... Edinburgh: Printed by Alexander Donaldson and John Reid.

(title)

1764: UK (Scottish)
James Buchanan

An Essay towards Establishing a Standard for an Elegant and Uniform Pronunciation of the English Language throughout the British Dominions as Practised by the Most Learned and Polite Speakers. By James Buchanan. London. Printed for E. & C. Dilly.

(title)

1775: UK (Scottish)
William Perry

The Royal Standard English Dictionary... By W[illiam] Perry. Edinburgh: Printed for the author, by David Willison; and sold by J. Wilkie, T. Evans, and J. Murray, London; J. Bell, W. Creech, J. Dickson, C. Elliott, R. Jamieson, Edinburgh; Charnley, Newcastle; Etherington, York; Norton, Bristol; Frederick, Bath; and by the Author. MDCCLXXV.

(title)

1788: UK (Scottish)
James Beattie

The language... of the most learned and polite persons in London, and the neighbouring Universities of Oxford and Cambridge, ought to be accounted the standard of the English tongue, especially in accent and pronunciation.

(*The Theory of Language*, no. 88 in the series *English Linguistics 1500–1800*, ed. R. C. Alston (Menston: Scolar, 1968), p. 92)

1799: UK (English)
James Adams

Refined English is neither the received standard of that country [Scotland], and its most eminent scholars designedly retain the variation; retain it with dignity, subject to no real diminution of personal or national merit.

(*The Pronunciation of the English Language,* no. 72 in the series *English Linguistics 1500–1800*, ed. R. C. Alston (Menston: Scolar, 1968), p. 158)

1808: UK (English)
Anonymous

The common speech of the United States has departed very considerably from the standard adopted in England.

(review of John Marshall's *Life of Washington*, in *The British Critic*, April)

1816: US
John Pickering
[American usage] has in so many instances departed from the English standard, that our scholars should lose no time in endeavouring to restore it to its purity, and to prevent further corruption.

(*A Vocabulary, or Collection of Words and Phrases which have been supposed to be Peculiar to the United States of America.* Introduction reproduced in M. M. Matthews (ed.), *The Beginnings of American English*, Chicago, 1931)

1836a: UK, OED citation
Anonymous
It is, however, certain that there were in his [Higden's] time, and probably long before, five distinctly marked forms, which may be classed as follows: – 1. Southern or standard English, which in the fourteenth century was perhaps best spoken in Kent and Surrey by the body of the inhabitants.

(*The Quarterly Review*, Edinburgh, February, 1836, p. 356, writer not named.)

1836b: UK (English)
B. H. Smart
The common standard dialect is that in which all marks of a particular place of birth and residence are lost and nothing appears to indicate any other habits of intercourse than with the well-bred and well-informed, wherever they may be found... It may be that a person cannot altogether reach this standard; but if he reach it very nearly, all the object of a complete uniformity may be gained. A person needs not blush because he cannot help betraying that he is a Scotchman or an Irishman; but it may nevertheless be an object of ambition to prove that his circle of intercourse has extended much beyond his native place.

(*Walker Remodelled: A New Critical Pronouncing Dictionary*, London)

1846: US
Joseph Worcester
[Johnson's] dictionary, from the time of its first publication, has been far more than any other, regarded as a standard for the language.

(preface, *A Universal and Critical Dictionary of the English Language*, Boston)

1859: UK (English), OED citation
Richard Chenevix Trench
As soon as a standard language has been formed, which in England was the case after the Reformation, the lexicographer is bound to deal with that alone.

(*A Proposal for the Publication of a New English Dictionary by the Philological Society*, London)

1869: UK (English)
Alexander J. Ellis

[T]here prevailed, and apparently still prevails, a belief that it is possible
to erect a standard of pronunciation which should be followed
throughout the countries where English is spoken as a native tongue,
and that in fact that standard already exists, and is the norm
unconsciously followed by persons who, by rank or education, have
most right to establish the custom of speech.

(*On Early English Pronunciation*, London:
Early English Text Society)

1878: UK (Scottish), OED citation
James A. H. Murray

Chaucer's language is well known to be more southern than standard
English eventually became.

(article in the 8th edition of the *Encyclopaedia Britannica*.
[Murray was the chief editor of the *OED*.])

1907: UK (English)
Henry Cecil Wyld

(1) The difference of spelling in 'cord/gnawed,' of course, shows us that
at one time these words were not pronounced alike; indeed, provincial
and old-fashioned speakers still make a difference between them, but
the majority of speakers of Standard English at the present day do
pronounce them alike.

(2) It is believed that from these two great types of speech – that
of London, the centre of Law, Government, and Commerce, and
that of Oxford, the centre of learning and culture – the Standard
English which we all write, and which we all try, at any rate, to
speak, has grown up.

(*The Growth of English*, London: John Murray,
pp. 107 and 121)

1908: UK (English), OED citation
Henry Sweet

Standard English, like Standard French, is now a class-dialect more than
a local dialect: it is the language of the educated all over Great Britain...
[Not in *OED*:] The best speakers of Standard English are those whose
pronunciation, and language generally, least betray their locality.

(*The Sounds of English,* Oxford University Press,
pp. 7–8)

1909: UK (English), OED citation
Daniel Jones

1 Standard Pronunciation.

(heading, in Jones, *The Pronunciation of English*,
by Daniel Jones)

1912: UK (American)
Logan Pearsall Smith

It was, then, this East Midland [dialect in the late Middle Ages], spoken in London and in Oxford and Cambridge, which was adopted as our standard speech.

(*The English Language*, Oxford University Press, p. 39)

1917: US
Fred Newton Scott

In fine, the idea that somewhere, in some linguistic Utopia, there exists a standard English which all cultured Englishmen use alike and cannot help using and to which distracted Americans may resort for chastening and absolution, is a pleasing hallucination, which a single glance into Mr. Henry Sweet's *Primer of Spoken English* should have dissipated forever.

('The Standard of American Speech', *The English Journal*, 6:1–15, January)

1919a: US
H. L. Mencken

I think I have offered sufficient evidence in the chapters preceding that the American of today is much more honestly English, in any sense that Shakespeare would have understood, than the so-called Standard English of England. It still shows all the characters that marked the common tongue in the days of Elizabeth, and it continues to resist stoutly the policing that ironed out Standard English in the Seventeenth and Eighteenth Centuries. Standard English must always strike an American as a bit stilted and precious.

(*The American Language*, New York: Alfred A. Knopf)

1919b: US, OED citation
George P. Krapp

The Pronunciation of Standard English in America.

(title)

1921a: UK (English)
Henry Bradley

The wiser sort among us will not dispute that Americans have acquired the right to frame their own standards of correct English on the usage of their best writers and speakers... But is it too much to hope that one day this vast community of nations will possess a common 'standard English', tolerant of minor local varieties...? There are many on both sides of the ocean who cherish this ideal and are eager to do all in their power to bring it nearer to fulfilment.

(*The Literary Review*, 3 December, p. 224)

1921b: UK (English)
Henry Newbolt

It is emphatically the business of the Elementary School to teach all its pupils who either speak a definite dialect or whose speech is disfigured by vulgarisms, to speak standard English, and to speak it clearly, and with expression... We do not advocate the teaching of standard English on any grounds of social 'superiority', but because it is manifestly desirable that all English people should be capable of speaking so as to be fully intelligible to each other and because inability to speak standard English is in practice a serious handicap in many ways... We do not, however, suggest that the suppression of dialect should be aimed at, but that children who speak a dialect should, as often happens, become bi-lingual, speaking standard English too.

(*The Teaching of English in England: the Newbolt Report*,
pp. 198, 204, 205)

1925: US, OED citation

The informal or local speech will often seem more penetrating, more genuine than the standard speech.

(*The English Language in America*, writer not named)

1927: UK (English)
Henry Cecil Wyld

From the beginning of its career in these islands, English was not a uniform language, but existed in several different forms, or *Dialects*... Fortunately, at the present time, the great majority of the English dialects are of very little importance as representatives of English speech, and for our present purpose we can afford to let them go, except in so far as they throw light upon the growth of those forms of our language which are the main objects of our solicitude, namely, the language of Literature and Received Standard Spoken English.

(*A Short History of English*, 3rd edition, London: John Murray,
p. 16; first edition, 1914)

1928: UK (English)
Ernest Weekley

(1) For the student of language it is a matter of regret that the old dialects, the historical descendants of Anglo-Saxon, should give way to an artificial standard, which is little more than a century old, its absurd spelling having been fixed by printers, its current pronunciation by pedants.

(2) At the present day every educated Englishman uses, or at least is familiar with, three separate types of speech. First, the jerky, chiefly monosyllabic, almost telegraphic language which he uses with his family and intimates... Secondly, the more formal and correct language required in intercourse with strangers and in business or official transactions... Lastly, there is the literary language of the great masters of verse and prose. The second of these languages is most representative of 'standard English,' *i.e.* the general means of spoken and written communication, with great but ever decreasing variations in pronunciation, intonation, fullness of vocabulary, and power of expression. In the mouths of those who have by birth or education the restraint which is characteristic of the best type of Englishman it

becomes what is sometimes called 'public school English,' a type of speech usually condemned by those who do not happen to possess it. From this it grades downwards, by imperceptible degrees, to the raucous clamour of the soap-box orator. Now that education and access to literature are the right of all, it is chiefly by intonation that spoken 'standard English' may still be divided into a number of 'class dialects.' Written 'standard English' is much more uniform.

> (*The English Language*, London: Ernest Benn (Fleet Street),
> pp. 27 and 76–7.)

1932: UK (English)
R. W. Chapman
Standard English is, in essentials, the best of the English dialects, and therefore – though foreign languages may excel it in this or that quality – one of the most subtle and most beautiful of all expressions of the human spirit.

> (*Oxford English*, quoted in Jeff Wilkinson, *Introducing Standard English*, Harmondsworth: Penguin, 1995.)

1934: UK (English)
Henry Cecil Wyld
Everyone knows that there is a type of English which is neither provincial nor vulgar, a type which most people would willingly speak if they could, and desire to speak if they do not. It is unnecessary to particularize RS [Received Standard] farther than I have done in the preceding sentence, beyond saying that it is the type spoken by members of the great Public Schools, and by those classes in society which normally frequent these. I suggest that this is the best kind of English, not only because it is spoken by those often very properly called 'the best people', but because it has two great advantages that make it intrinsically superior to every other type of English speech – the extent to which it is current throughout the country, and the marked distinctiveness and clarity in its sounds... How different are the conditions with Modified Standard. Here all is variety. Every province, every town, nay, almost every suburb, and every class, has its own idiosyncrasies of pronunciation.

> ('The Best English', Tract XXXIX of the Society for Pure English,
> London: 1934)

1942: US
Albert H. Marckwardt
We have seen enough of the relationships between dialects and the ways in which they differ from one another, to realize that the acceptance as a standard of one type of speech over another is based not upon linguistic considerations but rather upon political, cultural, and economic factors. As a tool of expression, London speech was probably no better, neither more efficient nor more effective, than Gloucester speech, Nottingham speech, or Canterbury speech... London English is a satisfactory standard for most southern English speakers, but there is no excuse for its adoption in New York, Chicago, Atlanta, or

San Francisco, when these cities in themselves constitute powerful centers which affect in many ways the behavior and culture of the inhabitants within their spheres of influence.

(*Introduction to the English Language*, New York: Oxford University Press)

1947: UK/NZ, OED citation
Eric Partridge

Standard English and Standard American are the speech of the educated classes in the British Empire and the United States.

(*Usage and Abusage*)

1949: UK (English)
C. L. Wrenn

'Good English' may be described as the English of the educated classes used without self-consciousness... It must also be remembered that we can only speak of a 'received standard English' when referring to the educated language of England, as far as pronunciation is concerned. There are many types of 'good English' as described above outside of England – that of Edinburgh in Scotland, for example, or that of Philadelphia or Boston in America. In the written language, however, there is relative uniformity among the more educated users of English the whole world over. The answer, then, to the question 'What is correct', is 'what educated speakers say', not what they ought – according to some notions of grammar or dictionary – to say... English and the speech of the United States are one language: but in the more than three centuries that have passed since the first settlements, each has developed in divergent ways – both in its generally accepted 'standard' forms and in dialects.

(*The English Language*, London: Methuen, p. 188)

1962a: UK (English), OED citation
P. H. Johnson

Had spoken standard English varied by a few fancies such as 'crorss' for 'cross' and 'poyt' for 'poet' [*sic*].

(*Error of Judgment*)

1962b: US
Lincoln Barnett

Many features of standard American speech – so-called 'Americanisms', words and idioms which purists on both sides of the Atlantic have noted and often deplored – were inventions contrived to meet the necessities of a new existence and made possible by the virtuosity of the English tongue.

(*History of the English Language* (published originally in the US as *The Treasure of Our Tongue*): this quotation from the first UK edition, London: Sphere Books, p. 140)

1963: US
W. Nelson Francis

Educated or *standard English* is that naturally used by most educated people who fill positions of social, financial, and professional influence in the community. Some people learn it as their native speech, if they come from families that already belong to this social class. Others acquire it in the course of their schooling and later by conscious or unconscious imitation of their associates. Control of standard English does not, of course, guarantee professional, social, or financial success. But it is an almost indispensable attribute of those who attain such a success... The British version of standard English, RP, is the same for all speakers regardless of their place of origin. In America, however, there is no such thing as a single standard form of American English, especially in pronunciation. The nearest thing to it is the speech of anonymous radio and television announcers, which one linguist has aptly called 'network English'.

(*The English Language: An Introduction*, New York: W. W. Norton, 1967 edition, pp. 246–7)

1965: UK (English)
David Abercrombie

First let me make clear what I mean by Standard English. This phrase is used in a variety of senses. I shall use it, as many other people do, to mean that kind of English which is the official language of the entire English-speaking world, and is also the language of all educated English-speaking people. What I mean by Standard English has nothing to do with the way people pronounce: Standard English is a language, not an accent, and it is as easily recognizable as Standard English when it is written down as when it is spoken. It is, in fact, the only form of English to be at all widely written nowadays. There is, in Standard English, a certain amount of regional variation, perhaps, but not very much – it is spoken, and even more written, with remarkable uniformity considering the area which it covers.

('R.P. and local accent', in his *Studies in Phonetics and Linguistics*, Oxford University Press, p. 10)

1968: UK (Manx)
Randolph Quirk

Standard English [is] that kind of English which draws least attention to itself over the widest area and through the widest range of usage. As we have seen, this norm is a complex function of vocabulary, grammar, and transmission, most clearly established in one of the means of transmission (spelling), and least clearly established in the other means of transmission (pronunciation). This latter point draws attention to one important factor in the notion of a standard: it is particularly associated with English in *written* form, and we find that there are sharper restrictions in every way upon the English that is written (and especially *printed*) than upon English that is spoken. In fact, the standards of Standard English are determined and preserved, to no small extent, by

the great printing houses... Standard English is basically an ideal, a mode
of expression that we seek when we wish to communicate with members
of the wider community of the nation as a whole, or with members of the
still wider community, English-speakers as a whole. As an ideal, it cannot
be perfectly realised, and we must expect that members of different
'wider communities' (Britain, America, Nigeria, for example) may
produce different realisations. In fact, however, the remarkable thing is
the very high degree of unanimity, the small amount of divergence.

(*The Use of English*, Harlow: Longman, 2nd edn, pp. 99–100;
1st edn, 1962)

1972: UK (Manx, English, English, Swedish)
Randolph Quirk, Sidney Greenbaum, Geoffrey Leech, and Jan Svartvik
By reason of the fact that educated English is thus accorded social and
political sanction, it comes to be referred to as Standard English, and
provided we remember that this does not mean an English that has been
formally standardized by official action, as weights and measures are
standardized, the term is useful and appropriate. In contrast with
Standard English, forms that are especially associated with uneducated
(rather than dialectal) use are often called 'substandard'... The degree of
acceptance of a single standard of English throughout the world, across
a multiplicity of political and social systems, is a truly remarkable
phenomenon: the more so since the extent of the uniformity involved
has, if anything, increased in the present century... What we are calling
national standards should be seen as distinct from the Standard English
which we have been discussing and which we should think of as being
'supra-national', embracing what is common to all... The United States
and Britain have been separate political entities for two centuries; for
generations, thousands of books have been appearing annually; there is
a long tradition of publishing descriptions of both Am[erican] E[nglish]
and Br[itish] E[nglish]. These are important factors in establishing and
institutionalizing the two national standards, and in the relative absence
of such conditions other national standards are both less distinct (being
more open to the influence of either AmE or BrE) and less
institutionalized.

(*A Grammar of Contemporary English*, Harlow: Longman,
pp. 16–18)

1975: UK, OED citation
Local names pronounced in [Chinese] dialects widely different from
'Mandarin' or, as it must now be called, Standard Speech.

(*The Times Literary Supplement*, writer not named)

1978a: UK, OED citation
There is also a kind of 'standard standard'. Some people call it
'broadcast' or 'publications' standard, because most newspapers and
television news shows use it.

(*English Journal*, December, writer not named)

1978b: US
Albert C. Baugh and Thomas Cable

[The *spoken standard*] is the language heard in the conversation of educated people. It is marked by conformity to the rules of grammar and to certain considerations of taste which are not easily defined but are present in the minds of those who are conscious of their speech. Whatever its dialectal coloring or qualities varying with the particular circumstances involved, it is free from features that are regarded as substandard in the region. To one side of this spoken standard lies the domain of the *written standard*. This is the language of books and it ranges from the somewhat elevated style of poetry to that of simple but cultivated prose. It may differ both in vocabulary and idiom from the spoken standard, although the two frequently overlap... The spoken standard or, as it is sometimes called, the *received standard*, is something which varies in different parts of the English-speaking world. In England it is a type of English perhaps best exemplified in the speech of those educated in the great public schools, but spoken also with a fair degree of uniformity by cultivated people in all parts of the country. It is a class rather than a regional dialect. This is not the same as the spoken standard in the United States or Canada or Australia. Each of these is entitled to recognition. The spread of English to many parts of the world has changed our conception of what constitutes Standard English. The speech of England can no longer be considered the norm by which all others must be judged.

(*A History of the English Language,* 3rd edn, New York: Prentice-Hall, pp. 313 and 315: 1st edn 1957)

1982: UK (English)
Peter Trudgill and Jean Hannah

The subject of this book is *Standard English*, the variety of the English language which is normally employed in writing and normally spoken by 'educated' speakers of the language. It is also, of course, the variety of English that students of English as a Foreign or Second Language (EFL/ESL) are taught when receiving formal instruction. The term *Standard English* often refers to grammar and vocabulary (*dialect*) but not to pronunciation (*accent*)... Traditionally, schools and universities in Europe – and in many other parts of the world – have taught that variety of English often referred to as 'British English'. As far as grammar and vocabulary are concerned, this generally means Standard English as it is normally written and spoken by educated speakers in England and, with minor differences, in Wales, Scotland, Northern Ireland, The Republic of Ireland, Australia, New Zealand and South Africa. As far as pronunciation is concerned, it means something much more restrictive, for the RP ('Received Pronunciation') accent which is taught to foreigners is actually used by perhaps only 3 per cent to 5 per cent of the population of England. The RP accent has its origins in the south-east of England but is currently a social accent associated with the BBC, the Public Schools in England, and with members of the upper-middle and upper classes. It is considered a prestigious accent in the whole of the

British Isles and British Commonwealth, but it is for the most part an
accent associated only with England.

> (*International English: A Guide to Varieties of Standard English*,
> London: Edward Arnold, pp. 1–2)

1983: US
Robert Claiborne

But when we are communicating with 'outsiders,' and especially if we
are communicating in writing, we will almost certainly do best with
colloquial Standard English. The reasons are not very obscure. To begin
with, though most English speakers *speak* some nonstandard dialect,
they almost certainly *understand* the educated speech of their region
and, if they're literate, written Standard English. (The latter, in fact, is
acceptable currency almost anywhere in the English-speaking world.)
The overwhelming majority of English-language publications –
newspapers, magazines and books – are written, apart from some
dialogue passages, in Standard English. The directions and manuals that
come with medicines, many foodstuffs, and the innumerable gadgets
that enrich or complicate our lives are in Standard English. And the
governmental and corporate bureaucrats that most of us have to
correspond with from time to time deal in Standard, if often heavily
jargonized, English. In short, Standard English is 'better' than other
dialects because – and only because – with it we can give information
to and get information from, many more sources than with any other
dialect.

> (*Our Marvelous Native Tongue: The Life and Times of the English
> Language*, New York: Times Books, p. 296)

1986: UK (Irish, English)
Loreto Todd and Ian Hancock

Standard English is the term given to the spectrum of Englishes taught in
schools, described in *grammars* and *dictionaries*, used by the media and
written with relatively little variation throughout the English-speaking
world... Standard English is not absolutely clearcut and discrete. It
comprehends varieties which allow a speaker to indicate friendship or
formality, casualness, intimacy or aloofness. Formal spoken styles are
often close to written norms, with fewer reductions and weak forms
than are found in colloquial speech.

> ('Standard English' in *International English Usage*,
> London: Routledge, pp. 440–1)

1987a: US
Thomas J. Creswell and Virginia McDavid

Standard English is revealed by observing the spoken and written
English of mature, socially responsible, literate adults. This procedure,
however, despite its apparent simplicity and straightforwardness, is
sometimes made difficult by the complexity and multiplicity of changes
and variations in actual usage. Lexicographers, in writing definitions and
assigning regional, social, stylistic, or other labels to words,

constructions, or senses, study large numbers of instances of, say, the use of an individual word and pose such questions as Who said or wrote this? Under what circumstances? To what audience? In what publication?

> ('Usage: Change and Variation', in *The Random House Dictionary of the English Language*, 2nd edn, New York: Random House, p. xxiii.)

1987b: UK (English)
Gerald Knowles

Standard English was for a long time essentially a written form of the language, but it did influence the use of grammar and vocabulary in speech, and even pronunciation. In all parts of the country [the UK], local forms and usages have been subject to displacement: as fashions have changed new forms have been accepted in the standard language and have gradually spread to local dialects... The vast majority of English speakers today have a standardized variety of English... Agreement on matters of pronunciation seems to have developed in the nineteenth century, especially in the public schools of the south of England. This has led to a widespread acceptance in England of one variety of pronunciation as a standard and this is the type that was adopted in the 1920s for broadcasting by the BBC. It is known as RECEIVED PRONUNCIATION, or more commonly as RP. (The word *received* is here used in the older sense 'generally accepted'.) An RP speaker is somebody whose speech belongs to England, but cannot be pinned down to any region of England. RP has had a powerful influence on all regional varieties, but relatively few people actually speak it.

> (*Patterns of Spoken English*, Harlow: Longman, p. 4)

1989: US
C. M. Millward

A *standard language* is a variety of a language that is socially and culturally predominant and is generally accepted as the most proper form of that language. Written Standard English is, with minor differences, primarily in spelling, the same the world over. However, with reference to the spoken language, the term Standard English must be further qualified. The Standard English of New Zealand is by no means identical to the Standard English of Ireland. Indeed, even within a given country, what is considered standard may vary from area to area... Diversity among the regional dialects of England, particularly in pronunciation, is greater than in any other part of the world where English is spoken as a native language. England is also the only English-speaking nation with an official or quasi-official standard dialect, which we can call Standard British English (SBE). This dialect is a social and educational, rather than regional, dialect. It is superimposed upon regional dialects; in effect, many of its users are bidialectal to some extent, able to speak both SBE and a regional dialect. SBE is the English taught in the public (that is, private) schools of England and Wales.

> (*A Biography of the English Language*, New York: Holt, Rinehart and Winston Inc., pp. 297 and 299)

1989: UK (English)
J. A. Simpson and E. S. C. Weiner (editors, *OED2*)

For native English words the variety of pronunciation represented is, broadly speaking, educated standard southern British, or 'Received Pronunciation' (RP). There could be no question, at this stage, of systematically registering non-RP (i.e. other British and Non-British) pronunciations; although of course those already included in the Dictionary have remained and have been augmented by a few analogous cases.

(Introduction to *The Oxford English Dictionary: Second Edition*, Oxford: Clarendon Press, 1989, p. xix)

1990: UK (English)
E. S. C. Weiner

Murray's model is unblushingly Britocentric... The implicit assumption [in the creation of *The Oxford English Dictionary* in the nineteenth century] was that Standard British English was identical with the standard version of English overseas. And this was probably correct in the 1880s. Britain's linguistic hegemony had not been questioned: good English, the English that all English-speakers had in common, was probably believed to be British English (the Queen's/King's English) in all communities, both in Murray's day and for many years afterwards.

('The Federation of English', in Christopher Ricks and Leonard Michaels (eds.), *The State of the Language*, London: Faber and Faber, p. 500)

1991: UK (English)
Sidney Greenbaum

In countries where the majority speak English as their first language one dialect is used nationally for official purposes. It is called *Standard English*. Standard English is the national dialect that generally appears in print. It is taught in schools, and students are expected to use it in their essays. It is the norm for dictionaries and grammars. We expect to find it in official typed communications, such as letters from government officials, solicitors, and accountants. We expect to hear it in national news broadcasts and documentary programmes on radio or television. Within each national variety the standard dialect is relatively homogeneous in grammar, vocabulary, spelling, and punctuation. Pronunciation is a different matter, since there is no equivalent standard accent (type of pronunciation). For each national variety there are regional accents, related to a geographical area, and social accents, related to the educational, socio-economic, and ethnic backgrounds of the speakers. In British English, Received Pronunciation (RP) is a non-regional social accent associated with public school education but it is not regarded as a standard accent to be learned in schools throughout the country. It is spoken by about 3 per cent of the population in Britain. Standard English has prestige because people connect it with education and with higher-income groups. It is not intrinsically better than other dialects, though many believe it is.

(*An Introduction to English Grammar*, Harlow: Longman, p. 4)

1992a: UK (English)
David Burnley

The rapid development in public broadcasting after about 1920 led in England and abroad to the establishment of BBC English as a *de facto* spoken standard. This standard, alternatively known as *Received Pronunciation*, is that of a social and educational élite.

(*The History of the English Language: A Source Book*, Harlow: Longman, p. 298)

1992b: UK (Scottish)
Tom McArthur

Standard English A widely used term that resists easy definition but is used as if most educated people nonetheless know precisely what it refers to. Some consider its meaning self-evident: it is both the usage and the ideal of 'good' or 'educated' users of English. A geographical limitation has, however, often been imposed on this definition, such as the usage of educated people in Britain alone, England alone, or southern England alone, or the usage of educated people in North America and Britain generally. Others still find standard English at work throughout the English-speaking world. For some it is a monolith, with more or less strict rules and conventions; for others it is a range of overlapping varieties, so that standard Am[erican] E[nglish] is distinct from but similar to standard Br[itish] E[nglish]. Although for some the term is negative, for most it appears to be either neutral or positive, referring to something important.

(first paragraph of the entry 'Standard English' in McArthur (ed.), *The Oxford Companion to the English Language*, Oxford University Press, p. 982)

1993a: UK (English)
N. F. Blake and Jean Moorhead

Many people regard Standard English as correct English. It is certainly the variety which is taught to foreign learners of English and, in its written form, it represents the form which is found in most types of writing – school text-books, government documents, newspapers and literature. But Standard English is only one variety among the many varieties of English, though it has acquired a special position among these varieties because it is used as the medium of education in England... Because of the position of Standard English it is often taken subconsciously as a norm in discussions of language acquisition, change and varieties... The effect of broadcasting has been to allow people to hear many different varieties of English from all over the world. Although this has not necessarily undermined the perceived status of Received Pronunciation, it perhaps has made it appear to speakers of the language that a high degree of variety exists and that many people, even quite distinguished ones, can use forms of spoken English which differ from those of Received Pronunciation.

(*Introduction to English Language*, Basingstoke: Macmillan, pp. xi and 85)

1993b: UK (English)
Godfrey Howard

About many words and expressions, there is general agreement. About others, even dictionaries take different views on whether a word or a phrase is slang or Standard English, how to pronounce some words and on what is good grammar. Outside linguistics, few people use the term Standard English; in any case, it seems more valid to spell it with a small *s*,... to suggest generally accepted good use of English instead of a prescriptive decree laid down by an absolute authority, since such authority does not exist.

(The Good English Guide: English Usage in the 1990s,
Basingstoke: Macmillan, pp. 58–9)

1993c: UK (English)
Charles Barber

There has been a rise in the prestige of *all* regional accents in Britain, and it is probable that we are moving towards the American position, in which it is normal and acceptable for a speaker to use an educated regional accent, and there is no supra-regional class-accent. There is consequently a tendency in present-day Britain to draw the boundaries of 'acceptable pronunciation', and indeed of 'Standard English' generally, rather wider than formerly, and to take into account the usages of a larger part of the population. Some of the changes that seem to be taking place in the language are therefore more apparent than real: they may be changes in acceptance, rather than actual substantive changes. What formerly existed as a usage in some group, but was considered non-standard, may now come to be accepted as standard, because of the changing definition of 'standard'.

(The English Language: A Historical Introduction,
Cambridge University Press, p. 266)

1994a: UK
Christiane Dalton and Barbara Seidlhofer

Distinctions within the code of a language are called *varieties*. Regional varieties which differ from the common core with respect to syntax, lexicon, morphology, and phonology are called *dialects*. Regional and/or social varieties which only differ with respect to phonology (sound level) have been termed *accents*. Thus, the speech of newsreaders on American, British, and Australian TV is likely to be the same dialect, i.e. Standard English, but different in terms of accent... British society seems to exploit differences in accent as social markers to a greater extent than American society... This probably explains why the prestige variety of British English (or, as Trudgill and Hannah (1985) point out, 'English English') is so well documented that it is the best described phonetic variety of any language on earth. This is also the reason why we draw on it more extensively than on *General American*... The term RP is customarily used to describe prestige 'English English' and stands for 'Received Pronunciation'.

(Pronunciation, Oxford University Press)

1994b: UK/NZ
Laurie Bauer

Even if standard English is not monolithic there are problems with defining a single standard for all dialects of English. English is spoken natively by over 300 million people all round the world, and the English used in broadcasting and the professions in, say, Washington DC is different in many ways from the English used in broadcasting and the professions in Canberra. That is, there is regional variation between varieties of English, each of which is recognized as a standard in its own sphere of influence. These spheres of influence usually (but not invariably) correspond to countries. So we might wish to distinguish between standard US English and standard Australian English, between standard New Zealand English and standard Canadian English. It is in this sense that there are a number of different standard Englishes. Certainly, these different standards have more features in common than they have distinguishing them, but they are none the less distinct. Once we accept that, it becomes an open question how many standard varieties there are in a given country. Should we distinguish a standard Norwich English from a standard Nottingham English, a standard Seattle English from a standard San Francisco English, a standard Sydney English from a standard Melbourne English? In principle, there seems to be no reason why we should not. In practice though this is not done, and one reason is that these various local standards are not codified.

(*Watching English Change*, Harlow: Longman, p. 3
(author a New Zealander))

1995: UK (Welsh)
David Crystal

Since the 1980s, the notion of 'standard' has come to the fore in public debate about the English language... We may define the Standard English of an English-speaking country as a minority variety (identified chiefly by its vocabulary, grammar, and orthography) which carries most prestige and is most widely understood.

(*The Cambridge Encyclopedia of the English Language*,
Cambridge University Press, p. 110)

1997: UK (Welsh)
David Crystal

Even if the new Englishes did become increasingly different, as years went by, the consequences for world English would not necessarily be fatal. A likely scenario is that our current ability to use more than one dialect would simply extend to meet the fresh demands of the international scene. A new form of English – let us think of it as 'World Standard Spoken English' (WSSE) – would almost certainly arise. Indeed, the foundation for such a development is already being laid around us. Most people are already 'multidialectal' to a greater or lesser extent.

('The future of global English', chapter 5 in *English as a Global
Language*, Cambridge University Press, pp. 136–7)

Panel 5.2 'Standard English' and the Atlantic divide

Henry Cecil Wyld in *A Short History of English* (1914) called the standard language spoken with a public-school accent *Received Standard (English)*, and usage which had been adapted towards it was *Modified Standard (English)*. Throughout the first half of the twentieth century, the Wyldian view dominated in Britain and its Empire (at least), so that *standard English* was taken to refer to the high British variety only, as in:

> [Discussing points of usage:] So also in modern standard English (though not in the English of the United States) a distinction which we feel, but many of us could not define, is made between *forward* and *forwards*.

> (Logan Pearsall Smith (a US scholar in the UK), in *The English Language*, Oxford University Press, 1912, p. 49)

However, in 1919, the Baltimore journalist H. L. Mencken challenged both the worth of this kind of English and its name:

> I think I have offered sufficient evidence in the chapters preceding that the American of today is much more honestly English, in any sense that Shakespeare would have understood, than the so-called Standard English of England... Standard English must always strike an American as a bit stilted and precious.

> (*The American Language* [the chapter 'English or American?'], New York: Alfred A. Knopf)

In the same year, the American linguist George P. Krapp brought out a book with the title *The Pronunciation of Standard English in America*. By 1919, therefore, Americans had two options regarding how to use and interpret the term *Standard English*: either as referring to something British (and admirable or otherwise) but *not* American, or as applying equally to comparable usage in the UK and US. In the latter case (which has become the dominant US point of view), American Standard English could not be Wyld's 'Received Standard English', but even so the assumption that only the British are entitled to the label 'standard' persists to this day in the UK and elsewhere (including on occasion the US), as in the following representative citations:

1989: UK/NZ
Robert Burchfield
> The rate of change in the twentieth century is not substantially different from that of earlier centuries, except in the sense that overseas varieties of English, in the United States, Australia, and elsewhere, are steadily moving away, in small matters and large, from Standard English, and from one another, at a somewhat accelerated rate.

> (preface of *Unlocking the English Language*, London: Faber and Faber)

1990a: UK
Mandy Loader

The British are quick to point out how different American English is from Standard English.

> (letter by Mandy Loader in *The EFL Gazette*, London,
> the April issue)

1990b: UK
John Carey

In some ex-colonial countries there are plans to recognise the local pidgins and creoles as languages in their own right, not just incompetent versions of the mother tongue. America had this idea back in the 19th century, when Noah Webster proclaimed a separate American language. But American speech offers few problems of intelligibility to users of standard English.

> ('Filthy English?', John Carey's review of Christopher Ricks and
> Leonard Michaels (eds.), *The State of the Language* (London:
> Faber and Faber), in *The Sunday Times*, 7 January)

1993: UK
Dennis Freeborn

Almost everyone can now hear Standard English, in a wide variety of its styles, every day, and a large amount of American English also.

> (*Varieties of English* (2nd edn), with Peter French and
> David Langford, Macmillan, p. 39)

1994: US
William Safire

What Americans call *rubber chicken*, the British call *function fish*; both refer to the food required to be consumed at large gatherings. The use of the noun *function* to mean "event," long a Standard English sense of the word, has been on the increase in the United States.

> ('Of Comparisons and Passed Mistakes', in the *New York Times*
> language column, as reprinted in the *International Herald Tribune*,
> 28 November)

6   Scots and Southron

Scots... *n* **1** the Scots language, the speech of Lowland Scotland ... [as] treated in this dictionary...

(definition, from Mairi Robinson
(editor-in-chief), *The Concise Scots Dictionary:
a new comprehensive one-volume dictionary
of the Scots language,*
Aberdeen University Press, 1985)

The status of Scots: *Dialect, language, or semi-language?*

The people of Scotland occupy a unique historical and cultural position in the English-speaking world. They use the standard language (with distinctive phonological, grammatical, lexical, and idiomatic features) in administration, law, education, the media, all national institutions, and by and large in their dealings with Anglophones elsewhere, but in their everyday lives a majority of them mix 'the King's English' with what in an earlier age was called 'the King's Scots'.

Gaelic, the Celtic language shared with Ireland and once used throughout the Highlands and the Western Isles (the Hebrides), is now largely limited to those islands. At one time, most speakers of Gaelic learned their mother tongue at home and Standard English at school, and in later life mixed it with the vernacular of the Lowlands. During much of the twentieth century, speakers of Gaelic have generally been bilingual from childhood; they now number some 80,000 in a population of about five million who in the main have little acquaintance with the language and its traditions, although everybody knows about it, and many have a feeling of loss because no one in their families speaks it any more. On the other hand, although the population at large also knows little about the traditions of Scots (the Germanic vernacular of the Lowlands), they use it widely as a matter of course and those who do not use it much or at all usually understand it well enough.

On the languagehood of Gaelic there can be no argument. On its status, however, there is much discussion but little action, official or otherwise, and it continues the decline shared with the Celtic languages of Wales, Ireland, France, Man, and Cornwall. On the status of Scots there is also much discussion, almost all of it ineffectual in official terms, and within that debate three broad points of view can be distinguished:

○ *A dialect of English*
For many, in Scotland and elsewhere, Scots is obviously an English dialect. However distinctive it may be (or may have been) in sound, spelling, syntax, and vocabulary, it is not different enough structurally and lexically to be a language in its own right (despite often being unintelligible to non-Scottish Anglophones) and has none of the socio-legal trappings of a language: no official status, no significant presence in schools, only a minor role in the country's legal system, and no role whatever in its administration. Many Scots who hold the 'dialect' view would probably have no objection – might indeed be pleased – if Scots *were* a clear-cut language, but they tend to think that people should accept the facts of life. In addition, for many the matter is a niggling distraction from the business of real life: English in Scotland is distinctive, but it is English, and being part of the English-speaking world is a plus – but if some people want to make a fuss about Scots they are welcome, and it may even be good for tourism.

○ *An independent language*
For many others, in Scotland and elsewhere, Scots is obviously a language, however attenuated and mixed with English it may have become. In favour of this position they point out that, among other things:

(1) It has a highly distinctive sound system, grammar, and vocabulary, dating from the Anglian kingdom of Northumbria over a thousand years ago, long before either Scotland or England was a state as understood in our times. (See panel 6.1.)

(2) It has a varied and unbroken orthographic and literary tradition from the Middle Ages to the present day, including two medieval epic poems, ballads and love poetry, and writers of standing who have used Scots on its own or with English. These include John Barbour, 'Blind Harry', William Dunbar, Gavin Douglas, Sir David Lindsay, Allan Ramsay, Robert Burns, Sir Walter Scott, John Galt, Robert Louis Stevenson, Christopher Murray Grieve ('Hugh MacDiarmid'), Edwin Muir, James Leslie Mitchell ('Lewis Grassic Gibbon'), and Neil M. Gunn.

(3) It has dialects of its own, ranging from the Borders (with ancient links in northern England) to the Northern Isles of Orkney and Shetland (with ancient links to a variety of Old Norse called Norn).

(4) It is now recognized as a language by the European Bureau of Lesser Used Languages, an agency of the European Union. (See also chapter 1.)

They therefore argue that, since equivalent forms in other countries have long been officially recognized as distinct languages, Scots should be so recognized and strengthened, and exponents resent what they see as neglect in schools and universities, and fear that it may be in terminal decline. Some puristically distinguish between traditional 'good' Scots (more or less the rural dialects and traditional literary forms) and contemporary 'bad' Scots (more or less the urban dialects), noting however that urban dialects in and around Glasgow are thriving like weeds (and have their own subliteratures).

○ *An area of confusion*
Finally, and significantly, many are uncertain about where Scots begins and ends in relation to conventional English, and what parts of it are 'good', 'bad', or anything else. They may as a result view it with an affectionate but sometimes embarrassed unease, perhaps feeling that somewhere along the line they are losing access to many handy – even fine – traditional usages. However, they are generally aware that Scots has its dialects, styles, and writers, pre-eminent among them Robert Burns (often considered on a par with William Shakespeare, if not indeed higher).

All three groups cut across the social classes, and the existence of Scots can have a profound effect, both intellectually and in terms of linguistic performance. At one extreme is the so-called 'inarticulate Scot' (usually working class and often male), who is uncertain about when to use what with whom, while at the other end of the continuum are people with exceptional linguistic dexterity (both working and middle class), their skills honed on a wide range of code-juggling options. The upper class is a landed RP-accented group educated in the main in public (that is, private) schools in England, for whom Scots is familiar but seldom if ever a sustained personal skill.

In 1808, the clergyman John Jamieson published in two volumes *An Etymological Dictionary of the Scottish Language*, yet despite the explicit title pan-British dialectologists have tended to regard his work as the first dictionary not of Scots as such but of a non-standard form of English; the definitions were after all couched in Standard English. However, Jamieson's volumes had an influence on the development of *The Oxford English Dictionary*, whose first and chief editor, James Murray, was a Scot and deeply interested in the vernacular, which however he treated in the *OED* as part of English at large. Yet despite the weight of English (as touched on in chapter 4), Scotticists have generally proceeded on the principle, explicit or implicit, that their subject is an entity distinct from (though related to) Southron (Southern), and recent published work in Scotland sustains this standpoint. Thus, the poet and critic Roderick Watson, of the Department of English Studies at Stirling University, observes:

Scots will take one form of a word from a Latin or French root when English takes another or leaves it altogether, as in *dispone* (dispose), or *dominie* (schoolmaster). Even common English words can be used in un-English ways, as in 'can I *get* to go' for 'may I go', or 'I *doubt* it's true' to mean 'I'm afraid it *is* true' – the opposite of what an English-speaker might assume. Even for Scots themselves the writing, spelling and speaking of their language can provide special problems, not the least of which is the number of apostrophes which are often added, quite wrongly, as if it were simply English with letters missing – thus *a'* for 'all' instead of the more correct *aa*, and *fa'* for *faa*, and so on.

('The Scots language', a section of chapter 1 in
The Literature of Scotland, London: Macmillan, 1984, pp. 16–17)

The view that Scots was once a distinct language but is now simply a dialect or group of dialects is long-established and currently widely accepted. The argument here is that before the Union of the Crowns (1603) and the Union of the Parliaments (1707), Scots – like many other Western European vernaculars – had begun to develop as a national language. However, the slow two-stage union with England enabled the language of the more powerful and populous south to overwhelm its northern relative, which had been under threat at the courtly and literary level for some time. By 1762, the English clergyman, grammarian, and scientist Joseph Priestley (fifty-five years after the Union and two years before receiving an honorary degree at Edinburgh University) could write that 'the English and the Scotch, had the kingdoms continued separate, might have been distinct languages, having two different standards of writing' (in *Theory of Language and Universal Grammar*, p. 129). (See also panel 5.1.)

A third view, mainly among scholars, and a variant of the dialect position, proposes that, as a consequence of how British history unfolded, Scots at a crucial stage came to occupy a limbo-like position between language and dialect. A. J. Aitken, former editor of *The Dictionary of the Older Scottish Tongue,* put it as follows in 1985:

The 'Older Scots' [of the fourteenth to seventeenth centuries], as it is now called, was an autonomous national language, with its own distinctive pronunciations, vocabulary and, very strikingly, spelling... The island of Britain then had two national languages of Anglo-Saxon origin, both sharing some of their features but noticeably different in others... Unfortunately, no sooner had the language attained its majority... than its long decline began. In its written form it now began to assimilate to the Southern English of Tudor literature and the Bible. The route by which the Reformation reached Scotland dictated that the Scots would adopt the Bible in English and not a separate translation into Scots. As a written language Older Scots ceased to exist in the 17th and 18th centuries... [However,] if Scots is not now a full 'language' it is something more than a mere 'dialect'. A distinguished German scholar once called it a *Halbsprache* – a semi-language.

('Is Scots a language?', in *English Today* 2, July 1985)

Two issues of *English Today* later, the Swedish linguist Eric Gunnemark replied with some heat to Aitken's closing remarks, representing what appears to be a strong international trend:

> I was horrified to read that Scots has been called a *Halbsprache* in German: *Halvsprak* in Swedish is worse than 'half a language'! ... My German university friends assure me that if Low German is a language (and who denies that?), then Scots is bound to be a language. They can't understand why Scots shouldn't be allowed to be called a language, just like Luxemburgish, which is not taught in the schools of Luxembourg as a German dialect but as a language. In my *Geolinguistic Handbook*, Scots will remain a language.

(from a letter to the editor, English Today 4, January 1986)

Despite the pejorative overtones of *halb* and *halv*, Aitken's translation 'semi-language' is intriguing and he certainly did not intend it to be disparaging. The usage fits the curtailment, displacement, and hybridization which any discussion of the history of Scots must deal with. Is such curtailment and displacement effectively the end of a language, or can it continue to be a language despite being reduced, as it were, to satellite status – or perhaps never having any other status? This is a question of some importance for many languages and 'near-languages' (if that is a safer term), including those in a tight embrace with English. (See chapter 1.) It can be considered again after exploring issues that may cast light on the problem of Scots conceived as (somehow) less than a language but more than a dialect.

Scots and English: *The same but different*

Generally speaking, the meaning of the word *bilingual* is clear enough: if people are bilingual they can speak (and write) two languages with roughly equal ease (although not necessarily in the same departments of life). It is usually not difficult to establish whether an individual or a community is unilingual or multilingual. Most Australians, for example, use only English at a significant level, and most Japanese use only Japanese. On the other hand, most people in Singapore are at least bilingual, in such pairs as English/Chinese, English/Malay, and English/Tamil, and the state reflects the usage of its citizens by having English, Mandarin, Malay, and Tamil as co-official languages, with English as the language of education, administration, and law – and, increasingly, as a key language of the middle-class home, regardless of ethnic background. (See chapter 1.)

Recognizing bilingualism is straightforward enough if the languages concerned are genetically or typologically very different. French, although historically closely linked with English, belongs to a different branch of the Indo-European language family, has had a distinct history, and is very different in its phonology and syntax, though not so much in its lexis (at least as written and printed). Tamil and English have had centuries of contact, but Tamil (a Dravidian language of southern India) is distinct from English at all levels, and has an utterly different orthography. There can be no doubt at all about bilingualism in terms of such pairs as English/French and English/Tamil.

Things are also generally straightforward if the systems of two languages of the same genealogical background are fairly distant from one another. Despite a common Germanic ancestry, the members of the pairs English/Dutch and English/German are mutually unintelligible, and speakers of both are as a result recognized as 'true' bilinguals. But linguists do not put Dutch and German in entirely separate boxes, because there is a speech continuum from the coast of the Netherlands across Germany to Switzerland and Austria, including the division of Low German (to which Dutch is closely related) and High German (which is close to Low German but not close to Dutch). Many years of schooling in Standard Dutch and Standard German have not eliminated the mutual intelligibility in Dutch/German border areas, and even within the standard languages resemblances are strong. Yet, nonetheless, people who use both Standard Dutch and Standard German are commonly considered to be 'true' bilinguals.

In Scandinavia, the three closely related and standardized Northern Germanic forms Danish, Norwegian (with two subforms), and Swedish have for political, social, and cultural reasons long been considered distinct. Because of their similarities, however, the citizens of Denmark, Sweden, and Norway experience a high degree of mutual intelligibility, despite certain areas of difficulty. As a result, people do not usually think in terms of Danish/ Swedish, Swedish/Norwegian, or Norwegian/Danish bilingual pairs. Rather, Danes, Swedes, and Norwegians generally understand one another well enough to agree (if pressed) that they all speak national variants of Common Scandinavian. Theirs are similar forms that for primarily political reasons are regarded as distinct languages.

However, within some of the nation-states of north-western Europe matters are complicated by minority forms with uncertain or disputed status, because of both their genealogical closeness and social subordination to majority forms traditionally recognized (at home and abroad) as 'proper' languages. One example is Frisian in the Netherlands, now widely agreed to be distinct from Dutch and regarded by the government as a language in its own right. Another is Faroese, on the Faroe Islands, which are part of Denmark; it is treated by the Danish government as a language in its own right and not as an offshore dialect of Danish, despite similarities. As a result, both Frieslanders and Faroese can assert – with a reasonable hope of being believed in international circles – that they are bilingual in terms of their local and their national languages.

Matters are sometimes even more complex. A country's minority languages may be as distinct from its state-endorsed language(s) as Tamil from English, or as similar as Frisian to Dutch. Basque, for example, is entirely different from Spanish, and so no one doubts the existence of Basque/Spanish bilinguals in northern Spain. In the case of Catalan, however, matters are less clear-cut. Catalan, as part of the Romance family, can be described as either a close cousin of Spanish (Castilian) or a divergent dialect. As a result, the many Catalans who insist on the distinctness of their language engage in publicity drives to establish that distinctness in world opinion – as when the Olympic Games were held in Barcelona some years ago. They often also insist on the distinctness of Catalonia from (the rest of) Spain, advocate the study of an extensive Catalan literature, develop Catalan for media use, and employ a standard form for administration and education.

The more sustained such a process, the more likely it will be that Catalan can acquire a status comparable to Portuguese, long an undisputedly distinct language which was however in the seventeenth century subordinated to Castilian Spanish during a brief union of Portugal and Spain. Spanish/Portuguese bilingualism has long been accepted internationally, while true Catalan/Spanish bilingualism is not yet accepted or much thought about. Catalan activists, looking nowadays at street names and other signs in their own idiom in Catalonian towns, may feel that the debate is over, but the international jury is apparently still out.

With the Union of the Crowns of England and Scotland, the Scottish nobility began to adapt their speech and attitudes towards those of the nobility of England. The attention of most aristocratic and many other Scots came to focus as the decades passed on London, Oxford and Cambridge and the way of life of leading families in the Home Counties. The prestige of the standardizing usage of the upper- and middle-class south-east in the seventeenth to nineteenth centuries had already been buttressed by the publication in 1611 of the Authorized Version of the Bible, which was dedicated to King James, himself a Scot. This translation was used in northern kirks as well as southern churches, one outcome being that Scottish congregations moved from Latin as their language of worship not to their own vernacular but to Southron, which became the prestigious medium through which one could hear and read about God, the prophets, Christ, and salvation.

A crucial synthesis took place from then on between the endonormative importance to Scots of such matters as religion and education and the exonormative influence of England on the language needed to make progress in such matters. Since the Reformation, Scots have notably sought to provide as solid an education as possible for as many of their young as possible. However, because of 1603 and 1707, the gravitational pull of England has meant that the medium of God's word in kirk and of instruction in schule has been the same standard language as in England, the United States, Canada, Australia, and other English-speaking countries.

Although some Scots are 'true' Gaelic/English bilinguals, the majority are taken to be as unilingual as most people in England. Many Scots unreflectingly share this viewpoint, probably because the last thing they wish is to be identified as *not* speaking a viable version of the prestige language. Yet at the same time many like to have their cake and eat it: to be different when it suits them, and the same when it suits them. As a result there is a widespread but unquantifiable tendency to enjoy being able to withdraw into a clublike national code while at the same time resenting any suggestion that one does not speak English as competently as any other Anglophone anywhere – and especially the English.

The Price Compromise: *Virtual reality*

To draw on the Iberian analogy again, one can compare speakers of Gaelic and English to speakers of Basque and Spanish, universally recognized as true bilinguals because their language pairs are far apart. Speakers of Scots, however, are analogous to speakers of Catalan, because both Scots and Catalan have their own dialects and literatures, and there is in both Scotland and Catalonia a sense of distinctness despite the existence of powerful politico-educational systems whose centres of gravity lie elsewhere. However, despite the similarities, the varieties of Scots have acquired such a shaky and often stigmatized status within Scotland that Scots-language activists can only sigh over the recent successes of Catalan. So uncertain indeed is the status of Scots, both socially and in the minds of many scholars, that the Welsh observer Glanville Price some ten years ago made the following comment – or confession – when writing about it:

> A problem faced by anyone seeking to discuss, or even merely identify, the languages of Britain is that of deciding how to cope with the form of speech and the written medium derived from it – for the moment I am deliberately avoiding using any such term as 'language' or 'dialect' – variously known as 'Scots', 'Braid (or Broad) Scots', or 'Lallans' (= 'Lowlands [Scots]'). The specific problem that confronts us is that of the linguistic status of Scots. In short, is it a distinct language from English, or is it merely a highly differentiated dialect of English?... There is no obvious answer, and the decision as to whether or not to accord to it the status of a 'language' is inevitably based to a considerable extent either on largely subjective criteria, or on practical considerations... In planning and writing this book, I have changed my mind four times, and, in the end, I devote a separate chapter to Scots not because I necessarily accept that it is a 'language' rather than a 'dialect' but because it has proved to be more convenient to handle it

thus rather than include some treatment of it in the chapter on English.

('Scots', chapter 14 of Languages of Britain,
London: Edward Arnold, 1984, p. 186)

This frank admission reflects the general uncertainty, yet at the very point where Price describes his doubts he gives Scots a chapter to itself in a book with the title *Languages of Britain*. Everything he says and does emphasizes the limbo-like condition of Scots while nonetheless testifying to its importance – and significantly he places the chapter in question in a set of three which constitute part IV of his book, whose title is 'The Germanic languages' (of Britain, past and present), these being English, Scots, and Norse. The other languages of Britain, as Price lists them, are: Irish (Gaelic) in early Britain (and, stretching a point, in Northern Ireland); Scottish Gaelic, Manx Gaelic, ancient British, Welsh, Cornish, Cumbric, Pictish, Latin, French in the Channel Islands, Anglo-Norman, and Romani. I think of this approach to Scots as 'the Price Compromise': eminently sensible and cautious – and not far removed from Aitken's 'semi-language'. But for comparative purposes Price has in his book given Scots the virtual status of an autonomous language.

A northern alternative: *The King's Scots*

The roots of Scots lie in Northumbria, a North Sea kingdom that in its hey-day – the seventh to ninth centuries – stretched from the Humber to the Forth. Throughout that period, the Northumbrians spoke and wrote 'Anglian dialects' or simply 'Anglian', as scholars call them or it: the north-ernmost variety of Old English. Eventually, northernmost Northumbria became south-east Scotland, while the rest became north-east England. And north of the border 'Inglis' (the language of the Angles) came increas-ingly to be known as 'Scots' (the language of the [Lowland] Scots), usurp-ing that name from Gaelic.

Anglian was the basis of what is sometimes called 'Northern English', a range of dialects that broke in two when the border between England and Scotland became more or less stable. Although the dialects of northern England have persisted strongly, in the last two centuries they have long been subordinate to the dialects of London and the south-east and pre-eminently to the standard form of English (derived from the East Midland dialect). The northern dialects of England never acquired a single unifying and defining name, whereas, because of the separate development of the kingdoms of Scotland and England, the group north of the border did. Like its more powerful 'sister' in England, Scots was influenced by Norse, French, and Latin, but in different ways, to different degrees, and under different conditions. For some six centuries, these sister languages ran in separate yet parallel courses, the Scots generally referring to the usage of England simply as 'Southron'.

A comparison with events in the Iberian peninsula can again be made here. Scots and English did not become as politically distinct as Portuguese and Spanish, although it may be argued that they are as linguistically distinct. Portugal and Spain, having briefly united, separated again permanently in the seventeenth century – a crucial time for the establishment of the standard languages of present-day Europe. Comparably, England and Scotland came together at about the same time, but that union has continued to the present day, despite ancient enmities as potent as those of Portugal and Spain. Just as Castilian Spanish would in all likelihood have dominated Portuguese if the Iberian union had continued, so Southron did dominate Scots, and has continued to do so. Indeed, it had already begun to do so before 1603.

Another, even more direct analogy, however, is with the period when Norway was controlled by Denmark and the Danish language greatly affected spoken and written Norwegian (so that one of the two standard forms of Norwegian today, Bokmal, is also known as Dano-Norwegian). However, as far as I know, the other form, Nynorsk, is not as liable to code-mixing and external influence as Scots has been, and indeed was created and fostered from the nineteenth century onward as a counterbalance to the influence of Danish. A. J. Aitken notes:

> By the mid-16c, Scots had begun to undergo the process of anglicization, in which southern English word forms and spellings progressively invaded written and later spoken Scots... By the late 16c, all Scots writing was in a mixed dialect, in which native Scots spellings and spelling symbols co-occurred with English borrowings: *aith/oath, ony/any, gude/good, quh-/wh-, sch-/sh*, Scots *ei*, English *ee, ea*, with the English forms gradually gaining in popularity. Scots elements virtually disappeared from published writings in Scotland before the end of the 17c, except for some vernacular literature, mostly verse. The elimination of Scots from unpublished writings like local records took some decades longer... Early in the 18c, Sir Robert Sibbald distinguished three sorts of Scottish speech: 'that Language we call Broad Scots, which is yet used by the Vulgar' ... 'in distinction to the Highlanders Language, and the refined Language of the Gentry, which the more Polite People among us do use.' That 'refined language', however, was no longer Scots but the ancestor of Scottish English.

> (from the entry 'Scots' in McArthur (ed.),
> *The Oxford Companion to the English Language*, 1992)

The outcome of the pressures on Scots from Southron – primarily in its written and printed form – have been the two developments discussed at the beginning of this chapter: the decline of autonomy and the growth of massive code-mixing and style-drifting, especially among the working class. This hybridization is generally drastically curtailed, however, when Scots leave Scotland, because it does not work well with other speakers of

English. In other words, in emigration or when working and travelling in England and elsewhere, Scots learn to shed their other grammatical system and put a wide range of distinctive expressions into storage. Such a loss of range is, I would argue (drawing on personal experience as well as observation), comparable to 'true' bilinguals giving up one of the two systems to which they have access. The greater the individual's early investment in the spectrum of Scots, the more closely the resultant loss through emigration approximates to that of one partner in a conventional language pair.

Shifts in perspective: *Different but the same*

Not long after I co-edited with A. J. Aitken the book *Languages of Scotland* (a collection of papers given at a conference at Glasgow University in 1977, published by Chambers in 1979), I left Edinburgh to become Associate Professor of English at the Université du Québec à Trois-Rivières. One of the first things I had to do on arriving at that highly politicized and very Francophone campus was to complete an official form in which, among other things, I had to list my language skills. And I unreflectingly put down, as I had done all my life, English and French (modern) and Latin and Greek (classical), and forgot about the matter.

This was unremarkable – except that I *had* just co-edited and contributed to *Languages of Scotland*, whose writers were collectively asserting that there were not two but three living languages in Scotland: English, Scots, and Gaelic. Indeed, this was, as far as I know, the first book ever to make such a joint assertion (however guarded some of the comments on the nature of Scots). The book was well received in Scotland and elsewhere, many noting its unexpected optimism, and continues to be widely cited. In addition, it has had an impact on attitudes, events, and publications in Scotland, especially in educational circles. Yet I had continued, despite this and despite having been immersed in two dialects of Scots from an early age – urban (Glasgow) and rural (Perthshire) – and also despite an interest inherited from my father (who spoke Scots all his life), I had continued to follow convention and take English as my first language: something which was of course expected of me as a British national engaged professionally in teaching Standard English to learners around the world.

The UQTR official form had to be up-dated annually. I dealt with it the second time much as before, knitted my brows the third time but made no changes, but by the fourth occasion I had grown a touch mutinous. Several years in a hotbed of language politics had made a difference, as I came to terms with tensions not only between French and English but also between the French of Quebec and the French of France – some activists (and some of their Gallic critics) insisting that Québécois is not French at all. So I thought once more about the paradox of Scots, and in my final bit of form-filling listed *anglais, écossais,* and *français* as my three modern languages. Nobody commented on the change; perhaps nobody noticed it. But fur masel, Ah'd cróssit a wee bit Rubicon aa ón ma lain – an, efter aa the years that separatit ma faither an me, Ah stertit tae feel a gey wheen shairer aboot ma ain owrelookit mither tongue.

My thinking was hardly complicated: Why acquiesce in the submersion (however long-standing, however overwhelming) of something so basic? Scots after all was not just my 'mother tongue': it was my mother's tongue. Her usage was not English as the world knows it except when she wrote letters, and it was at school that I acquired along with my friends a version of Standard English as a Second Something-or-other. The same is true for children raised in other distinct varieties of 'English', such as Newfoundland, African-American, Jamaican, Kamtok, and Tok Pisin, and to a lesser degree the 'conventional' dialect speakers of, say, the United States, Canada, Ireland, and very importantly England itself. These varieties have a comparable vigour and similar uneasy and unstable continua that shade into internationally accepted usage. They also have the same sense of an insider speech which those outside cannot easily follow, are unlikely to want to learn, do not need to learn, and are therefore not expected to make the effort to learn, except at the most superficial of levels.

The status of a language or a dialect is decided not only by systemic distinctness and institutional use but also by the sum-total of assumptions and decisions made about it – including, from time to time, shifts in perception. It was, for example, just such a slow shift in perception in South Africa, resting on major structural adaptations, which set Afrikaans apart from Dutch and eventually elevated it into a national and official language in its own right, displacing Dutch. The early stage of this variety was known as Cape Dutch, but no one would now think of describing Afrikaans as anything other than a language in its own right.

Filling in my form in UQTR was a small act of linguistic politics in the wrong place. But if in the meantime a general shift of perception regarding the status of Scots has been occurring, my act becomes instead a small straw in the wind. If a significant number of opinion-formers, among them scholars of Scots and English, in Scotland and elsewhere, were to see the matter in the same light, others might begin to re-see Scots as a distinct English language which with the Union shrank to the condition of a range of dialects, then towards the end of the twentieth century began to regain status. However, any political change in the condition of Scotland is unlikely to have a direct influence on the shaky condition of Scots or Gaelic, because the movement for Scottish autonomy (within the EU) does not have a linguistic dimension to it. Irrelevant in politics, Scots is also a minor issue in terms of the world's languages. But it is significant as the oldest of the Englishes beyond England, entirely distinct from standard usage: that is, it is 'the first of the rest'. Jack Aitken puts it as follows at the end of his *Companion* article:

> Nonetheless, despite stigmatization in school, neglect by officialdom, and marginalization in the media, people of all backgrounds have since the 16c insisted in regarding the guid Scots tongue as their national language, and it continues to play an important part in people's awareness of their national identity.

Scots is both close to and distant from the various Englishes of England and from International Standard English – whatever that may be. Because of this similarity yet separateness, Aitken has called it a 'semi-language' and Price has reluctantly given it a chapter to itself in his book. Once upon a time, Scots was known as 'Inglis', and so to call it 'the traditional English of Lowland Scotland' is accurate – as long as one notes that its Anglian roots pre-date both England and Scotland. Scots is markedly different from all other Englishes in the world save three: the dialects of Northern England, which share its Anglian origins; Ulster Scots in Northern Ireland, which is its sole overseas extension; and North American dialects which have Scottish and Scotch-Irish (Northern Irish) associations. Finally, it has a venerable on-going literature, dialects of its own, and a hybridizing relationship with Standard English in ways not far removed from Spanish, Malay, and Tagalog. (See chapter 1.) Thinking of Scots as one of an uncertain number of English languages – and the first of many to contrast with usage in England – could be a practical way of squaring this peculiar and persistent linguistic circle.

Panel 6.1 Some books and articles on Scots

Aitken, A. J. 1984. 'Scottish accents and dialects' and 'Scots and English in Scotland', in Peter Trudgill (ed.), *Language in the British Isles.* Cambridge University Press.

1985. 'Is Scots a language?', *English Today* 3, July.

1992. The articles 'Scots', 'Scottish dictionaries', 'Scottish English', etc., in Tom McArthur (ed.), *The Oxford Companion to the English Language.* Oxford University Press.

Aitken, A.J., and Tom McArthur (eds.), 1979. *The Languages of Scotland.* Edinburgh: W. and R. Chambers (Occasional Paper No. 4 of the Association for Scottish Literary Studies).

Bold, Alan. 1983. *Modern Scottish Literature.* Harlow: Longman.

Görlach, Manfred (ed.), 1985. *Focus on Scotland.* In the *Varieties of English Around the World* series. Amsterdam and Philadelphia: John Benjamins.

1991. 'Jamaica and Scotland – bilingual or bidialectal?', in *Englishes: Studies in Varieties of English, 1984–1988.* Amsterdam and Philadelphia: John Benjamins.

Graham, William. 1977. *The Scots Word Book*. Edinburgh: The Ramsay Head Press.

Jones, Charles. 1995. *A Language Suppressed: The Pronunciation of the Scots Language in the 18th Century*. Edinburgh: John Donald.

Kay, Billy. 1986. *Scots: The Mither Tongue*. Edinburgh: Mainstream.

McArthur, Tom. 1998. *The English Languages*, Chapter 6, 'Scots and Southron'. Cambridge University Press.

McClure, J. Derrick. 1975. 'The English Speech of Scotland', in *The Aberdeen University Review*, 46.

— 1988. *Why Scots Matters*. Edinburgh: The Saltire Society.

— 1994. 'English in Scotland', in Robert Burchfield (ed.), *The Cambridge History of the English Language*, Vol. V: *English in Britain and Overseas: Origins and Development*. Cambridge University Press.

— 1995. *Scots and its Literature*. In the *Varieties of English Around the World* series. Amsterdam and Philadelphia: John Benjamins.

MacLeod, Iseabail, and Pauline Cairns. 1993. *The Concise English-Scots Dictionary*. Edinburgh: W. and R. Chambers (with the Scottish National Dictionary Association Ltd.).

MacLeod, Iseabail, Pauline Cairns, Caroline Macafee, and Ruth Martin (eds.), 1990. *The Scots Thesaurus*. Aberdeen University Press (with the Scottish National Dictionary Association Ltd.).

Makins, Marion (ed.), 1995. *The Collins Gem Scots Dictionary*. Glasgow: HarperCollins.

Murison, David. 1977. *The Guid Scots Tongue*. Edinburgh: William Blackwood.

Price, Glanville. 1984. *The Languages of Britain*. Chapter 14, 'Scots'. London: Edward Arnold.

Robinson, Mairi. 1985. *The Concise Scots Dictionary: A New Comprehensive One-Volume Dictionary of the Scots Language*. Aberdeen University Press.

Watson, Roderick. 1984. *The Literature of Scotland*. London: Macmillan.

Watson, Roderick (ed.), 1995. *The Poetry of Scotland: Gaelic, Scots and English*. Edinburgh University Press.

Panel 6.2 Scots presented as a distinct language

The following quotations illustrate the extent to which Scots has been recognized as autonomous by grammarians, journalists, educational institutions, cultural groups, and advertising bodies in Scotland and elsewhere.

1789: US
Noah Webster

The northern nations of Europe originally spoke much in gutturals. This is evident from the number of aspirates and guttural letters, which still remain in the orthography of words derived from those nations; and

from the modern pronunciation of the collateral branches of the
Teutonic, the Dutch, Scotch and German.

('An Essay on the Necessity... of Reforming the Mode of Spelling ...',
an appendix to *Dissertations on the English Language*)

1907: UK (England)
Henry Cecil Wyld
Already in the fourteenth century that form of Northern English spoken
in Scotland had attained a sufficient degree of individuality to be
regarded as a separate group of dialects – Scots, as contrasted with
English. Scotland, therefore, henceforth develops a literary language of
its own, quite independent of England.

(*The Growth of English*, London: John Murray, p. 122)

1927: UK (England)
Henry Cecil Wyld
After the end of the fourteenth century, the other dialects, excepting
always those of Lowland Scotch, gradually cease to be the vehicle of
literary expression, and are no longer of importance to us as
independent forms of English.

(*A Short History of English*, London: John Murray, 3rd edition,
p. 17)

1958: Poland (US)
Margaret Schlauch
The dialect of medieval Scotland developed further towards a national
language... The success [of Robert Burns] was also in part explainable
by the fact that Scottish English had a long history as an independent
national language in its own right.

(*The English Language in Modern Times*, Warsaw: Panstwowe
Wydawnietwo Naukówe, the work of an American scholar with
Socialist views, pp. 62 and 153)

1972: UK (England/Sweden)
Randolph Quirk, Sidney Greenbaum, Geoffrey Leech, and Jan Svartvik
Scots, with ancient national and educational institutions, is perhaps
nearest to the self-confident independence of BrE and AmE, though the
differences in grammar and vocabulary are rather few... But this refers
only to official Scots usage. In the 'Lallans' Scots, which has some
currency for literary purposes, we have a highly independent set of
lexical, grammatical, phonological and orthographical conventions,
all of which make it seem more like a separate language than a
regional dialect.

(*A Grammar of Contemporary English*, Harlow: Longman, p. 18.
[Repeated verbatim on pp. 20–1 of their enlarged *A
Comprehensive Grammar of the English Language*, Harlow:
Longman, 1985.])

1977: UK (Scotland)
John Low

> Up to fairly recently the policy of suppressing the native languages has been successful: both Gaelic and Scots have declined in use and in social status... On the other hand, beyond the schools, we have had in the twentieth century, particularly since 1926, a resurgence of interest in Lowland Scots and in Gaelic through a new vigorous developing literature. A new race of writers, of whose existence many Scottish children have been kept in ignorance until recently, has used the old languages of Scotland (as well as English) and illustrated their power and potential as literary media capable of reflecting the contemporary and the universal.

> ('The case for linguistic devolution', *The Scotsman*, 29 December 1977 (writing from Moray House College of Education))

1978: UK (Scotland)
Tom McArthur

> *The Scots Language: Yesterday, Today and Tomorrow* (in conjunction with the Edinburgh Branch of the Scots Language Society), Tutor Tom McArthur: The aim of this course... is to examine the background and prospects of the Scots language and its on-going relationship with Standard English in Scotland. Part of each evening will be devoted to description, discussion and analysis, part to the actual use of Scots. The course will take advantage of modern language-study techniques and will be cultural as well as linguistic.

> (from a publicity leaflet issued by the Department of Extra-Mural Studies, University of Edinburgh)

Mid-1980s: UK (Scotland)

> The Scots Language Society exists to promote Scots in literature, drama, the media, education and in everyday usage. The Society in no way regards Scots, or Lallans, as *the* language of Scotland, but recognises that it should be able to take its place as a language of Scotland, along with Gaelic and English.

> (from the pamphlet *Scots Language Society: It's your ain Scots tongue – yaise it!*, issued mid-1980s)

1986: UK (Scotland)

> The Scots Language, Thursdays at 2 pm, starting 17 April 1986: This course is designed to complement BBC Scotland's TV series *The Mother Tongue* and Radio Scotland's *The Scots Tongue*. It will be helpful but not essential for participants to have seen/heard the programmes. Classes will cover the origins and development of Scots to its peak in the 16th century and its subsequent decline as a national language... Tutor: Dr Alex Agutter, University of Edinburgh.

> (from a publicity leaflet issued by the Department of Extra-Mural Studies, University of Edinburgh)

1988: France
Jean-Marc Gachelin

Trois langues sont actuellement parlées en Écosse, une langue celtique, le gaélique, et deux langues germaniques proches l'une à l'autre, l'écossais et l'anglais. [*Tr:* Three languages are spoken in Scotland at the present time, a Celtic language, Gaelic, and two closely linked Germanic languages, Scots and English.]

(Jean-Marc Gachelin, Université de Rouen, 'Traductions écossaises', in *Les problèmes d'expression dans la traduction biblique*, no. 1 of the Cahiers du Centre de Linguistic réligieuse)

1990: Germany
Manfred Görlach

(1) *Scots:* This is the one variety diverging from English ever to have achieved complete independence as a separate national language.
(2) The Scots language has a remarkably strong literary tradition.

(Manfred Görlach, (1) 'The development of Standard Englishes' (first published in 1988), (2) 'Scots and Low German: the social history of two minority languages' (first published in 1985), both in his *Studies in the History of the English Language*, Heidelberg: Carl Winter, pp. 43 and 148)

1992: UK (general)

The money's strange, the food's different and they speak three languages, but at least it's safe to drink the water... Although English is spoken throughout Scotland there is old Scots, the lowland language most commonly associated with Robert Burns, and Gaelic, which is widely spoken.

(from the headline of 'Undiscovered Scotland', an advertisement by the Scottish Tourist Board in the UK-wide *Radio Times*, 18–24 January)

1992/94: UK (Scotland)

Courses available to students in the Scots Language – and Literature – are increasing, and increasingly popular.

(from the University of Edinburgh Annual Report)

1993: UK (England)
Charles Barber

The separation of the Northumbrian dialect of Old English into the Scottish and Northern English dialects of Middle English is in part due to the political separation of the two regions, which led to the emergence of a Scots literary language in the course of the Middle English period... With the re-establishment of English as the language of administration and culture [in England] came the re-establishment of an English literary language, a standard form of the language which could be regarded as the norm.

(*The English Language: A Historical Introduction*, Cambridge University Press, pp. 138 and 144)

1995a: UK (Scotland)
Anne King

The acknowledgement of Scots needs now to be followed by an acceptance of it for what it is – a language without official status, but with at least nine different dialect areas; several written varieties – Lallans, *Sunday Post* Scots and Central Scots dialect (Liz Lochhead, Bill Herbert); a tremendously flexible, vigorous language whose speakers drift into English and back to Scots with ease. Scots, like all minority languages, is affected by media and American English influence, but is thriving.

('Oor Wullie in Beyond the Pail Scandal', an article about the status and condition of Scots, in *Edit: The University of Edinburgh Magazine* no. 8, Summer 1995)

1995b: UK (Scotland)

I agree with Alasdair MacInnes (Letters, 6 October) that a knowledge of Gaelic and its place in our culture is desirable for all Scottish people, and it is arrogant to suggest that we should all speak English alone; but there is an important element missing from this statement. It is also arrogant to assume that only Gaelic and English are spoken in Scotland. There is another language, which has had a literature and a history since the 14th century... and which the majority of Scots either speak in a variety of ways or at least understand. It is called Scots.

(Sheila Douglas, Scone, Perthshire, in the letter column of *The Scotsman*, 10 October. [Part of a detailed debate over months, typical of many in this Edinburgh-based newspaper.])

1996a: UK (Scotland)

A Language Suppressed: The Pronunciation of the Scots Language in the 18th Century

(title of a work by Charles Jones, Forbes Professor of English Language, University of Edinburgh, published by John Donald Publishers, Edinburgh)

1996b: UK (England)
Jeremy Smith

Scots has the longest attested history of any major language-variety derived from Old English outside the geographical boundaries of present-day England, and was the first non-English variety to begin developing a standardised form of the language... Furthermore, Scots has had an especially intimate contact with English throughout its history, and it thus provides an excellent laboratory for the study of language-contact.

(*An Historical Study of English: Function, Form and* Change, London: Routledge, pp. 165–6)

1996c: UK (general)

Scotland has not one but two indigenous languages: Gaelic and Scots. Both have been largely displaced by English over the past three hundred years. But displaced certainly does not mean destroyed. The languages have survived and produced considerable literatures... There are active campaigns to extend the use of both languages. Gaelic, with government assistance, has a presence on television, and is undeniably a language because it is distinctive. Scots, however, has a close relationship with English, with much common vocabulary, and so is easier to ignore.

(from the article 'Letter from Edinburgh' (unsigned in accordance with editorial policy), in *The Economist* (London), 10 February)

Panel 6.3 A Scots sampler

Below is a selection of Scots/English differences in three parts (Scots on the left, English on the right). All listed forms are in current use. As regards pronunciation, whatever their typical speech (more Scots, more English, or mixed), a majority of the Scottish people differ in speech from other Anglophones in two ways that are shibboleths of Scottishness: (1) A tapped or rolled alveolar *r* in such words as *breathe, world,* and *there* (minority pronunciations being a retroflex *r*, a uvular *r*, and the non-rhotic usage of England); (2) A voiceless velar fricative as in the *ch* of such words as *ach, loch, Bach, Munich, patriarch* (compare German *ach, Bach,* and *machen*).

(1) Pronunciation and typical spelling

hame, stane, sair, gae	home, stone, sore, go
hoose, oot, doon/doun, coo	house, out, down, cow
ba(w), ha(w), faut, saut	ball, hall, fault, salt
buit, guid, muin, puir	boot, good, moon, poor
licht, micht, richt, sicht	light, might, right, sight

(2) Grammar

lookit, mendit	looked, mended
tell/tellt, sell/sellt	tell/told, sell/sold
gae/gaed/gan	go/went
gie/gied/gien	give/gave/given
eye/een	eye/eyes
He'll no can come the day	He won't be able to come today
Ah micht could gae the morn	I might be able to go tomorrow
Ah dinna(e) ken	I don't know
We couldna(e) dae it	We couldn't do it
He'll no be comin	He won't be coming
That's me awa(w) hame	I'm going home now
Ah, it's yirsel	Ah, it's you

(3) Vocabulary

an ashet	a serving dish (from French *assiette*)
a bairn	a child
tae blether	to talk nonsense
a brae	a slope (of a hill)
braw	fine, beautiful, handsome
tae dicht	to clean, wipe
douce	sweet, especially in manner (from French *doux/douce*)
a dwam	a stupor; a dazed state
fantoosh	flashy
glaikit	stupid-looking
a howf(f)	a favourite haunt/pub
tae ken	to know
tae lowp	to jump, leap
(the) noo	now
sonsy	(of a woman) good-looking in a buxom way
tae speir	to ask
tae stravaig	to wander, roam, go about/around
a sybie/syboe	a spring onion (UK), scallion (US) (from French *ciboule*)
tapsalteerie	topsy-turvy
tae thole	to endure, tolerate
tae trauchle	to overburden or harass
a sair (= sore) trauchle	a great burden (= something hard to do or bear)

Panel 6.4 Orthographies for Scots

In 1977, two organizations, the Association for Scottish Literary and
Linguistic Studies (an academic group) and the Scots Language Society (a
cultural group) jointly sponsored a Scots Language Planning Committee, of
which I was co-convener, to look into the possibility of a standard
orthography for present-day Scots. After due discussion, the members each
rendered the same specimen of Scots poetry into their preferred
orthographies and then debated the results, which ranged from a system
only marginally different from Standard English to one as unlike Standard
English as possible. The chosen specimen was the first 12 lines of Robert
Burns's *Tam o Shanter*. Below are reproduced a traditional published
approach, then a version of the new near-English approach (the minimalist
position), and finally the form designed to be as unlike English as possible
(the maximalist approach).

○ **The traditional approach: taken from 'Poems & Songs of Robert
Burns', ed. James Barke (1955).**
The apostrophe of omission occurs only twice in this sample, both for *an'*
(the Scots for *and*), but is common elsewhere in Barke. It marks dialect
forms seen as departing from Standard English (*a'* for *all, wi'* for *with*, etc.)
and standard pronunciations which differ from standard spelling (*amaz'd*
for *amazed, tho'* for *though*). No such apostrophes appear in the re-creations
by the committee, because such marks were considered to imply a
subordinate and derivative status. The traditional sample is accompanied
by Standard English glosses for 13 Scots expressions. The text, a typically
Burnsian English/Scots mix, tends to buttress the view that Scots is no more
than a dialect of English:

When chapman billies leave the street,   *chapman billies* pedlars
And drouthy neebors neebors meet;   *drouthy neebors* thirsty
                                                                          neighbo(u)rs

As market-days are wearing late,
An' folk begin to take the gate;   *gate* street
While we sit bousing at the nappy,   *bousing* boozing; *nappy* ale
An' getting fou and unco happy,   *fou* full, drunk;
                                                                          unco mighty, very

We think na on the lang Scots miles,   *na* not; *lang* long
The mosses, waters, slaps, and styles,   *mosses* bogs; *slaps* pools
That lie between us and our hame,   *oor* our; *hame* home
Whare sits our sulky, sullen dame,
Gathering her brows like gathering storm,
Nursing her wrath to keep it warm.

○ **The minimalist approach: only just different enough**
The version that follows represents the position of the 'minimalists' on the
committee – myself among them – who sought a pragmatic system which
reflects the similarities and differences of Scots and Standard English. It is

my own current preference, and not identical with any of the original efforts, having adopted the acute accent over *o* (*ó*) to mark the vowel sound /o/ (compare the Lorimer New Testament quotation in chapter 1, which has *í* for the vowel sound /i/, as in *spírit*, 'speerit'):

> Whan chapman billies lea the street
> An drouthy neibors neibors meet,
> As mercat days are weirin late
> An fowk begin tae tak the gate,
> While we sit bousin at the nappy
> An gettin fu an unco happy,
> We thinkna ón the lang Scóts miles,
> The mósses, watters, slaps, an stiles
> That lie atween us an oor hame,
> Whaur sits oor sulky, sullen dame,
> Gaitherin her brous like gaitherin stórm,
> Nursin her wrath tae keep it warm.

○ **The maximalist position: as different as possible**

The version below positions printed Scots as far from English as possible – in my own view imposing an unnecessary burden on children who are already learning Standard English orthography in school. It rests on a phonemic analysis of a putative 'Common Scots' and adopts a reformist approach to spelling, which it makes as regular as possible (a position shared with various orthographies created for pidgins and creoles):

> Whan chapman bilys lei the streit,
> An drouthy neibors neibors meit;
> As mercat dais ar wieran laet,
> An fowk begin ti tak the gaet;
> Whiyl wei sit bouzan at the napy,
> An getan fou an unco hapy,
> Wei think na on the lang Scots miyls,
> The mosis, watirs, slaps an stiyls,
> That liy betwein us an our haem,
> Whaar sits uir sulky, sulin daem,
> Gethiran hir brous liyk gethiran storm,
> Nursan hir vraeth ti keip hit warm.

NOTE: J. Derrick McClure of Aberdeen University, a member of the short-lived planning committee, has written briefly about its work in 'The Concept of Standard Scots', *Chapman* 23–4, 1979, pp. 90–9, reprinted in his collection *Scots and its Literature*, 1995, in the series Varieties of English Around the World, ed. Manfred Görlach (Amsterdam and Philadelphia: John Benjamins), pp. 20–36, from which (p. 29) the immediately above maximalist version is taken.

7   Substrates and superstrates

> **pid.gin** ... *n* [C;U] a language which is a
> mixture of two or more other languages, esp.
> as used between people who do not speak
> each other's language: *pidgin English* – com-
> pare CREOLE, LINGUA FRANCA
> **cre.ole** ... *n* *(often cap)* **1** [C;U] an
> American or West Indian language which has
> grown through a combination of a European
> language with one or more other languages –
> compare PIDGIN
>
> (definitions, Della Summers (ed.),
> *Longman Dictionary of English Language and
> Culture*, 1992)

Pidgins and creoles: *A contentious topic*

Although the above definitions are well formed and indicate clearly the
links between the two words, present-day pidginists and creolists are
unlikely to consider them sufficient. This is not, however, necessarily an
adverse judgement on Longman's lexicographers; rather, scholars investigating the pidgin/creole phenomenon tend to have reservations about *any*
definitions of *pidgin* and *creole* – including their own – and there are at
least four reasons for this:

○ The etymology of the terms is problematic, and their current uses
  among both specialists and the general public are far from
  uniform, not always precise, and where precise are generally
  contentious.

○ The phenomena which the terms help identify are hundreds –
  probably thousands – of years old, and may indeed be basic to
  language itself.

○ Although progress has been made in understanding the pidgin/
  creole phenomenon, there is as yet no unified theory of the subject
  and its boundaries are far from clear.

○ The varieties of language which the terms cover traditionally have
  low prestige, and many people (including speakers of pidgins and

creoles) cannot understand why university people should bother with them. The American linguist John A. Holm has made the following comment on this point:

> What earlier generations thought of pidgin and creole languages is all too clear from their very names: *broken English, bastard Portuguese, nigger French, kombuistaaltje* ('cookhouse lingo'), *isikula* ('coolie language'). This contempt often stemmed in part from the feeling that pidgins and creoles were corruptions of 'higher', usually European languages, and in part from attitudes toward the speakers of such languages, who were often perceived as semi-savages whose partial acquisition of civilized habits was somehow an affront. Those speakers of creole languages who had access to education were duly convinced that their speech was wrong, and they often tried to make it more similar to the standard. With few exceptions, even linguists thought of pidgin and creole languages as 'aberrant' (Bloomfield 1933:471) if they thought of them at all – that is, as defective and therefore inappropriate as objects of study.

(*Pidgins and Creoles*, Cambridge University Press, 1988, p. 1)

Holm's observations can be compared with the following statement in a prominent British periodical, in a review (1996) of a book by Jean Aitchison, Rupert Murdoch Professor of Language and Communication at Oxford:

> An examination of Tok Pisin, Ms Aitchison claims, illuminates the general story of linguistic evolution. But her claim is arguably mistaken. Pidgins and creoles do not clarify that story because they do not recapitulate that process. They are, instead, examples of a different process, one that can begin only from an already evolved language. For pidgins are corruptions – in the sense of simplifying adaptations – of existing languages. They offer evidence of degenerative change in existing languages under certain pressures, not of how language evolved... [P]idgins [are] simple, clumsy languages incapable of nuance, detail, abstraction and precision. To get those things, a pidgin has to become a creole, and then begin the evolutionary ascent again into greater expressive power.

('Can you say what you want?', a review (unsigned, in accordance with editorial policy), in *The Economist*, 11 May 1966, of *The Seeds of Speech*, Cambridge University Press, 1996)

Part of the study of pidgin and creole languages at the present time is, as Holm implies, an understanding and evaluation of both the phenomenon and attitudes to it. Many people agree with contemporary language scholars that pidgins and creoles are viable entities worthy of detailed study, but many do not or are dubious about the project – and may as a result be dubious about contemporary language scholars.

The story of pidgin: *From jargon to language*

The Oxford English Dictionary (1928; 1989), having given the etymology
of *pidgin* as 'a Chinese corruption of English *business*', adds:

> Hence *pidgin-English*, the jargon, consisting chiefly of English words, often
> corrupted in pronunciation, and arranged according to Chinese idiom,
> originally used for intercommunication between the Chinese and
> Europeans at seaports, etc., in China, the Straits Settlements, etc.

The citations in the *OED* suggest that the spelling *pigeon* was commoner
than *pidgin* in the nineteenth century, when European traders were active on
the South China Coast, and appears to be the origin of the expression *That's
not my pigeon* ('That's not my business/concern'), which apparently has
nothing to do with birds. *Business*, however, is not the only China-related origin available for *pidgin/pigeon*; a second candidate is its Portuguese equivalent *ocupaçao*. Here, instead of losing just the *-ess* at the end of the word,
Chinese speakers would have had to lose two syllables at the start, *ocu-*.

The Portuguese, the British, and other trading nations on the China
Coast used a Babel of languages in their dealings with each other and the
Chinese, to whom all *gweilo* probably sounded alike. The Chinese as a
result may have extracted from the alien flux two syllables which sounded
the same *to them* and appeared to have the same signification in the two
most common and influential Western languages used in their ports:
something nasal sounding like *busin* and *paçao* (compare *Tok Pisin*). As an
individual word, *ocupaçao* is attractive as a source because, as the Irish linguist Loreto Todd has pointed out, 'the Portuguese were among the first
European traders in West Africa, Asia and the Americas' and were 'not
averse to using a simplified version of their language' in the course of their
travels and transactions (*Pidgins and Creoles*, London: Routledge, 1990,
p.19). But the adaptation of *business*, though still hard to believe, is marginally more credible.

In 1972, the British creolist Ian Hancock proposed the Portuguese word
pequeno ('small') as a source for *pidgin*, pointing out that the phrase
pequeno portugues has been used in Angola in the sense of 'broken
Portuguese'. This etymology correlates well semantically with other names
for makeshift languages, such as *petit nègre* ('Little Black' for Pidgin French)
and *baby hollands* ('Baby Dutch' for Pidgin Dutch), both suggesting child-
like usage. It also fits in phonologically with a usage in Sranan, a long-
established English-based creole in Surinam: the word *pitchee* (derived
from *pequeno*), meaning both 'little' and 'offspring'. A comparison can also
be made with *pikin* and *pikinini* in African pidgin usage and *piccaninny* in
American, Australian, and South African usage, words that apparently
derive from *pequeno* and its diminutive *pequenino* ('very small').

More exotic but equally plausible is the Hebrew word *pidjom* ('barter').

By 1700, three-quarters of the European population of the British colony of Surinam was Jewish and there were also subsequently many Jews in Jamaica. Intriguingly, the German writer Kurt Hassert wrote in 1913 that a 'Pidjom-Englisch' was spoken in what he called the 'London ghetto'. Little further information is available, as is also the case for the candidates *beachee* (a South Pacific pronunciation of *beach*) and *pidian* (a word meaning 'people' in a South American Indian language). We may well never know for sure where *pidgin* came from. For a fuller discussion of these matters, see Todd (*Pidgins and Creoles*, pp. 18–21), to which I am indebted here. In it, she concludes that 'it is probably naïve to think in terms of one specific origin' for *pidgin*, all of the suggested sources perhaps converging to crystallize the term. I tend to agree, having long suspected that more terms than *pidgin* have untidily multiple etymologies.

For over a century, *pidgin* has been used – pragmatically, condescendingly, humorously, or dismissively – as a label for any simplified hybrid language used in ports and on ships, and in garrisons, markets, mines, and the like. It is only in the later twentieth century that it has acquired the neutral, technical sense of 'a contact language which draws on elements from two or more languages' (*The Oxford Companion to the English Language*, 1992, p. 778) and 'a form of a language as spoken in a simplified or altered form by non-native speakers, especially as a means of communication between people not sharing a common language' (*The New Shorter Oxford English Dictionary*, 1993, vol II, p. 2204). Oxford has in both these instances stopped writing about 'corruption', but in the *NSOED* does not incorporate the perception of a pidgin as having more than one source language, a crucial point in any discussion of the subject. In the *Companion,* the American linguist Suzanne Romaine describes the emergence and growth of pidgins – and the various different scholarly approaches to them – as follows:

> This process of simplification and hybridization involves reduction of linguistic resources and restriction of use to such limited functions as trade. The term is sometimes extended to refer to the early stages of any instance of second-language acquisition when learners acquire a minimal form of the target language often influenced by their own primary language. There is, however, some disagreement among scholars over the number of languages in sufficient contact to produce a pidgin. Some investigators claim that any two languages in contact may result in a degree of linguistic improvization and compromise, and so lead to *pidginization*. Such a viewpoint includes in the category of pidgin *foreigner talk* and other classes of makeshift and often transitory communication. Other investigators argue that only in cases where more than two languages are in contact do true pidgins spring up. In situations where speakers of more than two languages must converse in a medium native to none of them, the kinds of re-structuring are more radical than in other cases and likely to be more durable.
>
> (from the entry 'pidgin' in McArthur (ed.), *The Oxford Companion to the English Language*, 1992, p. 778)

Sociolinguists typically identify a pidgin according to its locale and its *base language* or *lexifier language* (that is, the language from which most of its vocabulary is drawn). Thus, *West African Pidgin English* (or *WAPE*, also called *West African Pidgin* or simply *Pidgin*) refers to a broad band of usage from Gambia to Cameroon, its regional varieties having such names as *Ghanaian Pidgin (English)* and *Nigerian Pidgin (English)*, or again simply *Pidgin*. Because WAPE and such other forms as *Hawaii Pidgin English* and *Tok Pisin* in Papua-New Guinea draw the bulk of their vocabulary from English, they are referred to as *English-based pidgins*, as opposed to, say, French-based pidgins in Cameroon or Haiti. Some, however, gained their names well before linguists came on the scene, as for example *Aku* (technically known as *Gambian Pidgin English*), *Bamboo English* (a makeshift language associated with East Asia and the US military), and *Kamtok* (short for *Cameroon Talk*, whose technical label is *Cameroonian Pidgin English*).

The story of <u>creole</u>: *From local to global*

The etymology of *creole* is eminently transparent when compared with *pidgin*, but is convoluted. Ultimately, it derives from the Latin verb *creare* ('to bring into existence, beget'), the most notable of whose descendants for our purposes is Portuguese *criar* ('to nurse, breed'). When the Portuguese, Spanish, and French established colonies in the Americas, they used a noun from this or a cognate verb to refer to a person or animal born in the home, producing first Portuguese *crioulo,* then Spanish *criollo* and French *créole*, the French usage being adopted into English as *creole*. In the Caribbean and its hinterland in the seventeenth and eighteenth centuries, these co-generic words could refer as nouns and adjectives to: (1) a local descendant of European settlers (as in *a white creole* or *a creole white*); (2) a descendant of African slaves (as in *a Negro creole* or *a creole Negro*); and (3) a mixture of both, usually capitalized (as in *the local Creoles* or *the local Creole population*). In addition, their coverage extended in the course of time to the entire community, life, and culture of certain tropical and subtropical societies (as in *the French-speaking Creoles of Louisiana* and *Louisiana Creole cuisine*).

In the late nineteenth century, *creole* was extended to kinds of language used throughout the colonial and postcolonial tropics, primarily in the Americas but also in Australasia, the Indian Ocean, and elsewhere: kinds of language that differed markedly from certain European tongues to which they were related. As a result, people refer, for example, to *French Creole* or *Creole French* on Martinique or Mauritius, to *English Creole* or *Creole English* in Belize and Jamaica, to *Roper River Creole* in Australia, and to *Hawaii Creole English* in the Pacific. Although the idea of a Creole community as such is largely absent beyond the Americas, comparable stable, usually mixed-race communities have been a prerequisite in what is now seen to be the evolution of trade-and-plantation pidgins into mother tongues for which the term *creole* has proved to be suited. Generally, however, people of any background in a place where a creole is used are likely to speak it, whether or not it is in a strict sense their 'mother tongue' or they are part of the local ethnic majority.

Like pidgins, creoles are technically labelled in terms of their locale and their base languages: for example, *Jamaican Creole English* (also *Jamaican English Creole*, *Jamaican Creole*, or simply *Creole*, as well as *Jamaica Talk*, *Jamaican Patwa/Patois*, and *Nation Language*). Some creoles have also kept the names used when they were pidgins (for example, *Solomon Islands Pidgin English*, or *Solomons Pidgin*, commonly written as *Pijin*), while others have local names unlinked with either *pidgin* or *creole* (for example, *Bislama*, in Vanuatu, a term that syncopates 'Beach-la-Mar'). In addition, the use of both terms may occur side by side: for example, *Roper Pidgin* alongside *Roper River Creole*. Such a variety of nomenclature inevitably makes it more difficult to keep the terms *pidgin* and *creole* distinct from one another for clear-cut technical purposes.

Growing a mixed language: *Seven stages*

The term *pidgin*, along with its near-synonyms *makeshift (language)* and *(trade) jargon*, implies restriction, especially of lexis and grammar. The lexis is drawn in the main from the language or languages of a dominant group or groups – technically, the *superstrate language(s)* – while the grammatical structure derives in the main from several less powerful languages – the *substrate languages*. Thus, for Bajan, the pidgin (now creole) of Barbados, there is one superstrate, English, and the substrates are the languages which slaves took to the Caribbean from Africa. For Papiamentu, a pidgin (now creole) of the Netherlands Antilles, the superstrates are Portuguese and Spanish (with some Dutch), and the substrates are, again, the various African languages. The Latin-derived technical terms *superstrate* and *substrate* embody the same metaphorical contrast of socially 'high' and 'low' as the Greek-derived terms *acrolect* and *basilect* (as discussed and used from chapter 1 onwards).

In the situations in which pidgins emerge, people typically do not have access to, or are not free to use, the full resources of the languages involved. Because such people, whatever their standing, need quick and unsubtle communication for limited purposes, a pidgin at least in its earlier stages is a thoroughly stripped-down tool, about which Romaine notes:

> Non-pidgin languages generally have built-in redundancy and require the expression of the same meaning in several places in an utterance: for example, in the English sentences *One man comes* and *Six men come*,

singular and plural are marked in both noun and modifier, and concord is
shown in both noun and verb. However, the equivalents in Tok Pisin
(Papua New Guinea Pidgin English) show no variation in the verb form or
the noun: *Wanpela man i kam* and *Sikspela man i kam*. Because they lack
redundancy, pidgins depend heavily on context for their interpretation...
Pidgins are highly regular and have fewer exceptions than many other
languages, which makes them easier to learn.

(McArthur (ed.), *The Oxford Companion to the English Language*,
p. 779)

Linguists agree that there is a continuum of development from incipient
pidgins to fully-developed creoles which have their own print standards
and gain official recognition as languages in their own right. This continuum can be discussed in terms of seven stages or conditions:

1   A *makeshift language*, used by two or more groups of people with no
    language in common but the need to communicate, as with *Bamboo
    English* during the Korean War.
2   A *stable pidgin*, a limited means of communication which exists for
    years because of its social value, such as *Kitchen English*, used
    between domestic staff and employers in the early British Raj and
    continuing in India to the present day.
4   An *expanded* or *extended pidgin*, a more developed system which chil-
    dren begin to use, such as *West African Pidgin English*, used from
    Gambia to Cameroon.
5   A *creole*, the language, or one of the languages, of an established com-
    munity, such as *Roper River Creole* (increasingly simply *Kriol*), used by
    Aboriginal peoples in northern Australia.
6   An *independent language* with a standard form, whose makeshift ori-
    gins or creole status may be known but are essentially irrelevant, such
    as *Krio* in Sierra Leone, the mother tongue of c.250,000 people
    around Freetown and the second language of many more.
7   A medium which, whether it has independent status or not, interacts
    with and adapts towards its superstrate. Thus, creole speakers in such
    localities as Jamaica and Hawaii can engage in a range of usage similar
    to the play between dialect and standard in more traditional English-
    speaking communities (with the result that such creoles are often
    referred to as 'dialects'). The process of moving, in effect, from creole to
    'true' dialect status is *decreolization*, and the interplay between a former
    creole and its superstrate takes place within a *post-creole continuum*.
    Such a state exhibits degrees of mixing between the creole-cum-dialect
    on the one hand and the standard variety of the superstrate on the other.

A single variety may extend across the entire makeshift-to-dialect continuum. Tok Pisin, for example, is a lingua franca for many PNG tribes-
people, a mother-tongue creole for others, an officially recognized

national language, and a contributor to a hybrid whose other half is local Standard English. In addition, some creoles appear to have blended with dialects of their superstrates, as with Black English (African-American Vernacular English) in the US and London Jamaican in the UK. In addition, strong translinguistic links are possible in areas of complex language inheritance, as for example the Caribbean. In this region, all creoles have African substrates and also reflect centuries of contact among the European superstrates used on the islands, along the coasts, and aboard ship. The etymology of the word *creole* itself testifies to this, with its variants in four European diaspora languages.

An ancient pedigree: *Before and after Sabir*

The discussion of how pidgins emerge and evolve into creoles has two aspects: the more general (anywhere at any time among any languages), and the more specific (pidgins-cum-creoles whose superstrates are Western European diaspora languages). The *universalist* view proposes that human beings, in addition to having a fundamental propensity for speech, have the ability – in response to certain pressures – to re-structure and blend two or more pre-existing languages into simpler systems which can then, if the need arises, take on a life of their own, leading in due course, if conditions are appropriate, to new, fully functioning languages. Romaine observes:

> There is evidence for this hypothesis in the fact that baby talk, foreigner
> talk, and pidgins show certain similarities of structure. Baby talk
> expressions such as *Daddy go bye-bye* are similar to the reduced versions of
> language used to address foreigners.

> (McArthur (ed.), *The Oxford Companion to the English Language*,
> p. 790)

Pidginizing, creolizing, and hybridizing (as also discussed in chapter 1) have occurred many times in many places in many ways, and the fact that written and printed records are scarce is hardly evidence against them: such phenomena tend to occur among people who do not keep notes – in ports, on ships, in marketplaces, along frontiers: wherever they need a go-between jargon. And this general truth (which goes beyond pidgins as such) does not rule out occasions when miscegenation occurs in stable, even elegant conditions, as for example when, during the Renaissance, Latin served as a cultural superstrate for the vernaculars of Western Europe, and in the eighteenth and nineteenth centuries, when French had a similar role internationally, and filtered into many a fine lady's salon in England or elsewhere.

Pidgins and creoles with Western European superstrates and exotic substrates date from the fifteenth century, when the Portuguese and their successors began to sail farther from Europe than ever before, but this cannot be the whole story. Sailing the Atlantic and exploring its coasts and islands were novel undertakings of enormous significance but, even so, innumerable people in Southern Europe, North Africa, and West Asia – on ships, in armies, in caravans, as slaves, and so forth – had already for at least two millennia been travelling, trading, and generally communicating without formal instruction or trained interpreters. In ancient West Asia, Aramaic/Syriac served as a lingua franca in various empires for centuries and in the Indian subcontinent Urdu was the catch-all language of the Moghul armies from the sixteenth century, the name coming from Mongol *ordu*, 'camp' (also the etymon of *horde*). Aramaic probably and Urdu certainly have had pidgin-creole-hybrid continua as well as conventional dialects, as has the vast Hindi/Urdu/English complex used by millions in the subcontinent today.

Millennia ago, Phoenician and Greek traders, colonists, and expeditionary forces sailed far from home among both literate and non-literate peoples: the Phoenicians west to Carthage (in Tunisia), Tarshish (in Spain), and probably Cornwall (in Britain), the Greeks west to Sicily, Italy, and southern Gaul, north to the Black Sea, and south to Egypt, as well as east by land as far as Persia and India. Many 'bastard' and 'baby' speech forms must have come and gone in the process, especially for Greek after the conquests of Alexander of Macedon. As noted in chapter 5, a widespread variety known as the *koiné* (from *hé koiné diálektos*, 'the common language/dialect') was used for centuries after Alexander's death as a medium of trade and travel in the Mediterranean and West Asia. This was in effect a mesolect in relation to Attic Greek, the much-sought-after acrolect which served as a remote prototype for the standard languages of Europe. About the basilects we can only make guesses.

In the Roman world, equally, there were many forms of vernacular Latin, out of which in due course a range of 'Romance' derivatives emerged – their number varying depending on what one considers a 'language' and what a 'dialect'. (See chapter 9.) Although the major members of the Romance language family evolved in more or less regular ways from distinct kinds of spoken Latin (with some indications of substrates affecting them), the more basilectal Latins may well have been pidgin- and creole-like entities, including blends with kinds of koiné. Indeed, such jargons may well have been the base for Lingua Franca ('Frankish language'), the Romance-based Mediterranean makeshift attested since the Middle Ages.

Provençal (Occitan), with admixtures of Italian, was the primary superstrate of Lingua Franca, which was the shared language of the Crusaders, whom Muslims often (regardless of ethnic origin) called 'Franks', in certain West Asian languages rendered as *farangi* and *ferengi*, words which nowadays mean simply 'foreigner'. Lingua Franca endured from the eleventh to the early twentieth century – a thousand years of obscure but useful toil. Little of it survives. It was not much quoted or discussed in either script or print, much as European diaspora pidgins in their earlier stages went largely unquoted and undiscussed. Yet Lingua Franca cannot be ignored simply because its traces are few. Traces *do* exist, even (however tenuously) of its antecedents, as the British writer-translator Andrew Dalby indicates while describing his research for *Siren Feasts: a history of food and gastronomy in Greece* (London: Routledge, 1996):

> As is well known, in the medieval and early modern Mediterranean there was a widely used pidgin language known as *Lingua Franca* or *Sabir*, spoken on shipboard and in harbour towns wherever people of different languages needed to converse. It is also said to have been used among Christian slaves in Muslim countries. Some scholars believe that the *Lingua Franca* is the ultimate ancestor, through the early Portuguese West African pidgin, of most of the creoles and pidgins in use today. Apparently based originally on Provençal, it drew vocabulary from many sources. Although little of the *Lingua Franca* is recorded directly, its importance is confirmed by the many examples of cross-Mediterranean word borrowing that took place in medieval times – quite often between languages that were not directly in contact. A likely explanation is that the words in question belonged to the *Lingua Franca*, and were borrowed onwards from this. As I pursued the names of foodstuffs through medieval languages of the Mediterranean, in Latin, and in early Greek, I became aware that I was looking at the prehistory of the *Lingua Franca*: the remarkable mixing of words that took place in the four great centuries of the Roman Empire. For the first and last time in history, the whole Mediterranean was then open for travel and trade under the aegis of a single political power.

(Andrew Dalby, 'Ancient Feasts – and an Ancient Lingua Franca?', *The Linguist*, journal of the Institute of Linguists, London, 35:1, 1996, pp. 14–15)

Proponents of the *monogenetic* theory, which seeks to account for world-wide similarities among pidgins with Western European superstrates, argue that they all originated in the fifteenth-century Portuguese nautical jargon used by sailors of many backgrounds, and known, like Lingua Franca, as *Sabir* ('to know': perhaps because it was what sailors, traders, and travellers needed to know in order to get their work done). In spreading beyond the Mediterranean area, this constantly re-miscegenated makeshift could in course of time have acquired fresh lexical material from such new superstrates as French, Dutch, and English (depending on the home ports and crews of particular ships) as well as such new substrates as Asian, African, and Pacific languages, forming an indefinite range of makeshifts and potential creoles. It is noteworthy, for example, that the Romance form *sabe/save* (with its roots in Latin *sapere*, 'to know') is the word for 'know' in many such pidgins: compare also the colloquial English *savvy*, used as both verb and noun, and listed in the *NSOED* (2:2697) as late eighteenth-century 'Black & pidgin Eng. after Sp. *sabe usted*, you know' – as venerable an ancestry as any classical loanword in English.

Unfortunately, links cannot be firmly established between hypothetical ancient pidgins (with Phoenician, Greek, and Latin as their superstrates), one Mediterranean pidgin (with the superstrates Provençal and Italian), and the many pidgins of the Atlantic, Pacific, and Indian Oceans (with the superstrates Portuguese, Spanish, French, Dutch, and English). Nor am I asserting here that such links are ever likely to be established from existing sources. However, I would argue that a six-point *prima facie* case can be made for a tradition of makeshift languages from ancient through medieval times to the present day:

1   In general terms, similar situations are likely to produce similar outcomes.
2   The similar situations here are not isolated one from another but are part of a single long sea-faring tradition in whose middle and later centuries the emergence of pidgins is known to have taken place.
3   This suggests that pidgins comparable to those in the Mediterranean, Atlantic, and Pacific in medieval and recent times also arose in earlier times.
4   There has been a geographical and historical overlap among the various possible and actual superstrates as sea-borne traffic moved west through the Mediterranean into the Atlantic and beyond.
5   There is a just-discernible shading into recorded history of ancestral forms of Sabir (Lingua Franca) before Sabir itself shaded into the maritime pidgins (which, because of their far-flung miscegenative dynamism, retain few traces of the linguistic influences originally operating on Sabir).
6   Because the sea unites them, it is far more likely that the pidgins of the Western European diaspora languages had ancestor superstrates in the Mediterranean than that they leapt into unprecedented existence more than halfway through the 3,000-year-old maritime adventure of the Mediterranean and coastal European peoples.

Such possibilities, however, relate to language at its most fluid, ephemeral, illiterate, unscholarly, and *pragmatic*, a state of affairs that flies in the face of tidy, ivory-tower analysis. Philologists understandably can do little if there is no textual evidence to hand, and unfortunately for the comprehensive study of language there has never been enough textual evidence to hand.

English and Gaelic: *Hybrids in Ireland and Scotland*

In the general discussion of language, a gulf is often taken to exist between creoles and the dialects of their superstrates, even though creoles have drawn on the dialects of languages such as English rather than on their standard varieties; after all, aboriginal peoples and transported slaves came more into contact with dialect-speaking sailors, traders, and plantation overseers than with their upper- and middle-class employers and officers. A case in point is Gullah (also called Sea Island Creole), which is spoken in coastal and insular South Carolina, Georgia, and north-eastern Florida:

> [Gullah] developed on 18c rice plantations after British colonists and their African slaves arrived in Charleston from Barbados in 1670, in an encounter among African languages such as Ewe, Hausa, Ibo, Mende, Twi, and Yoruba, the English of overseers from England, Ireland, and Scotland, and the maritime pidgin used in some West African forts and aboard slavers' ships. It shares many features with other Atlantic creoles.

> (from the entry 'Gullah', by Salikoko S. Mufwene, in McArthur (ed.), *The Oxford Companion to the English Language*, Oxford University Press, 1992, p. 456)

Regardless therefore of its low social status, Gullah is complex: African languages on one side, English dialects on the other, and a ship-borne pidgin in the middle. One does not, however, have to travel as far from Britain as the Carolinas to find something similar at work. Loreto Todd has examined a variety of Irish English that is usually perceived as a dialect, spoken in County Tyrone in Northern Ireland, about which she concludes:

> In summary, one finds among Tyrone Catholics a spectrum of Englishes, ranging from a variety not immediately or easily intelligible to speakers of SE [Standard English] through to a variety which approaches the international norm. The strongly Gaelic-influenced variety is the mother tongue of most Catholics in the community and, although it has not been used in formal, state education, it is used in story-telling, songs and poems. Partly because of its exclusion from the schools, partly because of its association with Catholics, it has tended to be regarded as 'inferior' English, yet, at the moment, in the present political strife, it is used to gauge an individual's loyalties, and as a mark of solidarity. TE [Tyrone English] has much in common with other Gaelic-influenced dialects of English [in Ireland] and such dialects share many characteristics of such creole Englishes as Sierra Leone Krio. They differ from such creoles in that only one known language came into contact with, and was replaced by, English. Again, like Krio, TE is under constant and unceasing influence from SE... [Such] varieties of English have so much in common with creoles of the Krio type that they are, in this paper, referred to by a related name, 'creoloid'.

> (Loreto Todd, 'Dialect or creole: the case for the "creoloid"', unpublished paper, International Conference on Pidgins and Creoles, Hawaii, 1975, pp. 18 and 1)

And John Harris made the following observations in 1985, covering a wider range of Irish usage:

> To varying extents, [Irish dialects of English] bear the marks of two major historical inputs: an early Gaelic-English contact jargon, and the non-

standard English and Scots dialects which were transported to Ireland during the main period of British colonisation in the 17th century. Some of the most saliently nonstandard features of HE [Hiberno-English] can be attributed to phenomena that are common to most situations of language contact and shift, e.g. transfer from the substrate language, over-generalisation of superstrate rules. Others are widespread throughout the English-speaking world and reflect patterns that were current in standard and vernacular forms of Early Modern English. Still other features are in all likelihood due to the mutual reinforcement of substrate transfer and general nonstandard English characteristics. At many points HE shows a deep-seated structural divergence from standard norms. This brings with it many of the educational and communicative problems that are a familiar feature of conditions of interface between standard and vernacular varieties of English throughout the world.

> ('Hiberno-English', the focus article in *Standard English as a Second Dialect: Newsletter*, January 1985, Vol. 4, No. 1, published by TESOL (Teaching English to Speakers of Other Languages), Georgetown University, Washington D.C., p. 1)

In the same issue of the *SESD Newsletter* there was a 'call for papers' for a conference at Trinity College Dublin, 1985, in which 'it is anticipated that sessions on the following topics will be arranged: *language contact* (Irish [Gaelic] interference in HE, general questions of contact-induced change, creolisation); *historical perspectives* (issues in the history of HE and English, HE influence in North America and the Caribbean, theoretical issues in historical linguistics);... [and] *educational issues* (educational implications of the linguistic differences between HE and standard English, questions of a "regional standard", issues in language planning', etc.

What once happened between Irish Gaelic and English has also happened between Scottish Gaelic on the one hand and both Scots and English on the other; as most Scots know, it is not difficult to detect the Gaelic substrate in Highland English. For example, in pronunciation, *just* may be devoiced as 'chust', *pleasure* as 'pleashure', and *whatever* as 'whateffer'; in sentence structure, cleft sentences are common, as in *It's led astray you are* and *Isn't it her that's the smart one?*, as are present continuous rather than simple present forms, as in *Don't be learning bad English to the bairn* [child] and *If you can be waiting till the morning, our sale will be starting then.* Gaelic-in-English vocabulary includes *athair* 'father', *mo ghraid* 'my dear', and *duine bochd* 'poor fellow'. (Examples from A. J. Aitken's entry 'Highland English' in McArthur (ed.), *The Oxford Companion to the English Language*, 1992.)

Such substrate effects have hardly gone unnoticed, but in the nineteenth century descriptions of usage in the Celtic areas of Britain and Ireland were being formulated on a straightforwardly philological and dialecto-logical basis, and no one thought in terms of makeshifts, pidgins, creoles, or other such exotica. The Celtic languages might have historically been viewed with doubt and disdain by speakers of English and Scots, and the

Catholic Irish and Highland Scots may have been beyond the sociolinguistic pale, but they were nonetheless Europeans who duly took as large a part in the diaspora of English as the English and Lowland Scots. In addition, pidgins and creoles were not considered worth the attention of scholars until the close of the nineteenth century and have only gained ground academically in recent decades. It is not surprising therefore that it has taken time for insights from pidgin and creole studies to be applied to language in the Old World – and even nearer the heart of English than the Celtic Fringe.

English, Danish, and French: *Hybrids in England*

Scholars have for centuries discussed and written about the uniquely mixed linguistic inheritance of English, 'the mongrel tongue', but it was only in 1984 that the British linguist James Milroy made – could make? – the following comment on linguistic events within England a thousand years ago:

> Scandinavian place names in the Midlands and east of England (in some areas in the order of 90%) show that Danish settlement was extensive in the Danelaw (east of a line from London to Chester) in the tenth and eleventh centuries. The place-name evidence suggests that in some areas (e.g. North Yorkshire), a form of Danish must have been generally used for some time. However, as it is most unlikely that OE [Old English] and ON [Old Norse] were fully mutually comprehensible, contact forms (Anglo-Danish pidgin) must have been used to some extent in trade and commerce. As the bilingual situation receded, the varieties that remained must have been effectively Anglo-Norse creoles with a tendency in the post-creole situation to restore some of the grammatical distinctions lost in pidginization.

> (James Milroy, 'The history of English in the British Isles',
> in Peter Trudgill (ed.), *Language in the British Isles*,
> Cambridge University Press, 1984, pp. 11–12)

Turning his attention next to contact between Old English and Norman French, Milroy presents this later encounter as very different, because the Normans in England were fewer in number than the Danes, held positions of power, and remained in close touch with Normandy until 1204, after which the use of French in England declined. He argues, however, that between 1066 and the early thirteenth century pidgin-like 'interlanguages' were used in everyday Anglo-Norman life, extending those tendencies to structural simplification already at work in Anglo-Danish areas. He paints a picture therefore of a land in which two distinct kinds of contact were at work, for both of which he uses such terms as *pidgin, pidginization,* and *creole.* Of the relative flexibility of the term *creole,* Suzanne Romaine notes:

The term is also applied to cases where heavy borrowing disrupts the continuity of a language, turning it into a creole-like variety, but without a prior pidgin stage. Some researchers have argued that Middle English is a creole that arose from contact with Norse during the Scandinavian settlements (8–11c) and then with French after the Norman Conquest (11c). In addition to massive lexical borrowing, many changes led to such simplification of grammar as loss of the Old English inflectional endings. It is not, however, clear that these changes were due solely to language contact, since other languages have undergone similar re-structurings in the absence of contact, as for example when Latin became Italian.

> (from the entry *creole* in McArthur (ed.), *The Oxford Companion to the English Language,* 1992, p. 271)

We see here the terminology of pidgin and creole studies being stretched to areas where previously only the insights of philology applied. This is not, however, to minimize the capacity of earlier historians to note the massive changes at work when Old English came into contact with other languages. C. L. Wrenn, for example, writing at a turning point between the pre-eminence of an older philology and a newer linguistics, observes in 1949 on the 'Scandinavianizing' of English:

> [Middle English: *c.* AD 1100–1450] is marked by the sweeping changes in vocabulary caused first by the Scandinavian invasions and then by the Norman Conquest. For though the Norse invasions must have caused a general Scandinavianizing of the dialects in which they most operated, yet since the language of Northumbria and East Anglia and other lesser areas where Norsemen settled was scarcely written down in Old English times, it is only in Middle English documents that the real force of the Norse influence on the language becomes perceptible... [T]he natural affinities between Saxons and Norsemen [all referred to loosely as 'Danes'] – of race, Germanic tradition and language – asserted themselves, and the blending of the languages became inevitable.

> (Wrenn, *The English Language,* London: Methuen, 1949, pp. 25 and 65)

Wrenn also notes (p. 25) that 'the effects of the Norman Conquest and of the consequent French cultural influences later, were to deprive English finally of its homogeneous character'.

Although there is a strong similarity between the observations of Wrenn in 1949 and Milroy in 1984, some investigators of the history and nature of English and of the diaspora creoles have not acquiesced in the use of cre-olist terms and concepts to account in part for the rise of 'Middle English', regardless of universal agreement that vast hybridizing upheavals occurred between the eleventh and thirteenth centuries. Thus, Manfred Görlach in his article 'Middle English: A Creole?' lists four current uses of the term *creole* (with its derivative *creoloid*) as mutually incompatible:

1   The 'strict definition' that 'a creole evolves from a pidgin', as with the Caribbean creoles.

2   The proposition that a creole may develop in an existing language through reduction, as with the French Indian Ocean creoles.

3   The proposition that a 'creoloid' may emerge 'through fossilization of inadequately learnt language', with no actual pidgin involved, as proposed for Northern Ireland by Loreto Todd and Singapore by John Platt.

4   The proposition that 'creolization' may occur, again without a preceding pidgin, through the massive mixing of several languages, as proposed for a mélange of four languages in Kupwar in Southern India by John Gumperz.

Görlach adds:

> A long line of scholars... has ascribed the noteworthy changes in morphology and syntax that make ME [Middle English] so markedly different from OE [Old English] to the impact of the coexistence of Anglian and Scandinavian dialects in the Danelaw area... As far as we know, the drastic break that is probably the most distinctive feature of pidgins never happened within the history of English. If Anglians and Scandinavians made successful attempts at communication, their children and grandchildren would not have had any difficulty in understanding them... This is not to deny that English has changed more than, say, German in the course of its linguistic history and that these changes have to do with the frequency of language contact. But this alone is not enough; to call every mixed language a 'creole' would make the term useless. Yiddish, French, Albanian and Middle English (and many others) are composed of elements from various sources – but they are not creole languages.

> ('Middle English: A Creole?', in *Studies in the History of the English Language*, Heidelberg: Carl Winter, 1990, pp. 75, 77
> (original paper, 1977))

It is not hard to sympathize with Görlach, especially when he notes in a postscript that 'the concept of what constitutes a creole has continued to widen, and this could make the hypothesis [of creolization in Middle English] plausible to those who hold that extreme changes in the grammar and lexicon, together with regularization, are enough to justify the claim... I feel that my narrower definition is still called for, if the term is to retain sufficient precision' (p. 78). However, it is equally easy to sympathize with Todd, Platt, and Milroy, sensitized through studying pidgins and creoles to similar language phenomena in other places and times. Todd's and Platt's use of *creoloid* seems to me to be justified, because they are saying that something *like* creolization has occurred in Ireland and Singapore. I would add, similarly, that something like – but *not* – creolization occurred in medieval England.

My preference is to identify *hybridization* as a systemic phenomenon of which the pidgin/creole continuum is only one aspect. The prime feature of all hybridization is that wherever it happens nothing is the same afterwards; the blending of languages changes the system of at least one (and maybe more than one) of those languages, as has happened massively on three distinct occasions in the history of the complex we call 'English':

1   With contact between Old Norse (Danish) on the one hand and Anglian (a variety of Old English/Anglo-Saxon) on the other, in the ninth to eleventh centuries: two similar languages with more or less the same status.

2   With the dominance of Norman French over vernacular English between the eleventh and the thirteenth century, a case of political inequality in which influence passed largely 'downward' from French to English.

3   With the massive inflow of lexical material from Latin (and with it Greek) into a 'high' standardizing stratum of English from the sixteenth century onward, so that at some point (perhaps the nineteenth century) the vast Greco-Latin contribution came to be seen, by and large, as a natural part of the language (however intimidating for many).

Although none of this is pidginization or creolization as such, certain insights formed in pidgin and creole studies have strengthened our capacity to see this process as waves of hybridization rather than of 'borrowing' (a neat and conscious selective process often attributed in the earlier twentieth century to 'the genius of the language'). Because of such insights, I have in this study deliberately extended the terms *basilect*, *mesolect*, *acrolect*, *substrate*, and *superstrate* from pidgin-and-creole studies so as to be able to make certain points about language at large and the English language complex in particular. In some cases, as with such established creoles as Tok Pisin and Krio, the question of whether they are languages distinct from their superstrate is settled: they are (whatever their additional hybridization with conventional English may be). In other cases, such as Gaelic-influenced English in Ireland and Scotland, their differentness need not be pressed too far: isolation has not made them too different (like Gullah) and history has not given them official roles (like Tok Pisin). As regards what happened to English in medieval England, and regardless of what technical terms one uses to describe what happened, it seems incontrovertible that 'English' before the Danish and French encounters and 'English' afterwards were as different languages as Latin and Italian – and should at last be recognized as such.

Panel 7.1 English-based pidgins and creoles worldwide

Africa
Gambian Creole or Aku; Krio and pidginized Krio in Sierra Leone; Liberian Creole; Ghanaian Pidgin; Togolese Pidgin; Nigerian Pidgin (creolized in urban areas); Kamtok in Cameroon (creolized in urban areas); Bioku Pidgin on Fernando Po.

North America (All in the United States)
Afro-Seminole Creole; Amerindian Pidgin (most varieties now extinct); Black English Vernacular (status controversial); Sea Island Creole, or Gullah; Hawaii Pidgin and Creole.

Central America, the Caribbean, and neighbouring South America
Bahamian Creole; Barbadian Creole; Belizean Creole; Costa Rican Creole; Guyanese Creolese [sic]; Jamaican Creole or Nation Language or Patwa; Leeward Island Creole(s); Nicaraguan Creole; Surinamese Djuka or Aukan, Saramaccan, and Sranan;Trinidad and Tobago Creole(s) or Trinibagianese or Trinbagonian; Virgin Islands Creole; Windward Island Creole(s).

Australasia-Pacific Ocean
Bislama (Vanuatu), Hawaii Pidgin and Creole, Pijin (the Solomon Islands), Kriol or Roper River Pidgin/Creole (northern Australia), Pitcairnese and Norfolkese (Pitcairn Island and Norfolk Island), Tok Pisin/Neo-Melanesian (Papua-New Guinea), Torres Straits Broken/Creole.

(For further examples of pidgins and creoles, see chapter 1, including panel 1.2.)

Panel 7.2 A select bibliography of works on pidgins and creoles, in chronological order

The academic study of pidgins and creoles began with the Austrian linguist Hugo Schuchardt who, between 1881 and 1914, published treatises on such contact varieties as Indo-Portuguese, Indo-English, Malayo-Spanish in the Philippines, Melanesian English, Saramaccan in Surinam, and Lingua Franca. In 1979, several of his papers appeared, translated into English, in T. L. Markey (ed.), *The Ethnography of Variation: Selected writings on pidgins and creoles* (Ann Arbor: Karoma). In 1980 appeared *Pidgin and Creole Languages: Selected essays by Hugo Schuchardt*, edited by G. G. Gilbert (Cambridge University Press), who also wrote 'The First Systematic Survey of the World's Pidgins and Creoles: Hugo Schuchardt, 1882–1885', in M. Sebba and L. Todd (eds.), *Papers from the York Creole Conference* (Department of Language, University of York, 1984). Some significant titles in the field are:

Churchill, W. 1911. *Beach-la-Mar, the jargon or trade speech of the Western Pacific*. Washington: Carnegie Institution (publication no. 164).
Weinreich, Uriel. 1953. *Language in Contact: findings and problems*. The Hague: Mouton.
Hall, Robert A. Jr. 1955. *Hands Off Pidgin English*. Sydney: Pacific Publications.
Cassidy, F. G. 1961. *Jamaica Talk: three hundred years of the English language in Jamaica*. London: Macmillan.
Hall, Robert A. Jr. 1966. *Pidgin and Creole Languages*. Ithaca: Cornell University Press.
Hymes, Dell (ed.), 1971. *Pidginization and Creolization and Languages*. Cambridge: University Press.
Dillard, J. L. 1972. *Black English: its history and usage in the United States*. New York: Random House.
DeCamp, David and Ian F. Hancock (eds.), 1974. *Pidgins and Creoles: current trends and prospects*. Washington: Georgetown University Press.
Todd, Loreto. 1974. *Pidgins and Creoles*. London: Routledge. (2nd edn 1990.)
Adler, M. K. 1977. *Pidgins, Creoles and Lingua Francas: A sociolinguistic study*. Hamburg: Helmut Buske Verlag.
Valdman, A. (ed.), 1977. *Pidgin and Creole Linguistics*. Bloomington: Indiana University Press.
Hancock, I. F., E. Polomé, M. Goodman, and B. Heine (eds.), 1979. *Readings in Creole Studies*. Ghent: E. Story-Scientia.
Day, R. (ed.), 1980. *Issues in English Creoles: papers from the 1975 Hawaii conference*. Varieties of English Around the World, G2. Heidelberg: Julius Groos Verlag.
Bickerton, D. (ed.), 1981. *Roots of Language*. Ann Arbor: Karoma.

Bailey, R.W. and M. Görlach. 1982. *English as a World Language*. Ann Arbor: University of Michigan Press.

Andersen, R. (ed.), 1983. *Pidginization and Creolization as Language Acquisition*. Rowley MA: Newbury House.

Todd, Loreto. 1984. *Modern Englishes: Pidgins and Creoles*. Oxford: Basil Blackwell.

Mühlhäusler, Peter. 1986. *Pidgin and Creole Linguistics*. Oxford: Basil Blackwell.

Gilbert, G. G. 1987. *Pidgin and Creole Languages: essays in memory of John E. Reinecke*. Honolulu: University of Hawaii Press.

Holm, John. 1988. *Pidgins and Creoles*. In the Cambridge Language Surveys series. Cambridge: University Press.

Romaine, Suzanne. 1988. *Pidgin and Creole Languages*. In the Longman Linguistic Library series. London: Longman.

Todd, Loreto. 1990. *Pidgins and Creoles, Second Edition*. London: Routledge.

Byrne, F. and J. Holm. 1993. *Atlantic Meets Pacific: A global view of pidginization and creolization*. Amsterdam and Philadelphia: John Benjamins.

Mufwene, Salikoko (ed.), 1993. *Africanisms in Afro-American Language Varieties*. Athens: University of Georgia Press.

8   The Latin analogy

○ As for the antiquitie of our speche, whether it be measured by the ancient *Almane*, whence it cummeth originallie, or euen but by the latest terms which it boroweth daielie from foren tungs..., it cannot be young. Onelesse the *Germane* himself be young, which claimeth a prerogatiue for the age of his speche, of an infinit prescription: Onelesse the *Latin* and *Greke* be young, whose words we enfranchise to our own vse.

(Richard Mulcaster, in chapter XIII of
The First Part of the Elementarie, 1582)

○ The two languages from which our primitives have been derived are the Roman and the Teutonick: under the Roman I comprehend the French and provincial tongues; and under the Teutonick range the Saxon, German, and all their kindred dialects. Most of our polysyllables are Roman, and our words of one syllable are very often Teutonick.

(Samuel Johnson, in the preface to
A Dictionary of the English Language,
London: 1755)

The future of English: *Another Latin?*

In the first issue of *English Today*, the British EFL textbook-writer and teacher-trainer Alan Maley observed with regard to the future of the language:

One possible scenario for English as an international language is that it will succumb to the same fate as Latin did in the Middle Ages. That is, that the regional varieties will develop independently to the point where they become different languages rather than varieties of the same language.

('The most chameleon of languages: Perceptions of English Abroad',
English Today 1, January 1985, p. 31)

The same year saw the publication of the paper which Randolph Quirk presented at the British Council conference in London in 1984 (as discussed in chapter 3). In it, Quirk considers the same possibility:

Few today would suggest that there was a single standard of English in the world. There are few enough (not least among professional linguists) that would claim the existence of a single standard within any one of the ENL countries: plenty that would even deny both the possibility and the desirability of such a thing. Recent emphasis has been on multiple and variable standards (insofar as the use of the word 'standard' is ventured): different standards for different occasions for different people – and each as 'correct' as any other. Small wonder that there should have been in recent years fresh talk of the diaspora of English into several mutually incomprehensible languages. The fate of Latin after the fall of the Roman Empire presents us with such distinct languages today as French, Spanish, Romanian, and Italian. With the growth of national separatism in the English-speaking countries, linguistically endorsed not least by the active encouragement of the anti-standard ethos..., many foresee a similar fissiparous future for English. A year or so ago, much prominence was given to the belief expressed by R. W. Burchfield that in a century from now the languages of Britain and America would be as different as French from Italian.

('The English Language in a Global Context', in Randolph Quirk and
H. G. Widdowson (eds.), *English in the World,*
Cambridge University Press, 1985)

And more recently, David Crystal has observed:

Inevitably, the emergence of new Englishes raises the spectre of fragmentation – the eventual dissolution of English into a range of mutually unintelligible languages (as happened when Latin gave rise to the various Romance languages, such as French, Spanish and Italian). This has not happened.

('The language that took over the world', in *The Guardian,*
22 February 1997, p. 21)

In my own article 'The English languages?' (*English Today* 11, July 1987, see also chapter 3), I used the phrase 'the Latin analogy' for the scenario discussed by Maley, Quirk, Burchfield, Crystal and others. Since writing that article in 1987, I have concluded that this issue can be viewed from three positions :

○ **A pessimistic perspective**
A Babelesque approach which combines a sense of decline in the use and value of Latin with fears about the death of English as we know it. Although people holding this view do not have strong feelings about the perceived death of Latin – it happened too long ago – they may regret the weak current position of its classical variety, which is less and less taught in the schools of the Anglophone world. However, because of their concern about English, a Latin which 'died' under barbarian assault 1,500 years ago offers a suitably dire analogue of mutually unintelligible 'post-English' languages. People who hold such views are usually conservatives in the Wyldian tradition, asserting a 'Received

Standard' to which all should adhere or aspire, and which is for them the true English language.

○ An optimistic perspective
An international and multicultural approach which accepts the emergence of 'world Englishes', whether mutually intelligible or not. From this point of view, the growth of the vernacular Latins of Imperial Rome, which led in due course to the Romance languages, is hardly tragic. Such optimists might also argue that the death of Latin has been greatly exaggerated, in that it was the universal medium of scholarship in Western Christendom till the end of the seventeenth century. The assumption that Latin 'died' with the Western Empire ignores its role as a widespread acrolect, much as Lingua Franca was for a similar period the most widespread basilect. Between them were innumerable Germanic, Romance, Slavic, or other mesolects, jostling for position and often hybridizing with Latin and one another; the result is still with us, the French and Latinate elements in English being a case in point. Standard English, the optimists might add, is unlikely to break up, and the other Englishes already exist. People with such views may see Standard English more as a practical tool than a hallowed institution.

○ A neutral and pragmatic perspective
An approach which seeks, as far as this can be done, to establish what *did* happen to Latin: whether it 'broke up' spectacularly or whether subtler processes were at work, including its already being diverse long before the Western Empire collapsed. Crucial to a neutral view is understanding the emotive imagery often used when discussing the 'fate' of Classical Latin, Standard English, or any other 'endangered' high language: contrast, for example, *broke up* and *disintegrated* with *gave birth to* and *was the mother (language) of*. The assumptions here are that: (1) investigating the background of Latin, English, and comparable languages might clarify our perceptions of what tends to happen to prestigious, widely-used languages; (2) natural languages have always changed and apparently always will; (3) present-day global linguistic conditions are unique, making it risky to use analogies with past events to warn about the future.

None of the major commentators on the state and fate of English is in the pessimistic camp. Neither Quirk nor Maley, for example, endorses the Latin analogy as a warning about tomorrow's Englishes, Crystal does not present his comment as a warning, and Burchfield considers that any parting of the ways between American and British is at least a century away; further, he sounds no call to rally and prevent such an event, but simply makes an observation. Quirk, commenting on Burchfield's suggestion, notes that Henry Sweet made the same prediction that 'England, America, and Australia will be speaking mutually unintelligible languages' in a century or so, adding that Sweet's hundred years have passed and Americans, Britons, and Australians still understand one another (by and large). It is also Quirk's view, along with most commentators, that a general mutual comprehensibility in Standard English will continue for as far ahead as anyone can safely see.

The consensus among scholars is therefore moderate and non-apocalyptic, although they are all, of necessity, aware of massive on-going change. In the following observation, Burchfield uses the imagery of disintegration but does not discuss loss of mutual intelligibility:

> At a time when the English language seems to be breaking up into innumerable clearly distinguishable varieties, it seemed to me important to abandon [the *OED's* first editor James] Murray's insular policy and go out and find what was happening in the language elsewhere.
>
> (preface to the fourth and final volume of
> *The Oxford English Dictionary Supplement*, 1986)

An observation almost a decade later on the unity of English by Manfred Görlach is also non-apocalyptic, and essentially opts like Quirk for unity:

> Whenever a language spreads geographically or socially, we can expect to see its varieties diversify both in their number and in their degree of diversification. And we expect that the diverse varieties may become in time separate languages, as Latin became Italian, Spanish, Portuguese, Romanian, and so on. The world varieties of English have certainly diversified, their diversity being a major subject of this book. However, the pattern of past linguistic history may not be repeated. New factors of electronic communication and air travel are likely to prevent the fracturing of English into mutually incomprehensible languages. Locally divergent forms of English may drift off into separate languages, but the core of English is likely to remain a varied, diversified, but recognizably 'same' language.
>
> (preface of Görlach: *More Englishes: New Studies in Varieties of English, 1988–1994*, 1995, in the *Varieties of English Around the World* series, Amsterdam and Philadelphia: John Benjamins, p. vii)

Görlach probably speaks for many: despite all the diversity and because of all the recent technological innovations the centre will after all probably hold.

A complex inheritance: *Latin and English*

Latin has existed in its various forms for over 2,500 years – at least a thousand years longer than English. For around half that time, it was a conventional mother tongue, the most successful of the Italic 'dialects' of Indo-European, and from c.100 BC to c.AD 400 it was a pre-eminent language of empire, administration, law, commerce, culture, literature, and in due course religion.

With the dissolution of the Western Roman Empire c.AD 400, 'high' Latin gradually ceased to be a mother tongue, while in the Eastern or Byzantine Empire (which survived for another thousand years) it was replaced as the imperial language by 'Romaic' Greek. From then till the eighteenth century, Latin was in the West a learned, classical, and scriptural medium, comparable to Sumerian in ancient Babylon and Assyria, and to Sanskrit in ancient, medieval, and modern India and South-East Asia: acquired in the main by men through formal instruction in childhood and adolescence. Latin became first the sole, and later the primary, religious, cultural, documentary, diplomatic, and scientific language of Western Europe and its overseas extensions. It was therefore also one of the diaspora languages, alongside Portuguese, Spanish, French, and English (as discussed in chapter 1), was in fact their touchstone language, deferred to by Catholic and Protestant alike. Remarkably, the Latin of the present day, in the Vatican and elsewhere, is closer to that of Cicero and Caesar after two thousand years than present-day English is to the usage of Shakespeare five hundred years ago. High cultural languages, it would appear, can be kept going for a quite remarkable length of time, if the will and motivation are there.

Formal education in the British Isles was closely associated with Latin from the early Middle Ages to the beginning of this century. A 'classical education' was provided during and after the medieval period in the so-called 'grammar schools' of England – the grammar being Latin, because only the 'rules' of that language were described, labelled and *needed* as a formal tool before the seventeenth century. Grammar schools in England in the sixteenth century can reasonably be compared to English-medium schools in, say, India and Malaya in the nineteenth and twentieth centuries. In addition, the established methods of teaching English in such countries as Japan and Korea today – explicit grammar, representative texts, and rote learning, with limited oral activity – strongly resemble the rigid and often restrictive ways in which Latin was conventionally taught during most of the last two centuries in English-speaking countries, displaying many of the shortcomings and frustrations associated with them.

As is widely recognized, both the terms and style of the grammatical study of English derive from post-medieval Latin education, and the parsing and clause analysis of English grammar (widely taught until the 1960s) owes a great deal to a Latin grammatical model and associated teaching techniques that derived in turn from the Greek model formulated by Dionysius Thrax. (See chapter 5.) The three Roman grammarians through whom the Alexandrian model was transmitted into medieval and modern times were Quintilian (born in Spain, taught in Rome, c.AD 35–96), Donatus (flourished c.AD 350 in Rome), and Priscian (flourished c.AD 500, born in Mauretania, and taught in Byzantium). Even though in the later twentieth century there has, in many educational systems, been much less emphasis on Latin and Latin-linked models of grammar, a strong residual influence continues. Latin language, literature, rhetoric, and grammatical traditions have had a formative influence over many standard European languages and their literatures, and Latin continues to be taught in its classical form in many schools in mainland Europe and its colonizing diaspora – although not so much in the so-called Anglo-Saxon world.

Although Latin is often described as a 'dead' language, the metaphor hardly fits the unbroken scholarly tradition associated with it or the usages adopted and adapted from it into so many languages worldwide. The vast majority of surviving texts in Latin date not from Roman times but the Middle Ages and later (when it was avowedly long dead), and many of the usages taken into other languages have been absorbed in recent centuries from those texts. It has therefore long been a lively and useful corpse.

In the fourth century AD, the Vulgate Bible of Saint Jerome (a pupil of Donatus) became the model for Christian writing in Latin. This model was developed by Saint Augustine of Hippo, himself a teacher of rhetoric, in the fourth and fifth centuries AD, in such works as *Civitas Dei* ('The City of God') and *Confessiones* ('Confessions', widely regarded as the first autobiography). Augustine's example as a Latinist was followed in England by such scholars as Aldhelm in the seventh, Bede in the seventh and eighth, Alcuin in the eighth and ninth, and Aelfric in the tenth and eleventh centuries, while translations from Latin into Anglo-Saxon by King Alfred of Wessex and his aides in the ninth century laid the foundation of prose writing in that language, whose prose tradition was unique in Europe at the time. Without a Latin model to copy, the West Saxon tradition could not have developed, and although it was eclipsed by the Norman Conquest in the eleventh century it was not forgotten.

The hierarchical yet fluid interplay of languages in medieval Britain is aptly illustrated by three works from the twelfth century, all associated with the cycle of myth and legend called the *Matière de Bretagne* or *Matter of Britain* – the cluster of themes and stories concerned with King Arthur, the Round Table, and the Holy Grail. The Oxford cleric called in Latin Galfridus Monemutensis and in English Geoffrey of Monmouth (an Englishman with Welsh and Breton connections) wrote in Latin the prose work *Historia regum Britanniae* ('History of the kings of Britain', *c.*1135). He claimed that he translated this work from an unrevealed old book 'in the British tongue' (that is, Welsh), much as James MacPherson in the eighteenth century claimed to have translated his epic poem *Ossian* from a unified Scottish Gaelic original which did not in fact exist.

Among other things, Geoffrey's *Historia* illustrates the potency and primacy of Greco-Latin culture in Europe, because it begins with the validating arrival in Britain of a great-grandson of the Trojan hero Aeneas, whose name was supposedly Brutus (from which *Britannia* was then presumed to derive). The account ends with Arthur, a Celtic hero adopted by the Anglo-Normans as – ironically – a unifying national symbol of the mainly Germanic kingdom of England. Geoffrey's *Historia* was then translated into local French and romanticized as the *Roman de Brut* (1155), by Wace, an Anglo-Norman cleric from Jersey. And finally, Wace's work was the source for *The Brut*, a late-twelfth-century alliterative poem in English by the Worcestershire priest Layamon, whose work was the first to tell the stories of the kings Arthur, Lear, and Cymbeline in that language. The process of transfer from Latin through French to English took about fifty years.

Whereas literary translations from Latin into French into English or in due course Latin directly into English, were not unusual in the Middle Ages, Latin used for scholarly purposes was not readily translated until the Renaissance and Reformation. The schoolmaster, historian, and royal herald William Camden (1551–1623) wrote in Latin by preference, considering that to use English was to write in sand; his early work *Britannia* (1580) was not translated until 1610, thirty years later, but in his old age his *Annales* (first part 1615, second 1629) was translated between 1625 and 1635: almost immediately. The statesman-philosopher Francis Bacon, although he wrote a great deal in English, used Latin when he wished to be read by his international peers, as with his *Novum Organon Scientiarum* ('New Instrument of the Sciences': 1620). Sir Isaac Newton (1643–1727) chose Latin as the medium for his *Philosophiae Naturalis Principia Mathematica* ('Mathematical Principles of Natural Philosophy', 1687), a seminal work not translated into English until 1729, forty-two years later. However, he wrote his other major work, *Opticks*, in English, and it was published in 1704, a watershed year for serious technical writing in the vernacular.

Over the next two centuries, writers of all kinds in English (including novelists) brought into their work the phrases, imagery, and allusions of Rome, assuming correctly that most of their readers were familiar with them. In the late twentieth century, however, a wider readership much less likely to have learned Latin meets fewer references of this kind, although Latin tags have so penetrated English and other Western European languages that some are common usages, like *etcetera* and *subpoena*, while others lurk on the edge of general awareness, as with the legal *habeas corpus*, *sub judice*, and *ultra vires*, and others still have been translated into common use, such as *Time flies* (from *Tempus fugit*, now in limited use) and *Never despair* from *Nil desperandum* (also still in limited use). Few writers now quote a Roman source at length without translation, as their predecessors freely did from Elizabethan to Victorian times. As Virgil put it, *Facilis descensus Averno*.

In *Literacy and Orality* (London: Methuen, 1982), the American Jesuit

Walter J. Ong describes the 'Learned Latin' of Europe as follows (*learned* apparently being pronounced whichever way one wishes):

> Learned Latin was a direct result of writing. Between about AD 550 and 700 the Latin spoken as a vernacular in various parts of Europe had evolved into various early forms of Italian, Spanish, Catalan, French, and the other Romance languages. By AD 700, speakers of these offshoots of Latin could no longer understand the old written Latin, intelligible perhaps to some of their greatgrandparents. Their spoken language had moved too far away from its origins. But schooling, and with it most official discourse of Church or state, continued in Latin. There was really no alternative. Europe was a morass of hundreds of languages and dialects, most of them never written to this day... There was no way to translate the works, literary, scientific, philosophical, medical or theological, taught in schools and universities, into the swarming oral vernaculars which had often had different, mutually unintelligible forms among populations perhaps only fifty miles apart. Until one or another dialect for economic or other reasons became dominant enough to gain adherents even from other dialectical [*sic*] regions (as the East Midland dialect did in England or Hochdeutsch in Germany), the only practical policy was to teach Latin to the limited number of boys going to school. Once a mother tongue, Latin thus became a school language only... a language completely controlled by writing.

A language 'devoid of baby talk' and 'a first language to none of its users', this Latin remained as close to a monolith as any language has ever been, and derived its power and authority – like Sanskrit at the same time in India – from *not* being ordinary, *not* being natural. Also like Sanskrit, it became canonically fixed, and all the more honoured for that. When printing was invented in the fifteenth century, Latin was the first language to appear in the new medium, its long-established scribal conventions helping to establish a print standard for all subsequent languages that use the Roman alphabet.

We know little about the Latins spoken in the Roman Empire, but have before us today a living laboratory of English, with its hard-to-delimit international, national, and other standards and all its dialects, creoles, nativized varieties, and burgeoning hybrids. International Standard English has much in common with Learned Latin: it is a minority form within the complex, but crucial to everyone (even those who do not use it) because it is the increasingly global vehicle of education, research, the media, communication, transportation, commerce, and technology. The varieties of educated and professional spoken and written English around the world, buttressed by the print standard, are mutually intelligible, but many other Englishes are not. They therefore have much in common with the Latins of the late Empire, but because of the media some have lately become more widely accessible than in the past and are less likely therefore to part company with one another and the standard, as for example the everyday Englishes of London and Los Angeles. In the case of other varieties, however, from Scots to Tok Pisin to Taglish, prospects are uncertain and the gulf between them and the international standard remains wide.

A complex inheritance: *Latin in English*

By Samuel Johnson's time, the vocabulary of English had more or less settled into the condition we know today, but a hundred years earlier matters were different. In the early seventeenth century, the makers of the first dictionaries of English were not at all like Johnson in style or aims. His primary concern was recording and where possible 'fixing' the precise and proper meanings and uses of established words; theirs however was creating words entirely new to English and explaining others which were becoming current in high society. The majority of these new words of English were old words of Latin and Greek, adapted into the vernacular in regular ways. The early lexicographers of English included Robert Cawdrey with his small *Table Alphabeticall* (of 3,000 'hard vsuall English wordes', 1604: the first true English A–Z dictionary, though not so named), John Bullokar's *English Expositour* (1616: a veritable word factory), Henry Cockeram's *English Dictionarie* (1623: the first A–Z compilation to have this name), and Thomas Blount's *Glossographia* (1656: with 9,000 headwords). Their work marks a watershed in the growth, nature, and listing of the rapidly expanding vocabulary of acrolectal English.

Bullokar, to create his *Expositour*, appears (among other things) to have gone systematically through Thomas Thomas's bilingual *Dictionarium linguae latinae et anglicanae* ('Dictionary of the Latin and English languages', 1588, 1606). As he did so, he converted Latin words *en masse* into a Frenchified English, turning *alacritas* into *alacritie*, *catalogus* into *catalogue*, and *rumino* into *ruminate*. His justification was that others had already for some time been decanting Latin into English, so that he could safely assert that 'it is familiar among our best writers to usurp strange words'. For generations learned men, accustomed to speaking and writing Latin in their professional lives, had taken its words, phrases, and sentences into everyday usage; that is, they code-switched and code-mixed. As a consequence of both this everyday hybridization and the work of the so-called 'hard word' lexicographers, thousands of Latinisms were carried over ('transferred') into English in order to raise it up ('elevate' it), just as thousands of present-day English words (with their etymological baggage) are transfused into Bahasa Malaysia, Japanese, and other non-European languages. (See chapter 1.)

By the nineteenth century, this exotic vocabulary and the processes for adding to it had become so naturalized that purists like William Barnes (1801–86) – who wished to reduce the weight of Latin and restore the vigour of 'Saxon' – received scant support from either scholars or the public at large.

In consequence, a new kind of public vehicle became first an *omnibus* (Latin: '(something) for all') then was clipped to *bus*. Few people at the time took seriously Barnes's alternative recommendation *folkwain* ('people wagon'), which did however foreshadow the German *Volkswagen* a century later. In our own time, the box in the corner of the room is not a Saxon *far-sighter* but a Greco-Latin *television*. Present-day users of English, native or foreign, must be able to handle the dual system which Johnson called 'Roman' and 'Teutonick', whether or not they are aware of its existence. And of this dualism two observers have said:

> English and French expressions [in English] may have similar denotations but slightly different connotations and associations. Generally the English words are stronger, more physical, and more human. We feel more at ease after getting a hearty welcome than after being granted a cordial reception. Compare freedom with liberty, friendship with amity, kingship with royalty, holiness with sanctity, happiness with felicity, depth with profundity, and love with charity.
>
> (Simeon Potter, *Our Language*, Harmondsworth: Penguin, 1950/66, pp. 37–8)

> Apparently the Elizabethans discovered the possibilities of etymological dissociation in language: amatory and love, audition and hearing, hearty welcome and cordial reception: these quasisynonyms offer new opportunities for semantic differentiation. Two terms for the same denotatum; new connotations can arise, stylistic, poetic possibilities are offered when the new word is liberated from the restricted use in the language of science.
>
> (Thomas Finkenstaedt, *Ordered Profusion*, Heidelberg: Carl Winter, 1973, pp. 64–5)

Where Johnson pointed to two general sources of vocabulary, Potter and Finkenstaedt have drawn attention to special semantic relations within certain pairs of words. One member of such a pair is vernacular, like *hearty* and *happiness*, generally Anglo-Saxon in origin, but often from Scandinavian or Norman-French, and occasionally even from Latin or Greek, having been long since naturalized into Old or Middle English. The other is Latinate, like *cordial* and *felicity*, perhaps filtered through French, like *receive*, or with Greek links, like *cardiac*, or indeed both. Above, Potter talks about 'association' (the closeness of the two kinds of usage), while Finkenstaedt talks about 'dissociation' (the separateness of the two kinds of usage), a paradox which needs some thought. The words in the pairs which Potter and Finkenstaedt list are both alike and unalike: a *hearing* and an *audition* overlap semantically, but are worlds apart etymologically.

I would like to adapt and integrate the terms used by Potter and Finkenstaedt into one relationship with two aspects, and call it 'bisociation'. The term is general enough to include Johnson's two categories, the Teutonic and the Roman (that is, vernacular and Latinate), and particular enough to cover the points of detail raised by Potter and Finkenstaedt. In bisociate pairs like *freedom* and *liberty*, although meanings and uses are semantically linked, because the pair members are near-synonyms, they are distinct morphologically, stylistically, and collocationally, with the result that interchangeability is restricted. We may be *at liberty* to do something, but not **at freedom* to do it; we may be given *the freedom of a city* by its mayor but not **the liberty of the city*. The Statue of Liberty might, one supposes, have been called the Statue of Freedom, but it would have lost a *soupçon* of something in the process. Similarly, this parallel-but-different quality is apparent in the pairs *sight/vision* and *go up/ascend*. Consider the contrasts in 'What a sight she looked as she went up to bed' and 'In his vision, she ascended into heaven'. 'What a vision she was as she went up to bed' is entirely possible, but means something quite different, while 'In his sight, she ascended into heaven', is not clear but certainly isn't the same as 'In his vision'.

Bisociation is a powerful feature of English, but is by no means unique to it. Such *lexical parallelism* can occur when any vernacular language borrows so freely from a prestigious source that it gains a more or less well-defined extra stratum of vocabulary, as in Persian and Tamil, which have borrowed from Arabic and Sanskrit respectively. Latin has been bisociative with Greek, with such pairs as *circumlocutio/periphrasis, coordinatio/ parataxis, subordinatio/hypotaxis,* and *transformatio/metamorphosis*. These pairs have in turn entered English, providing it with a further doubleness at an even 'higher' socio-academic level, in which *circumlocution* contrasts with *periphrasis* (and both are glossable in the vernacular as 'talking-around'), *co-ordination* with *parataxis* ('ranking-together'), *subordination* with *hypotaxis* ('ranking-under'), and *transformation* with *metamorphosis* (*shape-shifting*, an actual usage whose meaning is comparable but distinct). English would appear therefore to have more than the two great sources identified by Johnson. There is: (1) a vernacular stream or stratum (which descends in the main from Germanic sources, but has a range of early Greco-Latin and French adoptions in it); (2) a Latinate stream (in which Latin and more recent French are closely linked); (3) a Greek stream that has for centuries been processed into English in any of three ways: indirectly through Latin and French, or directly (but generally using a Franco-Latin orthography). (See panel 8.1.)

This triple relationship is not so immediately obvious as the pairs on which Potter and Finkenstaedt commented. Nor have such complexities been planned; even word-makers as bold as Bullokar would not have attempted such an adventure. Like Topsy, these lexical relationships just growed, and are particularly apparent when we consider word bases. For example, the free vernacular base *bird* (in *birdie, birdman, bird-like*) is matched by the bound Latinate base *avi-* (in *avian, aviary, aviation*) and also the bound Greek base *ornith-* (in *ornithology, ornithopod, ornithopter*).

Similarly, the vernacular *earth* (in *earthy, Earthling, unearthed*) is paralleled by *terr-* (as *terrestrial, territory, subterranean*), and *ge-* (in *geography, geology*, and *geostationary*). More complexly, the vernacular *fire* (in *afire, firelight, firefighter*) is matched by Latin *ign-* (in *igneous, ignite, gelignite*), and by both the Greek base *pyr-* (in *pyromania, pyrolatry, iron pyrites*) and the free word *pyre* (whose meaning has specialized to something that can be set on fire for such a purpose as cremation).

Much of the diversity, range, and fertility of English vocabulary arises from this multiple condition, which can be called 'trisociation'. To demonstrate the abundance, we can look at the triset *ant, formic-, myrmec-*. The first member of the set, like *fire, bird,* and *earth*, is a free vernacular word, with such derivatives and compounds as *ant-eater, ant-like, ant-hill, driver ant, soldier ant*, and *worker ant* – all relatively transparent, because an *ant-eater* (whatever else it is and does) eats ants, and *soldier ants* attack and defend. The Latinate base *formic-* occurs in *Formicidae* (the biological 'ant family'), and *formicarium* or *formicary* (an ant-hill or colony of ants). Few people, however, routinely make the connection between everyday *ant* and technical *formic-*, and usually only the inkhorniest pedant would bring a *formicary* rather than an *ant-hill* into everyday chat. Finally, we have the Greek *myrmec-*, in such technical – and intimidating – words as *myrmecology* (the scientific study of ants), *myrmecophagous* (feeding on ants), and *myrmecophobia* (fear of ants).

This is only one among scores of such trisets that semi-formally operate in English. (See panel 8.2 for one possible formalization of what appears to be going on.) In such sets, there seems to be a core of more or less accessible, more or less regular (indeed predictable) contrastive material, and a periphery of irregular or etymologically distant items. In the case of ants, a literary and historical example from the periphery is Homer's *Myrmidons*, warriors who 'swarmed like ants' as they followed Achilles into battle.

Three lexical streams: *Vernacular, Latin, and Greek*

As indicated above, the vernacular members of such sets are mainly Germanic, but they are not exclusively so. For example, in addition to such Old English items as *house* and *home*, the vernacular includes *beef* from Old French *boef* (and therefore from Latin *bos/bovis*), as well as Old English *church* and Norse *kirk*, which are doublets descended from Greek *kyriakón* ('the Lord's [house]'). Although the language of origin is often a fundamental feature in the relationships among streams of vocabulary like these, in many instances that source is so far removed in time that all associations with it are lost. No one save an etymologist thinks of *beef* and *church* as other than 'ordinary' (and Johnson might have added, 'monosyllabic') words of English. The proof of this special ancient assimilation is the way in which such words form their derivatives: vernacular *beef* provides *beefy* and Latinate *bov-* provides *bovine*, in ways that follow distinct, ancient, and regular traditions of word-formation. Neither has, on the one hand, **beefal* (like *legal*) and **beefine* (like *aquiline*) or, on the other, **bovish* (like *waspish*) and **bovy* (like *catty*).

The vernacular level includes the words that children tend to learn first but that foreigners may well learn last, if at all, as for example phrasal verbs: *do away with, do down, look down, look down on, make away with, put up, put up with, shut up*. Most vernacular bases are free words and have many senses, such as *get*, whose main senses can be glossed as *become, grow, receive*, and *obtain*. Vernacular words also tend to be used informally, figuratively, and idiomatically, and to feature strongly in slang (*beef up, do for, get lost*) and do indeed include many monosyllables.

The Latinate element tends to be cultural and technical, educational and commercial, and is used in written reports and formal discussions. In vernacular terms, its constituents are often 'big', 'long', 'high-brow', or 'bookish' words, quite different from *big, long, high, brow*, and *book*. Some, however, with more or less French-derived forms, operate on the everyday level (as with *form, derive, report*, and *operate*), while others have a more polysyllabic, technical quality closer to the original Latin (as with *aggregate, arbitrary, collaboration, corroboration, disjunctive*, and *pejorative*). Most word elements on this level have cognates in the Romance languages, some of which are similar in visual form and general use, but not so similar in pronunciation (as with French *civilisation*), while others are *faux amis* whose forms may be similar but whose meanings are different (as with French *déception*, which may translate as 'disappointment', and has nothing to do with misleading people).

Material adapted from Greek into Latin, French, and English tends to be analytical and specialized, is generally not everyday usage except for specialists, and is common in such registers as medical and scientific English. The technical words of medicine are often swallowed whole, but can be glossed into everyday usage (the result often being a Saxonism of which William Barnes might have approved), as in: *adenoma* ('gland-thing'), a tumour of glandular tissue; *arthritis* ('joint-condition'), inflammation of the joints; *cardiology* ('heart-lore'), the study of the heart; *cardiopathy* ('heart-feeling'), disease of the heart; *cytostomy* ('cell-mouthing'), physically opening up communication between cells; *hysterectomy* ('womb-out-cutting'), the surgical excision of the uterus; *necrosis* ('death-state'), the localized death of tissue; *osteopath* ('bone-feeler'), a manipulator of bones; *phlebotomy* ('vein-cutting'), surgical incision into a vein; and *rhinoplasty* ('nose-shaping'), plastic surgery of the nose.

From plain to arcane: *A lexical bar*

The Oxford lexicographer Robert Burchfield has noted in a newspaper column:

> It is easy enough to construct an English sentence in which all the words except articles and prepositions are of external origin, e.g. *Invading armies impose exotic political systems on conquered countries*. Or one in which every word is of native origin, e.g. *Hardly any horse-drawn ploughs are found on English fields now*.

> (from the column 'Words and Meanings', the *Sunday Times*, London 1 April 1990 [my italics])

Certainly, this is not difficult if one is in the business of words, and has a sense of what constitutes 'internal' and 'external' sources (usually helped by a grounding in other languages and familiarity with etymological dictionaries). However, two writers at least, Victor Grove in *The Language Bar* (London: Routledge, 1950) and his successor in spirit David Corson in *The Lexical Bar* (Oxford: Pergamon, 1985), both drawing on the analogy of *the colour bar*, have argued that for large numbers of native users of English the kind of thing that Burchfield describes is not only far from easy but in their schooling they have had little help in crossing the 'bar' between the vernacular and the classical: that is, in terms of this study, in managing the long-term (?fossilized, institutionalized) hybridization inherent in Standard English.

In the past, a classical education was the privileged norm, and it was assumed that students from the 'right' backgrounds would acquire an understanding of, and some facility with, the Latin and Greek elements in the standard language. And if the classical languages were less studied, or not so fully studied, or even not studied at all, then the Latin and Greek roots and affixes listed in textbooks and dictionaries could be studied, assimilated, and put to use. But this has not always been the case, and many otherwise adequately educated people do not feel at ease with words whose natures and ultimate origins are in all truth 'Greek to them'.

Even so, however, as Burchfield implies, the levels can be syntactically distinctive (in terms of the registers being used), despite the fact that generally they flow smoothly into one another in many conversations and contexts, and certainly there are no hard and fast divisions in speech, writing, or print into a Neo-Latin English on the one hand and a Vernacular English on the other. Nevertheless, the following set of five deliberately manufactured sentences, each consisting of twenty words, indicates how an increasing density of Neo-Latinate material can affect the assimilation of information while at the same time altering the linguistic and sociocultural quality of that information:

1   *All 20 words vernacular*
    The cunning old fox sat under the tree, waiting for the silly crow to
    start singing and drop the cheese.
2   *17 vernacular, 3 Latinate words*
    He picked up the gem, inspected it carefully, put it in his pocket, and
    escaped before anyone could stop him.
3   *13 vernacular, 6 Latinate, 1 Greek*
    Most of the students who were involved in the project were enrolled
    for one semester in the world history course.
4   *9 vernacular, 10 Latinate, 1 Greek*
    In order to test their hypothesis, the investigators conducted a series
    of complex experiments that were rigorously planned and executed.
5   *7 vernacular, 9 Latinate, 4 Greek (compounds)*
    Abundant evidence exists, in both histological and radiological terms,
    of increased osteoblastic and osteoclastic activity, as indicated by
    osseous rarefaction.

'Real-life' equivalents of this sample can be found by ranging from the
children's and general sections in a library through to such specialized
areas as anthropology, biology, medicine, philosophy, and sociology,
where technical usage from the classical languages abounds. It is often not
just the message of such sections that is hard to grasp, but the medium
itself. Appropriate courses introducing the layers of the language at the
right time and in manageable doses (the kind of thing that Grove and
Corson were hoping for) could help bridge the gaps, but do not exist.
Books listing Latin and Greek roots separately do exist, are popular in the
US especially, and can without doubt be useful, but currently the histori-
cal-cum-functional groupings of vocabulary in Standard English are not
the subject of close analysis nor are they perceived as suitable for direct
instruction in schools and colleges.

There may never be a time when a majority of users of International
Standard English are comfortable across the entire spectrum of usage
inherited from its Anglo-Scandinavian, French, Latin, and Greek sources.
Part of the reason for this is the sociolinguistically high/low dimensions of
all languages with traditions in which some go to school and some do not,
or if all go to school some get fuller educations (and better instruction)
and some do not, while some are able to benefit more fully and some are
not. At present little weight is placed on an educated awareness of how the
history of Standard English affects its nature and use today – not only in
terms of its lexis (as discussed here) but also its grammar and prose styles
(not discussed here). However, this state of affairs may change, and if it
changes the kind of lexical analysis made above may find an appropriate
place. If nothing else, instruction of this kind would serve to acquaint
native-speaking students with the degree to which English has been pene-

trated by masses of material from other languages, and make it easier for them to appreciate why and how in its turn a mass of material from English is currently passing into other languages.

Regardless of any such developments, however, the standard language will continue to co-exist with other Englishes of greater or lesser congruity, and will continue to have within it the tripartite lexical system just discussed, whether it is transparent or opaque to users or discussed or ignored by teachers. English also shares much of this range of vocabulary in various ways and to varying degrees with other languages, such as French and Spanish (with their Romance origins, their own Greco-Latin inheritance, and their Anglicisms) as well as Swedish and Dutch (with their Germanic origins, *their* own Greco-Latin inheritance, and *their* Anglicisms), and *par excellence* both Malay (with its earlier lexical influxes from Sanskrit and Arabic and its current influx from English with its Greco-Latin inheritance) and Japanese (with its earlier influx from Chinese, its more recent receipts from Dutch, German, and French, and its current deluge of English). In such a world, no language can conceivably be an island, entire unto itself.

Panel 8.1 A linguistic flow chart of Greek, Latin, and French into English

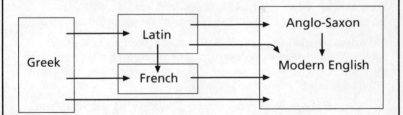

The chart represents the principal ways in which expressions from Greek, Latin, and French have moved into English over more than a thousand years. It originally appeared in McArthur, *Worlds of Reference: Learning, language and lexicography from the clay tablet to the computer*, Cambridge University Press, 1986.

Panel 8.2 Some Vernacular, Latin, and Greek sets

(1) Below are fifteen 'trisets' each introduced by a vernacular word beginning with B. In each set, this word is followed by associated bound bases of first Latin then Greek origin. Each set is followed by a selection of words formed in various ways from their bases. The meanings and uses of these words are distinct, but even so they have the same 'core' meanings. By and large, vernacular terms are more general and casual, Latinate terms more literary and cultural, and the Greek-derived terms more academic and technical. There is, however, nothing absolute about these relationships: we are dealing here with tendencies which may be stronger or weaker in certain contexts and registers. The patterns do, however, appear to be broadly consistent, as one might expect from the ways in which Greek, Latin, and English traditionally relate to each other.

bad, mal-, caco-	badly, malign, cacophony
be, ess-, ont-	being, essence, ontology
beast, besti-, therio	beastly, bestial, theriomorphic
belly, ventr-, gastr-	pot-bellied, ventral, gastritis
best, optim-, aristo-	bestseller, optimal, aristocrat
big, magn-, mega(lo)-	big-headed, magnitude, megawatt/megalomania
bird, avi-, ornitho-	birdsong, aviary, ornithology
birth, nasc/nat-, gen/gon-	birthday, nascent/native, genesis/cosmogony
black, nigr-, melan-	blacken, denigrate, melanin/melancholy
blood, sanguin-, (h)aem(at)/(h)em(at)-	bloody, sanguinary, an(a)emic/h(a)emorrhage
body, corpor-, som(at)-	bodily, corporeal/incorporate, psychosomatic
bone, oss(e)-, osteo-	raw-boned, ossify/osseous, osteopath
book, libr-, biblio-	bookish, library, bibliography
breast, mamm-, mast-	double-breasted, mammography, mastitis

(2) Below, the triset *air, aer-, atmo-* is laid out vertically with a wider selection of derivatives, compounds, and fixed phrases formed from it and in regular use. The patterns occurring here are repeated in scores of such informal parallels in Standard English.

Air airy, airiness, airily, airy-fairy; airborne, airtight, airworthy; airbase, airbus, airflow, airline, airmail; airplane (AmE); air-traffic control, Air Vice Marshal; Air Canada, British Airways, USAir

aer(i), aero- aerate, aeration; aerial, aerialist; aerial survey, aerial tramway; aeriform; aerify; aerobatic, aerobatics; aeroballistics; aerobic, aerobics, anaerobic; aerobiology; aeronaut, aeronautical; aeroplane (BrE), aerosol, aerospace, aerodynamic, British Aerospace

atmo- atmolysis; atmometer, atmometry; atmosphere, atmospheric, atmospherics; atmospheric braking, atmospheric electricity, atmospheric inversion, atmospheric pressure, Atmos Clock

9   The shapes of English

International English [Late 20c: with or
without a capital *I*]. The English language, usually in its standard form, either when used,
taught, and studied as a lingua franca throughout the world, or when taken as a whole and
used in contrast with *American English, British
English, South African English*, etc.

(Tom McArthur (ed.), *The Oxford Companion
to the English Language*, 1992)

Black English 1. Also called **Afro-
American English.** a dialect of American
English characterized by pronunciations, syn-
tactic structures, and vocabulary associated
with and used by some North American blacks
and exhibiting a wide variety and range of
forms varying in the extent to which they differ from standard English. **2.** any of a variety
of dialects of English or English-based pidgins
and creoles associated with and used by black
people. Also, **black English.**

(Sol Steinmetz (ed.), *Random House Compact
Unabridged Dictionary*, 1996)

English or not English? — *The Ebonics outbreak*

On the 18th December 1996, as business was winding down for Christmas
in the city of Oakland in California, the local school board unanimously
passed a resolution. Although hardly routine, it *was* in tune with other
decisions made in US educational circles in recent times regarding educational achievement, classroom language, and Standard English, so the
board members apparently did not expect it to raise much interest beyond
the immediately affected schools – and maybe not even there. Oakland
has a large black population, and its teachers and educational administra-
tors have long been concerned with the low level of achievement among
African-American children. The board, therefore, decided to change its
existing policy regarding children's everyday language and competence in
the standard language. However, the decision was swiftly reported in the
local media and public reaction was instant and widespread, despite

197

Christmas and the New Year. As two Californian journalists put it shortly
afterwards:

> Saying it has failed to adequately educate black youngsters, the Oakland
> Unified School District has declared black English a second language,
> making it the first district in the nation to give the dialect official status in
> programs targeting bilingual students. The move to recognise the black
> vernacular – called 'Ebonics' by some educators who consider it a distinct
> language spoken by the descendants of slaves – was approved
> unanimously by the Oakland school board. The vote was called historic by
> some educators and policymakers, who said it opened the possibility that
> Oakland could vie for federal funding available to help students who speak
> languages other than English.

> ('California Educators Give Black English a Voice', by Elaine Woo and
> Mary Curtius of the *Los Angeles Times,* in the *International Herald
> Tribune,* 21 December 1996)

In early January, the *Economist* in London noted:

> They never meant to do it, but on December 18th the local school board in
> Oakland, California unleashed the liveliest educational debate for several
> years. On that day, the board proposed a new approach to the teaching of
> standard English to black children in elementary grades. There are 28,000
> black pupils in the Oakland school system, around half of the total. Many
> of them do badly in school. Blacks account for 71% of the children from
> Oakland in 'special' (remedial) education, 61% of the children who are
> required to repeat a grade, and 80% of those who are suspended; their
> grade point average is 1.8, on a scale of 4, compared with the district
> average of 2.4... The school board thought it might help if the slang these
> children used at home were recognized as a distinct primary language,
> separate from English, and if teachers showed respect for this language
> and used it in the classroom, as a means to bridge the gap between
> standard English and the speech of the ghetto... The quasi-language in
> question has been christened 'Ebonics', a lumpish blend of 'ebony' and
> 'phonics'. Supporters of Ebonics say it derives from the structures of Niger-
> Congo African languages and marks the persistent legacy of slavery. Other
> linguistic scholars note that some usages have appeared only recently, as
> the ghettos have become more isolated from mainstream American life.

> (*The Economist,* unsigned (in line with editorial policy),
> 4 January 1997)

I was in San Francisco when the Ebonics story broke, and for several
days was able to follow it almost by the hour in the newspapers (local and
national), on car radio, on television, and in conversations. There was no
shortage of other local happenings (such as rivers bursting their banks) so
it was not a question of the media 'inventing' news. Suddenly everybody
seemed to be talking about it, first in the Bay Area then across the nation,
after which it became an international nine-day wonder. What I particularly noticed, however, in the letter columns of newspapers, in radio
phone-ins, and on TV talkshows was polarization and outrage. (See panel

9.1.) For a time, opponents on the issue seemed to be talking (or shouting) past one another, before discussion became more balanced and relaxed – allowing even for humour, as when at the end of the month Spanish English in southern Florida was nicknamed 'Cubonics'.

The term *Ebonics* was unknown to me before this development. Commoner names for the variety in question have included *African-American English, Afro-American English, Afro-American, American Black English, Black English, black English, Black English Vernacular*, and *BEV.* I listed these in *The Oxford Companion to the English Language* in co-operation with the African-American linguist John Baugh of Stanford University (not far from Oakland), who after the school board's resolution became closely involved in the debate. A more recent term than those we listed is *African-American Vernacular English* (*AAVE*), and this was the most widely used academic term at the time of the Ebonics outbreak. The earliest major publications on the subject with which I had been acquainted prior to the Oakland move were J. L. Dillard's *Black English*, published in New York by Random House, and William Labov's *Language in the Inner-City: Studies in the Black English Vernacular*, published in Philadelphia by the University of Pennsylvania Press, both in 1972, but I later learned that a work by Robert L. Williams entitled *Ebonics: The True Language of Black Folks*, was published in 1975 by the Institute of Black Studies in St Louis, Missouri. Williams coined the term in 1973, blending *ebony*, a euphemizing synonym for *black*, with *phonics*, a method of teaching reading and spelling based on regular sound/spelling correspondences: probably a unique approach to naming a language variety. Whatever the name(s) used for it, however, the English of the majority of African-Americans has long been caught in a negative triangle whose points are 'slang', 'dialect', and 'creole'. As Baugh noted in 1992:

> The most non-standard varieties [of African-American English] are used by poor blacks with limited education, who have restricted social contact beyond their native communities. Standard varieties are influenced by regional norms: black standard English in the South is different from the African-American standard in the North, and each in turn reflects colloquial usage among educated whites in the same areas. Considerable style-shifting occurs between blacks talking to non-blacks and especially on less formal occasions when blacks prefer to use vernacular speech among themselves. The corresponding variation is pervasive, occurring with phonology, intonation, morphology, syntax, African-American slang, idioms, and ritualized verbal confrontations. American Black English was born of slavery between the late 16c and mid-19c, and followed black migration from the southern states to racially isolated ghettos throughout the US. According to J. L. Dillard (1972...), some 80% of black Americans speak the vernacular, and he and several other commentators stress its African origins. The pidginization and creolization that resulted from slavery linger on the tongues of Americans of African descent.
>
> (from 'Black English Vernacular', in McArthur (ed.) *The Oxford Companion to the English Language*, 1992, p. 133)

At the close of the century, as the Oakland uproar suggests, the US in particular and English-using territories in general have achieved neither compromise about their socio- and ethnolinguistic constituents nor balance as regards Standard and other kinds of English, with the result that for many Anglophones anything that isn't 'standard' is 'dialect' if lucky and 'slang' if not. From the comments of many Americans on Ebonics it is clear that Standard English as they variously conceive it is the only credible, viable, and desirable English, despite the fact (which they concede, often in despair) that there's a lot of the other stuff around.

Linguistic insecurities: *The politics and realities of language*

At first sight, the Ebonics issue might seem like a flash in the pan, inspired primarily by the pressures and economics of minority education in the United States – and doomed to mockery and loss of face. After all, the Oakland school board *did* back down when so many public voices fiercely told them that African-American English is not – cannot be – a separate language. Yet the dust had not settled on the board's revised resolution before another such issue was raised in the media: the status of Spanglish as a distinct language. The journalist Lizette Alvarez, after describing and illustrating the mixed English-Spanish conversation of two Hispanic-American women (an actress and a media executive) on a late-night TV talk show, made the following comment in March 1997:

> Never mind that the talk show, 'Later,' appears on NBC and is geared to an English-speaking audience. Ms. Galan, born in Cuba and reared in New Jersey, and Ms. Torres, Puerto Rican and raised in Hell's Kitchen in Manhattan, were speaking the hybrid lingo known as Spanglish – the language of choice for a growing number of Hispanic-Americans who view the hyphen in their heritage as a metaphor for two coexisting worlds. 'I think Spanglish is the future,' said Ms. Galan, 32, ... 'It's a phenomenon of being from two cultures. It's perfectly wonderful. I speak English perfectly. I speak Spanish perfectly, and I choose to speak both simultaneously. How cool is that?'... As millions of Hispanic-Americans, first, second, and third generation, take on more prominent roles in business, media and the arts, Spanglish is traveling right along with them.
>
> ('It's the Talk of Nueva York: The Hybrid Called Spanglish',
> the *New York Times*, 25 March)

The *New York Times* then invited the Hispanic-American writer Roberto González Echeverría to comment on this report, which he did on 28 March, in a piece headed 'Is "Spanglish" a language?' His response was sincere, traditionalist, and worried, asserting that Spanglish was essentially a language of the poor and that Hispanic-Americans should keep their Spanish and English apart, noting that 'Spanglish treats Spanish as if the language of Cervantes, Lorca, García Márquez, Borges and Paz does not have an essence and dignity of its own', and that a dissemination of Spanglish beyond the US into Latin America 'would constitute the ultimate imperialistic takeover'. He adds that Hispanic-Americans should remember that they are a special immigrant group whose own diverse Spanish-based cultures are located near at hand, not on the other side of the world (like Italian, Chinese, or Hindi cultures), and urges them therefore not to create 'a Babel of hybrid tongues'.

Such matters as the nature of Ebonics and Spanglish within the complex of English are patently emotive and contentious, as are many such issues, regardless of the language complexes involved. A dramatic instance is what has happened to Serbo-Croat(ian), the Yugoslav national language which, in the wake of the (re-)establishment of Serbia and Croatia as separate political entities in 1991, has for most purposes become (or reverted to being?) Serbian and Croatian, forms which are closer than English and Scots, and perhaps as close as (or closer than?) American and British. What does such a development indicate about the perception, politics, and permanence of many of the entities we think of as single distinct languages? Could we suppose, for example, that, if the Serbs and Croats got together again in a re-union fifty years from now, the currently resuscitated two languages would as quickly become one again as the one has become two again? Or are they (and will they be) as much one or two as they ever were, the key things to change being labels and social perceptions? It certainly seems likely that, no matter how hard they try, Serbs and Croats (and other South Slavs) will go on understanding each other linguistically, whatever language they say they speak and however many minor differences there may be – and for many people there and elsewhere what they speak is still going to be Serbo-Croat.

This state of affairs points up the paradox at the heart not only of English but of most languages: that they are monolithic and multiple at the same time. People can couple, uncouple, and recouple entities which are closely related, calling them for one purpose dialects of one over-riding language and for another purpose a set of related but distinct languages, depending on how socially significant the varieties are and whether or not they have standard systems of writing, print, and broadcasting – or can acquire them. So yes, Serbian and Croatian are different, and yes, they are also Serbo-Croatian. Equally, traditional Scots and conventional English are manifestly different, and yes, they are the same, because of their history; and yes too, they are sufficiently different for clear-cut hybridization to take place between them, just as it takes place in a more extreme form between English and Spanish – a state of affairs regretted as much by purists on both sides in Scotland as on both sides in the US. And yes, conventional English and Tok Pisin are very different, and are socially and officially recognized as distinct languages; yet yes, they are closer to each other than Tok Pisin is to many of the other languages of Papua New Guinea – so close that, if one calls Tok Pisin a wholly different non-English language (as some creolists do), its manifest sociohistorical links with English have no place to go.

As we saw in chapter 3, many Anglicists have adopted the once-radical concept *Englishes* and some (implicitly or explicitly) incline towards the even more *outré* concept *English languages*, although none has worked out – or at present *can* work out – all the ramifications in such a shift from singular through plural to family. It is worth emphasizing that here we are dealing primarily with scholars' *perception* of the English language complex and not the complex itself, which is what it is regardless of what we call it and how we conceive it – much as the universe proceeds regardless of physicists' theories about it, but physicists (and maybe the rest of us) gain if they have better theories of physics. Languages are of course different from the phenomena of physics, in that we can institutionalize them, legislate for them, and consciously develop sets of guidelines for orthography, style, and the like, but in the main the analogy holds, because language is a mass activity and no individual or group has total control over it or complete awareness of what is happening to it at any time.

Although re-perceiving *English* as *the English languages* (for some or all purposes) may influence attitudes and policies, part of the re-perception is awareness that English has always been multiple and that the longstanding perception of it as monolithic has had little impact on that multiplicity. One should not therefore assume that re-perceiving it as multiple is going to produce much of a change in people's ideas and behaviour in the short term, even with today's rapid dissemination of information. But massive change is in any case under way, and towards even greater multiplicity than in the past, and will affect us however we perceive the complex, as the brouhahas over Ebonics and Spanglish demonstrate. The groundswell of awareness that African-American is different will not dissipate because the Oakland school district over-presented its case then retreated in alarm, nor will the vigour of Spanglish be diminished by pleas to remember the glories of Castilian literature. Such processes have their own momentum, and language is primarily what people do rather than what they say or think they do, or what they are told to do, say, or think – although these social aspects have their place in both everyday life and scholarly debate.

I have sought to show that informed observers have for decades teetered on the edge of pluralism, more or less asserting the languagehood of at least one English language other than English as conventionally understood: for example, diachronically, with Anglo-Saxon before 1150 and Scots before 1603, and synchronically with Tok Pisin and Jamaican

Creole, etc. (See panels 3.3 and 6.2.) It is only in the last two decades that scholars have been asked – or have asked themselves – to be more explicit about what they and their peers have been saying about multiplicity. If there is a solid case for the existence of just one English language other than 'conventional English' in its standard ('good') and non-standard ('bad') forms, then it must be thoughtfully noted. If a solid case can be made for two or more, then the paradigm has shifted – and may also shift for other languages of wide distribution, past as well as present.

Finally, I have tried to show that there is no absolute way of deciding which of a range of related systems within a language complex are separate enough to be 'officially' registered as distinct languages, especially if the complex has an emotionally loaded name that is applied freely and vaguely to both the (high) standard variety or varieties and the complex as a whole (high, low, and medium). Thus, where a complex is called *Turkic* or *Germanic* and the keystone entity within it is *Turkish* or *German*, the small difference in naming is just enough to limit confusion and contention. But where the complex is *English* and the keystone entity within it is also *English*, confusion and contention are inescapable. At the same time, however, it is clear that when emotive debates occur about unity-versus-diversity among English, Scots, Tok Pisin, Ebonics, Spanglish, and the like, both sides in any argument generally do accept the following paradox: that there is a shared Englishness among all the members of the complex (however difficult it may be to pin down) alongside a mutual alienness (ranging from the awkward but manageable to the unintelligible and baffling).

For this reason alone it seems to have become necessary (at least some of the time and for certain purposes) to regard a range of standards, dialects, creoles, nativized varieties, and hybrids as actual or potential members of a new philological family, the English languages, which would be as real as, say, the Romance or Turkic families, Certainly, as we have seen, numbers of Anglicists are edging in this direction. The members of this English (Anglic?) family are distinct yet linked, usually with overlap and interplay, in ways that are comparable to members of the Romance and Turkic families. Some are more distinct than others, some are defunct, some are in earlier and some in later stages of 'development' (however judged), and some may be losing distinctness while others are gaining it – all, again, much like Romance and Turkic. Consider, for example, how the number of Romance languages varies according to several conventional criteria and categories used to establish them:

- ○ *Status as a national language* French, Italian, Portuguese, Romanian, Spanish/Castilian, and Romansch/Rhaeto-Romanic (a national language of Switzerland): 6.
- ○ *Possession of a significant orthographic and literary tradition* The

above plus Catalan and Gallego in Spain and Occitan/Provençal in France: 9.

○ *Significant geographical, social, and structural distinctness* The above plus Andalusian in Spain, Friulian and Ladin in northern Italy, Sicilian in southern Italy, Sardinian and Corsican in the western Mediterranean, and Judeo-Spanish (the Romance equivalent of Yiddish): 16.

○ *Defunct but distinct*, such as Dalmatian in Yugoslavia and Mozarabic, the language of Christians in Moorish Spain: add at least 2, making a minimum of 18.

○ *Pidgins and creoles* (if their languagehood and Romanceness are conceded) varieties such as Papiamentu, a Portuguese-Spanish creole in the Netherlands Antilles, and Haitian Creole French: an indeterminate number, but add a representative 12, making 30 Romance languages in all (plus a range of disputes among linguists and others).

Taken together, the present-day Romance languages are spoken by around 400 million people, a number that compares well with the 350-plus million 'native speakers' of English at large. The organization known in English as the Latin Union exists to strengthen ties among these languages, especially in the face of an ever-advancing English, which is however itself so lexically Frenchified and Latinized that a case could be made for giving it associate membership.

Because it is the nature of languages to be fluid, variable, and interactive it is not possible to list in any absolute way the members of any complex-cum-family: they are not after all mothers and daughters, etc. It is even harder with English than Romance, because English is itself a member of the Germanic/Teutonic family, and such well-established constructs as language families are not easily disturbed. (See chapter 4.) There are few controversies regarding Germanic: the peoples of Scandinavia speak similar languages and are not usually troubled if Norwegian, Danish, and Swedish are called kinds of Scandinavian (or North Germanic), and Germans agree that Low German is a distinct language from High German, despite the fact that High German is known to the world simply as German (subsuming Low German much as English subsumes Scots). Within the English 'family', however, the public discussion of major diversity is so unexpected, even unnerving, that debate can be emotional, vehement, and confused, as with Ebonics and Spanglish – and where it is easily agreed among Germans that, within the same overall family, (High) German is a major language while Low German is minor, it is not easily agreed in the Anglophone world or in Scotland itself that conventional English is a major language while Scots is a minor language. (See chapter 6.)

Single or multiple, same or different? – *Scholarly inconsistency*

In such a complex, controversial, and emotive matter as agreeing the status, names, and associations of languages, dialects, creoles, and hybrids, etc., it is hardly surprising that confusion can also arise in the statements of scholars who seek to describe what is going on. An example is Barbara Rosen's article 'Is English Really a Family of Languages?' in the *International Herald Tribune* of 15 October 1994, which discusses my own work and among other things describes my circle model of English (as displayed in panel 4.8). Rosen quotes me as saying that the 'way in which scholars now look at language has radically changed. It is very unlikely that people will ever go back to thinking of English as one entity', followed immediately by Randolph Quirk's counter-quote: 'It's a gross exaggeration.' Rosen notes later in the text that 'Even McArthur's detractors agree that some of his examples are indeed distinct languages, but they reject the idea of calling them English', after which she provides and comments on a further quotation from Quirk:

> 'In common sense terms, there is only one English language... [Tok Pisin] could indeed become a separate language, but it wouldn't be English. It's not English now. I suppose it would be a dialect of English, you could say. It's broken English.
>
> 'People have been so silly about these things... Every language on Earth has recognizable dialects.' He says the difference may be only that 'a language is a dialect with an army and a flag and a defense policy and an airline,' but calling a dialect a language doesn't make it so. 'Nobody in Mexico would say "I'm speaking Mexican." [And] very, very few Americans would describe themselves as speaking American.'
>
> (Rosen, as above)

In journalistic terms, Rosen has represented my position fairly, as also (it seems to me) the positions of the sociolinguist Peter Patrick and the Anglicist Manfred Görlach, both of whom consider that the English-based creoles are indeed languages, but not English languages. I conclude from this that she has also represented Randolph Quirk accurately, give or take a subtlety or two, which leads to the following points, the first concerned with self-contradiction, the second with 'American'.

First: It can be difficult to talk about imprecise concepts like *language* and *dialect* while having to use those self-same concepts to carry the message – especially by phone to a journalist who is new to the issues and will get limited space on a page. I am not therefore too surprised that Quirk is quoted as saying that: (1) there is only one English (of which Tok Pisin is a part which might separate off, despite the fact that it is already separate and officially recognized as such, and Quirk knows this); (2) Tok Pisin is

not English but could be called a dialect of English (which is not what
Quirk would normally call it); (3) Tok Pisin is 'broken English' (using without qualification a term generally recognized as pejorative). This brief at-
odds-with-itself statement embodies the entire spectrum of views about
English, high and low, from c.1750 to the present day. (See chapters 5 and
7.) Comparably, Manfred Görlach is at odds with himself in an article in
the journal he edits, from which the following three extracts are taken:

○ Although pidgins and creoles are historically outside English (and, even if
they function in an ESD [English as a Second Dialect] framework, are
considered by many linguists distinct languages rather than varieties of
English), the evidence from them on lag and innovation may serve to
throw into perspective the interpretations gained from, in particular, ESL
communities.

○ In spite of all typological divergence, PCs [pidgins and creoles] behave like
other varieties of English when it comes to expanding their lexis in order
to designate non-English objects of material culture (such as plants and
animals, etc.): speakers tend to transfer words from their native languages
or make up new compounds from English elements.

○ Pidgins and creoles are marginal to my discussion: they are not properly
part of English.

(all from Manfred Görlach, 'Innovation in New Englishes', in *English
World-Wide*, 15–1, 1994, pp. 107–8, 108, and 116)

The tensions among these quotations are intensified further by the
name and nature of the journal itself, a scholarly vehicle for (among other
things) the discussion of English-based pidgins and creoles – whether or
not they are 'historically outside English' and despite the journal's full title
English World-Wide: A Journal of Varieties of English. It is because of such
contradictions and confusions (of which Anglicists are only too aware)
that I have not only tried here to explore the concepts and implications of
singularism and pluralism but also argued that certain fundamental para-
doxes should be accepted in our models. Pidgins and creoles *are* outside
English if *English* is taken to mean the conventional (largely standardized)
language in which for example this book is written, but they are inside it
if *English* means both the conventional variety and all the non-conventional varieties which have been historically and culturally identified with
the name. By and large, the paradox arises because it is inherently difficult
(?impossible) to separate off conventional English from the rest, because
all varieties exist within a continuum and not in neatly labelled sociolinguistic boxes. Non-conventional English manifestly includes all those pidgins and creoles described by scholars as 'English-based' and known to the
public at large as kinds of 'Pidgin English' – not Pidgin-anything-else.

Second: In his comment to Rosen, Quirk states that Mexicans do not
refer to themselves as speaking 'Mexican' and few Americans talk about

speaking 'American'. This may or may not be true for Mexicans, but Americans have long had a wide range of names for their primary language, including *English, the English language, American English, American, the American language,* and *the American tongue* – and non-Americans have also used them all. To demonstrate this, I list below some fifty instances of *American, American language,* and *American tongue* occurring on both sides of the Atlantic in significant texts over more than 200 years. (See panel 9.2.) These citations I regard as representative: if these writers have used them, many others must also have used them in speech as well as print to indicate (for whatever reason) that the primary language of the US is distinct, autonomous, and self-sustaining – not simply a migrant dialect of something else. I also looked for comparable uses of *Australian, British,* and *Canadian,* and found that *Australian* has had its own tradition since the 1890s, which suggests that there has long been an inclination to acknowledge such distinctness, either through ellipsis (*British* for *British English*) or by analogy (between *American* and *Scots* as geopolitical terms, comparable to the coining in 1781 of *Americanism* on the analogy of *Scotticism* by the Reverend John Witherspoon). (See panel 9.3.)

Scholars seeking to avoid or minimize inconsistency (their own or anyone else's) may get into worse trouble by seeking for too great a consistency, because neither the phenomenon itself nor the theoretical terminology by means of which we describe and account for it is consistent: one expert's dialect or group of dialects is another's language or semi-language; one grammarian accepts split infinitives and *hopefully* as a sentence adverbial, while another rejects them both. Too determined a drive for consistency, strict categorization, and postcolonial liberation may incline creolists to claim (regardless of the continua that link most creoles with English) that such forms are distinct languages *and therefore not (and no longer to be thought of as) English.* Ironically, there is a sense in which both the creoles and the Standard English used to describe them have been built out of a mass of English and other languages: on the one hand, French in an elegant London salon; on the other, West African tongues in the huts of slaves.

A case may be made here for a *principled inconsistency,* which for example recognises that American can for some purposes (political, legal, rhetorical, stylistic, editorial, etc.) be a distinct language, but for others is a variety within the complex at large – and manifestly continuous with the rest. Thus, 'English' is certainly the name of a working language of the United Nations, but in documentary terms it is not just any English: it follows British conventions. Americans submitting a document to the UN do so in American, but any commentary on that document for UN purposes, by any person whatever (including Americans), will be printed in British.

World languages: *A recurring pattern*

In early 1997, I spoke to a conference at the University of Sfax in Tunisia on
the subject of this book. Not long before I went there, and while I was thinking about how to tailor the talk to the interests of Arabic-speaking teachers
and learners of English, I read an article by the Lebanese linguist Hassan
Mneimneh entitled 'Arabic: One Language or Many?', in which he observes:

> It is useful to think of Arabic not merely as a *language*, but as a
> *language system*. Indeed, linguists refer to Arabic speakers as diglossic –
> using one variety of the language for speaking in everyday life, and
> another for reading, writing, and ceremonial speech. The former is
> referred to as 'colloquial' Arabic, and varies from one place to another,
> while the latter is 'Classical' Arabic, and is relatively constant across the
> Arab world... Classical Arabic – having become a language of learning
> and scholarship – was thoroughly documented, standardized, and
> formalized by native speakers of a multitude of languages in the Islamic
> realm. It is almost appropriate to consider the resulting formal
> language, with its codified unchanging morphological and syntactic
> rules, as a quasi-artificial language, fit both for rigorous scientific and
> philosophical discourse and for literature.

(*Language International* 9.1, 1997, pp. 18–19 and 42,
Amsterdam and Philadelphia: Benjamins)

Mneimneh argues that Arabic diglossia pre-existed the Qur'an rather
than emerged as a consequence of it, and that its language and style served
to enhance an existing division. During and after the expansion of Islam,
colloquial Arabics (Egyptian Arabic, Lebanese Arabic, Moroccan Arabic,
Sudanese Arabic, Syrian Arabic, etc.) were later infused with material from
other languages, and other languages (Berber, Malay, Persian, Swahili,
Turkish, etc.) were infused with material from Arabic. In addition, the
Classical language, 'while itself anchored on the Qur'an, exhibited noticeable variations as a result of dialectal influences'. He then proposes:

> The diglossic Arabic language system can be best visualized as an arc of a
> circle, with the language of the Qur'an at the center, and the points of the
> arc as the dialects. The orientation of the language according to the view of
> each dialect-point is along the radius linking it to the center, the other
> dialects being [perceived as] more or less off course... However, with the
> emergence of nation-states early in this century, a process of 'coagulation'
> was initiated, tending towards one common colloquial per country. It thus
> became practical to speak of Tunisian Arabic or Lebanese Arabic. However,
> this country-by-country homogenization has not obliterated the regional
> commonalities. It is thus possible to study a regional Arabic, such as Gulf
> Arabic, North African Maghribi Arabic, or Near Eastern Levantine Arabic,
> and expect a reasonable level of verbal communication in the relevant
> region. Furthermore, the proliferation of radio, television, and satellite
> exposure to other Arabic dialects, has recently weakened the
> aforementioned process of coagulation... Somewhere on the radius

connecting each dialect-point to the center lies an intermediate form of Arabic that approximates the formal language, and that is used for business communications, newspaper articles, and radio and television news.

(as above, p. 42)

At the Sfax conference, I incorporated elements of Mneimneh's perspective into my talk, drawing some parallels between world English, world Arabic, and indeed world French, because of the trilingual environment in which many members of that audience live. The discussion that followed was lively, and well-disposed from personal experience to the idea of language complexes. Shortly afterwards, I witnessed an incident in the hotel reception area which says a great deal about languages that are widely distributed and highly significant. A Syrian presenter, unhappy about the conference schedule, got into a vigorous public discussion about it with one of the Tunisian organizers. Their encounter, however, was conducted not in Arabic but in English because, as I later learned, the Syrian could not understand Tunisian Arabic. The Tunisians could generally understand Syrian Arabic, however, because television and films from Damascus are staple entertainment in Tunisia, while Tunisian Arabic is rarely encountered in the Levant. So the only solution was the shared external medium, which some decades ago might have been *le français international*, but is now International English.

Several points arise from Mneimneh's article, as excerpted and described above. First, the model he has created for his Arabic language system is markedly similar to the McArthur and Görlach circle models of English discussed in chapter 4. (See panels 4.8, 4.10, and 9.4.) Second, his term *language system* seems to serve the same end as my *language complex*. Third, in order to discuss the complexity of Arabic he at times calls the varieties within his system 'dialects' and at times 'languages', because (like Quirk, Görlach, and the rest of us) he is slave to an established vocabulary and perspective. Fourth, he emphasizes flux and imprecise boundaries among the kinds of Arabic, as I have been doing for kinds of English. Fifth, he describes formal Arabic as 'a quasi-artificial language', a description which works equally well for Standard English, after the two centuries or more of polishing it has undergone. And sixth, the parallelism between what he says about Arabic and what I am saying here about English (and Spanish, French, etc.) suggests that it may be possible to reach beyond such instances towards a larger model of *world languages* as a group.

By *world language* I do not here mean a complex which spreads across the entire planet, but one that has extended across either the known world of a certain time and place or a significant part of the world we know now. Thus, Greek reached the territorial limits accessible to it at the time of Alexander the Great, and Sanskrit spread during its long heyday throughout *its* known world: the South Asian subcontinent, Indochina, the Malay archipelago, and with less direct impact China and Japan. In chapter 7, I speculated about a current of languages (acrolectal, mesolectal, and basilectal) which at one time circulated in and around the Mediterranean, then flowed out through the Straits of Gibraltar, eventually circling the planet in a tide of adapting forms. This flow was from Sumerian c.3,000 years ago through Babylonian, Assyrian, Aramaic, Phoenician, Greek, and Latin to the Western European diaspora languages, the foremost of which, Portuguese, Spanish, French, and English, spread throughout the world and influenced many further languages, many of them relatively minor while others are world languages in their own right, such as Arabic, Hindi, Malay, and Mandarin.

At each stage in the emergence of such languages the requirements for world status have become more demanding. When Sumerian began the process, its script and scribal élite were unique and immensely effective. But in due course many societies in and around Mesopotamia acquired scripts and social skills, so that the stakes were raised for future world-language stature. Phoenician, Greek, and Latin (among other languages) became successful over a wide area because of trade, colonies, and empires, along with the development of more efficient scripts, texts, and writing materials, ranging from reeds and clay to pen and paper. The European diaspora languages came to the fore because of further inventions that included gunpowder, the magnetic compass, and the printing press (as Francis Bacon pointed out in his *Novum Organon* in 1620), and the English complex (in terms of its foremost political and institutional languages, British and American) gained precedence because of success in colonizing and frontier-building, ship-based commerce, the industrial revolution, military success, mass education and publishing, as well as such Euro-American technologies and services as the telephone, photography, the cinema, television, the computer, and the Internet.

The passage from one world language to the next appears to follow either of two routes: (1) Inheritance by a wholly different language, as when Babylonian succeeded Sumerian and Latin followed Greek (with massive resulting sociocultural changes); (2) Inheritance by a derivative or a variant of the language in question, as when French and Spanish, etc., succeeded Latin (establishing themselves as new languages with no continuity of name), or, more recently, as when American English began to displace British English in global terms (linguistic variation and cultural disturbance being minimal and name continuity being preserved). This last is a controversial assertion because the two politically distinct forms are linguistically very similar and such a situation may never have happened before – with the possible exception of Pali becoming a successful rival of its close relative Sanskrit when it became the primary medium of Buddhism, Sanskrit having already long been the primary medium of Hinduism.

It also seems to be the case that a world language has always developed a regularized and institutionalized 'high' variety identified as the language in its best or proper form, the 'best' Greek in the Hellenized world being Attic, the 'best' Latin being that of the Roman nobility, and the 'best' seventeenth-century French the usage of courtiers, writers, and academicians. Among objective indicators that the high form or forms of a language have been regularized and institutionalized are printed grammars, dictionaries, and a literary canon, and it was proof positive of the success of French as a national and international language that by 1700 it had all three. The same was the case in the eighteenth and nineteenth centuries with British and in the nineteenth and twentieth centuries with American, which by 1940 had caught up with British and begun to pass it. The assessment and adjudication of usage in the US, like that of the UK, has for most purposes long been endocentric, with a thoroughly novel exception for both developing in the 1980s and 90s: questions of international intelligibility. When Mikie Kiyoi, a Japanese executive of the International Energy Agency, wrote about international English three years ago in Paris, she put the matter as follows:

> It is incontestable that English is the world's most accepted working language. Several centuries of Anglo-American economic and cultural predominance have contributed considerably to the language's status today... I work in an international organization where English is a main working language. Native English speakers have a double advantage at such organizations: Even though they are required to speak a language other than English, that other language is frequently French. And compared with the remoteness of English from my native language – Japanese – the difference between English and French is negligible. I have to live with this unfortunate fate: My native tongue is remote from European languages. Yet I believe I have the right to request that my Anglo-American friends who are involved in international activities not abuse their privilege, even though they do not do so intentionally. First of all, I would like them to know that the English they speak at home is not always an internationally acceptable English... I sincerely believe there exists a cosmopolitan English – a lingua franca, written or spoken – that is clearly different from what native English speakers use unconsciously in their daily life... We non-natives are desperately learning English; each word pronounced by us represents our blood, sweat and tears. Our English proficiency is tangible evidence of our achievement of will, not an accident of birth. Dear Anglo-Americans, please show us you are also taking pains to make yourselves understood in an international setting.

> ('Dear English Speakers: Please Drop the Dialects',
> *International Herald Tribune*, 3 November 1995)

Such non-native points of view are increasingly being heard, and as the reasonableness of their case becomes apparent, further efforts are likely to be made to regularize whatever we mean by International/World Standard English, with more and more of its users (ENL, ESL, and EFL) discussing the best ways of managing this acrolect of acrolects: for example, everybody (native and non-native speakers alike) seeking to speak distinctly at optimal speed, politely taking turns and not interrupting unnecessarily, seeking to be aware of different cultural conventions, and taking care in the use of slang, jargon, idioms, jokes, allusions, and foreignisms. In the same way that dictionaries, grammars, and manuals of style and usage have been developed to regularize and confirm the stature of British, American, and now Australian, so the first transnational works are currently being compiled for worldwide reference. Because at least three national standards are now institutionally established, it has in the late 1990s become necessary (and increasingly attractive for publishers) to transcend them. English, the first geographically true world language, is now so large and varied that its current standard varieties and usages appear no longer to be quite standard enough.

'My name is Legion': *An immense and intricate reality*

In the fifth chapter of the Gospel of St Mark (as told in chapter 1 in Lowland Scots, Oxbridge English, Jacobean English, and Tok Pisin), Jesus came ashore in the country of the Gerasenes or Gadarenes, where he met a man with an unclean spirit who lived among tombs and wandered the hillsides, gashing himself with stones. When Jesus, intending to cast out the spirit, spoke directly to it and asked it what its name was, the answer came, 'My name is Legion: for we are many' (5:9). Jesus then cast the devil(s) out of the man and into a nearby herd of pigs, which rushed headlong into the lake and were drowned.

The Gadarene story is not inappropriate here. After all, a single language which encompasses British, American, and Australian, Anglo-Saxon and Middle English, Middle Scots and Modern Scots, Tok Pisin and Ebonics, Spanglish and Taglish, and Krio and Kamtok, and so on, does look like a case of multiple personality disorder – one voice after another asserting its distinctiveness within a most improbable whole. Some voices are new, others old, and most have been silent in the halls of power since at least the days of Samuel Johnson, for whom they were 'the corruptions of oral utterance' and part of a 'wild and barbarous jargon' (Preface, *A Dictionary of the English Language*, 1755). Or, as the Guyanese poet David Dabydeen has put it:

> It's hard to put two words together in creole without swearing. Words are spat out from the mouth like live squibs, not pronounced with elocution. English diction is cut up, and this adds to the abruptness of the language: *what* for instance becomes *wha* (as in *whack*), the splintering making the language more barbaric. Soft vowel sounds are habitually converted: the English tend to be polite in *war*, whereas the creole *warre* produces an

appropriate snarling sound; *scorn* becomes *scaan, water wata,* and so on...
In [the collection of poems] *Slave Song* I speak of the brokenness of the
language which reflects the brokenness and suffering of its original users.
Its potential as a naturally tragic language is there in its brokenness and
rawness, which is like the rawness of a wound. If one has learnt and used
Queen's English for some years, the return to creole is painful, almost
nauseous, for the language is uncomfortably raw.

('Nigger Talk in England today', in Christopher Ricks and
Leonard Michaels (eds.), *The State of the Language: 1990 Edition,*
London and Boston: Faber and Faber, pp. 3–4)

Like other commentators on West Indian English, Dabydeen draws
attention to Shakespeare's *Tempest* and particularly Caliban, the beastman
whose name shares an etymology with both *Caribbean* and *cannibal*. For
these observers, Ariel is the docile house slave of the aristocratic magician
Prospero while Caliban is the surly field nigger who lusts after Prospero's
beautiful, cultivated daughter Miranda. Caliban shouts at Prospero, 'You
taught me Language, and my profit on't is, I know how to curse: the red-
plague rid you for learning me your language!' (1:2, c.1611). Dabydeen
adds that nowadays, in an act of self-assertion, 'Caliban is tearing up the
pages of Prospero's magic book and repasting it in his own order, by his
own method, and for his own purpose' (p. 9). Certainly, West Indians are
asserting their own language, whether as an independent Creole or a unifying continuum from creole to standard, the usage about which Mervin
Morris insists, 'Is English we speaking'. (See chapter 1.) And all such West
Indian usage has recently been strengthened (empowered? validated?
made less raw?) by the publication of the magisterial *Dictionary of
Caribbean English Usage* (Oxford University Press, 1996), compiled by
Richard Allsopp, who was born in Guyana and lives in Barbados, and
wrote the definitions, like many another regional lexicographer before
him, in impeccable Standard English.

Morris is both right and wrong. There *is* one English, used by untold
millions, a vast mass lit with flashes of standardness that blends at many
points with other languages, some also world languages, some of more
modest range, and some barely clinging to life. And there *are* so many
Englishes, 112 of which, based on territoriality, are listed in panels 2.1 and
2.2. These have legal status either on their own or alongside one or more
other languages, and each is defined and empowered locally, not from outside, a condition that differentiates it from every other English in the
world – no matter how similar its high variety may be to other such varieties elsewhere. And within these and other territories are further
Englishes that are neither conventional nor validated by orthographies,
dictionaries, and other devices, except here and there a Scots or a Tok
Pisin. Some are traditional dialects and 'semi-languages', others are pidgins and creoles, and others still are hybrids, but all are in a state of flux

continuous with the authorized usage of territorial government, court, and school as well as with all other Englishes elsewhere.

Informed Anglophones tend to have points of view on English as a worldwide phenomenon that broadly correlate with their positions on the standard language (as discussed in chapter 5). Such responses may be represented as follows:

1   *The strongly authoritarian and traditionalist response*
    Resolutely monolithic, asserting that English is and always has been one thing, despite its diversity, because it is held together by a standard variety ('good' or 'proper' English) that should be defended at all costs as a key achievement of Anglo-Saxon civilization. Substandard dialects, creoles, and the like may be important in heritage terms and could be good for culture and tourism, but ultimately they are an obstacle to personal and social development, and in any case are fading under the influence of education and the media – or would fade if teachers and journalists did their jobs properly.

2   *The mildly traditionalist and pragmatic response*
    More or less monolithic, considering that the many varieties of English (standard, near-standard, substandard, non-standard; national, regional, local), while they cannot be called languages as such, should be acknowledged (and respected within the relevant pecking order). The standard language sustains the unity of speech, writing, and print throughout the homeland and the world, throughout which good English is immensely valued and valuable, while substandard, broken, fractured, and hybridized English are not. People gain in social and cultural terms from diversity, but the centre must hold, and the proper aim of education is to inculcate the best and most effective usage possible.

3   *The eclectic, liberal, and pragmatic response*
    Both monolithic and pluralistic, depending on circumstance, and maybe with a bias towards pluralism. From one point of view, English *does* indeed encompass everything that has been identified with it, and from another, certain varieties are (or can be regarded as) languages in their own right: either as legal-cum-political entities or simply because they are unintelligible to outsiders. Standard varieties (national and international) are vital tools in education, the media, law, government, business, science, and technology, tend to be sustained by such activities, and change with time and place, and are best approached descriptively rather than prescriptively (although prescription in certain areas and for certain purposes may be necessary).

4   *The libertarian, egalitarian, and progressive response*
    Monoliths are part of an out-dated worldview which has been (or ought to be) supplanted by a more multicultural and decentred perspective

that accepts diversity as good in itself. The Englishes (whether they are identified as autonomous languages or less radically as a range of variations) are part of a mass of usage which has arisen for a number of reasons, many of which are hegemonic and Eurocentric. Standard forms – local, national, or international – are (or need to be) constantly re-negotiated and should not encourage the prolongation of existing élites or lead to the rise of new ones.

5 *The uncertain and perhaps confused response*
Not sure what the debate is all about but by and large aware of the importance of communication and perhaps intimidated by people who seem to be too fluent about such things. Inclined to change according to situation and company and wishing everybody *did* speak the same language everywhere ('Isn't that what the schools are for?'). At times authoritarian, traditionalist, and judgemental, at times egalitarian, progressive, and even libertarian ('Live and let live') – theirs is a condition commoner than many hard-core traditionalists might like to admit.

It does, however, seem likely that the variedness of the English language complex will become increasingly obvious in the next quarter of a century, even as the currently rather vague entity International Standard English becomes more clearly defined and regularized. Varieties of English may be increasingly compared and contrasted as – or as if they were – separate languages, especially in the three main areas discussed in this study (none of which, of course, can be sharply marked off one from the other). These are, in sum:

1 *Territorially delimited English languages*
Such entities as British, American, Indian, and Nigerian, whose standard forms have legal or quasi-legal status and whose variations within the continuum from local to global have a set of identifying features that include accents, grammatical usages, and words and phrases, co-occurring with subvarieties such as dialects, creoles, and hybrids. At the higher end of the spectrum all such Englishes are more or less standardized and internationally transparent: that is, their distinctness as languages is legal and institutional, not a matter of unintelligibility to outsiders; at more diverse points on their spectrum, however, their languagehood is likely to be based on greater or less opacity to outsiders.

2 *Historically distinct English languages*
These include: (1) Precursors of present-day Englishes, such as Anglo-Saxon and Middle Scots; (2) Dialects or semi-languages with established names, traditions, orthographies, works of reference, literatures, and often supporting societies, such as the Yorkshire and Newfoundland dialects, which tend to be opaque to outsiders; (3) Pidgin-cum-creoles, which may or may not have orthographies and literary and media con-

ventions (many in fact being at various stages in such development), and may or may not be officially recognized as distinct languages. All the members of this group need to be studied to a greater or less degree as foreign languages, because that is in effect what they are.

3 *Anglo-hybrids*
These include Spanglish in the US, Frenglish in Quebec, Taglish in the Philippines, Hindlish in India, Malenglish in Malaysia, Singlish in Singapore, among many others, few if any of which are stable. Such forms can be classified in terms of both English and the companion language (as with *Frenglish* and *franglais*, *Italglish* and *itangliano*), and their futures, despite the large numbers of people who use them, are uncertain. In some contexts, hybridization may lead to a stable mix that is primarily English (as once happened in Ireland, bringing Hiberno-English into existence), in others a profound change may occur in the companion language (as happened to English when it massively absorbed Greco-Latin material from the sixteenth century onward).

It is difficult to put figures on the number of past, present, and potential English languages. However, there *are* 113 distinct territories (ranging in size and population from the United States to Ascension Island) in which English is currently used, each with its unique aspects and continuum of forms. In some of these territories there are highly distinct varieties, some of which are already recognized as languages in their own right, such as Scots (by the European Union) and Tok Pisin (official in Papua New Guinea), while others that may not be so recognized are opaque to outsiders, such as Kamtok in Cameroon and Spanglish in the US.

If we remove small territories such as Ascension Island, bringing the territorial number down to 70, then add a conservative 10 for cases like Tok Pisin, we would get 80 English languages in all – a number that seems ridiculous until one considers that some 400 million people have English as their mother tongue and around 300 million more use it as an essential second language, mostly in the territories in question: some 700 million in all. Ultimately, however, it doesn't matter what number we choose for the elements of this vast complex: its name would still be Legion.

Panel 9.1 Some reports and comments on Ebonics

From the *San Francisco Chronicle*, 21 December 1996

Tatum Willoughby, a fifth-grade student at Prescott Elementary on Campbell Street in West Oakland, used to cry because she had trouble 'speaking the right language,' as she calls it. The bright African American child tried hard to translate the phrases and words she uses at home – black English – into the standard English her teacher said would help her excel. But after months of being taught through a program that recognizes that African American children may come into the classroom using ebonics... Tatum reads her essays with pride. Occasionally, the 10-year-old slips into black English, such as saying 'dis' for 'this.' But she quickly corrects herself. 'Most people won't understand you if you speak (black English),' Tatum said.

(front page: from 'How Ebonics Works', by Thaai Walker and Nanette Asimov)

I think it's tragic. Here we have young black kids who are incapable in far too many cases of negotiating even the most basic transactions in our society because of their inability to communicate... We're going to legitimize what they're doing. To me it's just ass backwards.

(editorial section: quoted comment by Ward Connerly, a University of California regent)

If people are not willing to accept ebonics as a second language, then they should at least accept that African American students are not achieving at the level they need to, and we need to do something about that.

(editorial section: quoted comment by Alan Young, director of state and federal programs, Oakland school board)

Editor – I am absolutely thrilled at the Oakland school district's choice of ebonics as the language of choice in the classroom. I expect that very shortly we will see New York punks being taught in Brooklonics, Georgia rednecks in Ya'allonics, Valley girls in Bimbonics, chronic nerds in Siliconics and farm boys in Rubonics. But what most of us need to keep up with the bureaucrats is a thorough understanding of Moronics.

(letter section: Richard Ogar of Berkeley)

Editor – The real goal of those backing this move is multiculturalism, as opposed to the melting pot society which is what made this nation so successful. If the U.S. is to remain a leading economic and social force as we enter the 21st century, we must not allow the PC crowd to have its way in imposing multiculturalism on the nation. The action of the Oakland school board does a tremendous disservice to black students, and I hope it is soundly rebuked by higher authorities, without whose funding it cannot succeed.

(letter section: from Jack D. Bernal in San Francisco)

The Oakland Tribune, 21 December 1996:

The [board's] report offers sound goals – African-American students will become proficient in reading, speaking and writing standard English. It recommends greater involvement of parents and incentives for teachers who tackle these challenges. The Ebonics approach would presumably make African-American students eligible for state and federal bilingual funds, giving the district more resources to provide additional help for them. District officials deny the approach is a strategy to get more funding. There's nothing wrong with looking for additional ways to help a population that is struggling in the public school system. But making non-standard English a language undermines the very goals the board has embraced. It sends a wrong and confusing message to students. If what they are speaking is a language, what's the urgency of learning another language?

(front page: from 'English spoken here, by African Americans', by Brenda Payton)

The International Herald Tribune, 24–25 December 1996

The Reverend Jesse Jackson said Sunday that the school board in Oakland, California, was both foolish and insulting to black students throughout the United States when it declared that many of its black students speak a language distinct from traditional English... 'I understand the attempt to reach out to these children, but this is an unacceptable surrender, borderlining on disgrace,' he said. 'It's teaching down to our children'... Mr. Jackson said the Oakland school board had become a laughingstock, and he urged its members to reverse their decision.

('Jesse Jackson Ridicules Acceptance of Black English', by Neil A. Lewis (New York Times [News] Service))

The New York Times, 26 December 1996

A Tested Policy: To the Editor: The California State Board of Education endorsed ebonics in 1991, and the State Department of Education has financed research institutes and conferences that have studied the subject extensively. I spoke at two such conferences this year alone. Oakland's school board is not the first district to apply this policy. Los Angeles and San Diego have used it for years... Those like the Rev. Jesse Jackson who seek the quick headline will find themselves out of step with the legitimate demands for cutting-edge education.

(letter by John W. Templeton, Executive Editor, Aspire Books, San Francisco)

[Jackson said on 17th December that he would meet with the Oakland school officials to discuss their plan to recognize black English as a distinct language, appreciating that the board sought to secure additional government funds. The Clinton Administration then commented that it would refuse special funding for black English as a second language (source, *New York Times* 18th December). Jackson duly met with the Board and, in the words of Elaine Ray in *The Stanford Report*, 8 January 1997, 'the meeting... resulted in Jesse Jackson's conversion.']

Time Magazine, 13 January 1997

'African-American students come to school with a home language other than English. We're going to bridge that gap and make sure our children learn.'

(quoting Toni Cook of the Oakland School Board)
Time itself commented: 'A muddled plan to teach black English in the schools made outraged headlines, but the actual teaching methods may make sense.'

The New York Times, 14 January 1997

Hoping to quell the uproar set off by its resolution to treat black English as a second language in its classrooms, the Oakland school board will scratch parts of a plan that suggested it would offer instruction in the tongue that some linguists call ebonics, school officials said today. After almost a month of national debate and a weekend of sometimes tense meetings here, the Oakland schools task force that introduced the black English policy... produced a new resolution on Sunday that calls only for the recognition of language differences among black students in order to improve their proficiency in English. 'The debate is over,' the head of the task force, Sylvester Hodges, said. 'We are hoping that people will understand that and will join us.'... The many writers, educators and politicians who have attacked the school board's original plan have tended to agree that the issue is perhaps more about the symbolism than the specifics of what black children in Oakland might be taught.

('Oakland Scratches Plan To Teach Black English', by Tim Golden)

Panel 9.2 Citations of the terms *American* and *American language* used to refer to American English

NOTE: (1) Both *American* and *American language* are listed as alternatives to *American English* in the *OED*. (2) Such US dictionary publishers as Merriam-Webster and Random House routinely define one meaning of *American* (noun) as 'American English'. (3) For *American,* only citations of the unmodified word are given, excluding for example both *General American*, commonly used for an accent of the US taken by some to be (more or less) representative of the country at large, and *Southern American*, for usage in the southern states. (4) The distribution of the listed citations suggests that the practice of using *American* as shorthand for both *American English* and *the American language* is increasing, but fuller research may well indicate that the incidence has always been quite high (including in the under-represented nineteenth century).

1789: US
Noah Webster
> The question now occurs; ought the Americans to retain these faults which produce innumerable inconveniencies in the acquisition and use of the language, or ought they at once to reform these abuses, and introduce order and regularity into the orthography of the AMERICAN TONGUE?
>
> ('An Essay on the Necessity, Advantages and Practicability of Reforming the Mode of Spelling, and of Rendering the Orthography of Words Consistent to the Pronunciation', an appendix to *Dissertations on the English Language*, Boston)

1800: US
Anonymous
> 'On the Scheme of an American Language' [title]
>
> (title of a treatise, perhaps by Noah Webster)

1802: UK (OED citation)
> [A Latin verse] which my schoolmaster has translated into American.
>
> (from *Port Folio*, 28 August)

1838:US
James Fenimore Cooper
> The common faults of American language are an ambition of effect, a want of simplicity, and a turgid abuse of terms.
>
> (*The American Democrat* 24)

1889: UK (OED citation)
Rudyard Kipling
> The American I have heard up to the present is a tongue as distinct from English as Patagonian.
>
> (*From Sea to Sea*)

1906: UK
J. W. and F. G. Fowler
> Americanisms are foreign words, and should be so treated. To say this is not to insult the American language.
>
> (*The King's English,* Oxford University Press, p. 33)

1908a: UK (OED citation)
> English spoken; American understood
>
> (*Daily Chronicle*, London, 10 June)

1908b: US
Charles Whibley
> 'The American Language'
>
> (title of an article in the *Bookman* (New York) by an Englishman commenting on US usage (described by Mencken in *The American Language*, 1919, see below)

1917: US
Fred Newton Scott

I mean that almost everyone who touches upon American speech assumes that it is inferior to British speech. Just as the Englishman, having endured for a time the society of his equals, goes on to bask in the sunshine of aristocracy, so the American, when he has used the American language for business or for familiar intercourse, may then, for higher or more serious purposes, go on to the aristocratic or royal language of Great Britain.

('The Standard of American Speech', *The English Journal*,
6: 1–15, January)

1919: US
H. L. Mencken
The American Language

(title of a book published by Alfred A. Knopf,
New York)

I can write English, as in this clause, quite as readily as American, as in this here one.

(from the above)

I think I have offered sufficient evidence in the chapters preceding that the American of today is much more honestly English... than the so-called Standard English of England. It still shows all the characters that marked the common tongue in the days of Elizabeth, and it continues to resist stoutly the policing that ironed out Standard English in the Seventeenth and Eighteenth Centuries. Standard English must always strike an American as a bit stilted and precious.

(from the above)

1923: US

The official language of the State of Illinois shall be known hereafter as the American language, and not as the English language.

(from an Act of Legislature of Illinois, chapter 127,
section 178)

1928: UK
Ernest Weekley

The foreign language which has most affected English in our own time is contemporary American... The colloquial speech of the American is becoming, largely as a result of the foreign ingredients in the melting-pot, more and more remote from the spoken English of the educated Englishman, but, at the same time, the more slangy element in our language is being constantly reinforced by words and phrases taken from American, especially the type of American which is printed in the cinema caption.

(Ernest Weekley, *The English Language*,
London: Ernest Benn, 1928)

1947: UK/NZ
Eric Partridge
Too often are spoken English and spoken American criticized as though it were impossible for them to have any laws of their own.

Standard English and Standard American are the speech of the educated classes in the British Empire and the United States.

(*Usage and Abusage*, London: Hamish Hamilton
(quoted from the 1957 edition))

1949: UK
C. L. Wrenn
Many seventeenth century usages have survived in standard American, and far more in some of the dialects: and some of these, like *fall* for 'autumn', may well seem more attractive than their English equivalents. American has developed new ways of speech... The English of educated standard American, then, is just as much 'good English' as that of educated London: but the 'clipped syllables' which the American hears in Englishmen's pronunciation as against the 'drawl' and 'nasal tone' which the Englishman notices in American, are in reality differences of rhythm and intonation which shew the development of two types of English.

(*The English Language*, London: Methuen, pp. 190–1)

1950: UK
Simeon Potter
In nineteenth-century American may be found for the first time *blizzard* (from the storm of 1880), *bogus,* and *rowdy.*

(*Our Language*, Harmondsworth: Pelican (1966 revision),
p. 79)

1958: Poland (US)
Margaret Schlauch
Nor are the strictly morphological differences very great between English and American, when viewed on the level of standard usage.

(*The English Language in Modern Times*: Panstwowe
Wydawnietwo Naukówe, Warsaw, p. 200
[a US academic working in Poland])

1966a: UK (US)
Whitney Bolton
The order of selections [in this book] is chronological, but readers may find other arrangements which correspond to their interests, such as the idea of an English Academy, spelling reform, neologisms, the American language, ...

(Introduction to Bolton (ed.), *The English Language*, published in
the UK by Cambridge University Press)

1966b: UK (OED citation)
We have tried... to translate from French into American and vice versa.

(*The Listener*, London: 2 June)

1980: US
Stefan Kanfer
The rich have always liked to assume the costumes of the poor. Take the
American language. It is more than a million words wide, and new
terms are constantly added to its infinite variety. Yet as the decade starts.
the U.S. vocabulary seems to have shrunk to child size.

('80s-Babble: Untidy Treasure', *Time*, 28 January)

1983a: US
Success with Words: A Guide to the American Language

(title of a book published by the *Reader's Digest*, Pleasantville)

1983b: US
Robert Claiborne
This new land grab carried the U.S. boundary to the Pacific, and with it
the American language and its ever-growing vocabulary.

(*Our Marvelous Native Tongue: The Life and Times of the English
Language*, New York: Times Books, p. 214)

1984: UK
Anthony Burgess
I cannot believe that Simenon in French is as bad as he is in English,
American rather. The book exemplifies a problem unresolved and hardly
ever discussed – how far an American translator is justified in turning a
European into an American, equipped with the slanginess and slackness
that characterise so much transatlantic hack writing.

(review of *Intimate Memoirs*, by Georges Simenon, tr. Harold J.
Salemson, in *The Observer* (London), 26 August, p. 18)

1985: UK
Michael Davie
The output [in a programme on Worldnet called 'America Today']
contained, apart from news, features about Yosemite National Park,
business news, 'A Journey Through the Solar System,' and a sports
section ('Hi, everybody!'). There is also a daily teach-yourself-
American lesson.

(from the column 'Notebook', *The Observer* (London),
7 July, p. 44)

1986a: US
Otto Friedrich *et al.*
It was the British empire, on which the sun never set, that originally
spread English around the world, along with tea breaks, cuffed trousers
and the stiff upper lip. But when the imperial sun finally did set after
World War II, the American language followed American power into the
vacuum.

('A Language That Has *Ausgeflippt*', *Time*, 16 June)

1986b: US
Vivian Ducat
> Sociologists refer to the spread of the American language and culture –
> begun by GIs, bolstered by American commercial expansion and buoyed
> by advertising, movies and, of course, tourism – as 'cocacolonialism.'

> > ('American Spoken Here – and Everywhere',
> > in *Travel and Leisure*, October)

1988: UK
Stanley Reynolds
> The American language does not possess, aside from the homosexual
> world, the expression 'a bit of rough' or 'rough trade'.

> > ('Moonlighting', *The Listener*, 21 April)

1989a: UK
Robert Burchfield
> It may be true that there is a form of Standard American to which all
> Americans ultimately aspire. If there is I have not yet encountered it,
> though the several approximations to one standard spoken form tend to
> merge into one in the written form of the language.

> (*Unlocking the English Language*, London: Faber and Faber, p. 122)

1989b: US
Laurence Zuckerman
> George Bush is hardly known for his rhetorical gifts. But his speech at
> last summer's Republican Convention has already left its mark on the
> American language.

> > ('Read My Cliché', *Time Magazine*, 16 January)

1989: US
Jef Verschueren
> Considering the variety of English spoken by [Jesse] Jackson, we note
> that sometimes he clearly uses a version of Standard American, and
> sometimes a typical form of Black English.

> ('English as object and medium of (mis)understanding', in Ofelia
> García and Ricardo Otheguy, *English across Cultures: Cultures
> across English*, Berlin and New York: Mouton de Gruyter, p. 40)

1990: US
John Algeo
> *Bits and pieces*, if it is a Briticism, is so by virtue of frequency of use.
> The expression is normal in American, but is more popular in British.

> ('The Briticisms are coming! How British English is Creeping into
> the American Language', *Journal of English Linguistics*, 23:1,2
> (1990–95). [Algeo uses the term *American* extensively in contrast
> to *British*, as demonstrated here.])

1991: UK
Martin Spence

This central section of the book, despite being written in American, is almost clear, deriving, as it does, from secondary sources... He is a hippie, plain and very simple, believing that the only way forwards is backwards, and living in a green dream.

> (review of Max Oelschlaeger, *The Idea of the Wilderness*, in
> *The Times Saturday Review*, London, 25 May, p. 19)

1992a: US
William Safire

According to one theory, this talking *rap* came from British English into the American language, perhaps transferred through Caribbean English.

> ('Hopping Along the Hip-Hop Trail', New York Times News
> Service, in the *International Herald Tribune*, 9 November)

1992b: US
John M. Broder

But the state [Arkansas] has also contributed a wealth of colorful words and phrases to the American language.

> ('A Short Dictionary of Clinton Holler', in the
> *International Herald Tribune*, 11 November)

1992c: US
Russell Baker

Yet The Washington Post is making a determined effort to ram this abomination [the word *wonk*] into the American language.

> ('Honk Against Wonks', in the *International Herald Tribune*,
> 18 November)

1993: UK/US
William Safire

Whose English language is it, anyway? From the tone of the new 'BBC News and Current Affairs Stylebook and Editorial Guide', you'd think the Brits invented it. With unmistakable disdain, the broadcastocrats in London call what we speak 'American.' As a user of Murkin English, I rise to the defense.

> (in the column 'Language', *The New York Times,* as reprinted in the
> *International Herald Tribune*, 23 August)

1994a: US
James Fallows

Terms like 'cyberspace' and 'virtual company' were coined in sci-fi novels of a decade ago. They have survived in the American language because they describe real phenomena: systems that bind people together but are not based in any physical place.

> ('The Information Revolution', in the *International Herald Tribune*,
> 16 May)

1994b: UK
Iain Johnstone
Schwarzenegger has fulfilled [the American dream] and more, giving
hope to any immigrant who has ever done a press-up or been defeated
by the nuances of the American tongue or aspired to marrying into the
Kennedy family.

('Well, he said he'd be back', *The Sunday Times*, 14 August)

1995a: UK (US)
Bryson explores the countless varieties of English, from American to
Australian and Creole to Cockney, and exposes the perils of marketing
foreign brands with names like *Pshitt* and *Super Piss*.

(description of the American writer Bill Bryson's book *The
Mother Tongue: English and How It Got That Way*, in the *Softback
Preview* (a book-club magazine-cum-catalogue), London,
January, p. 9)

1995b: UK/US
Thomas Gustafson
*Representative Words: Politics, Literature, and the American Language,
1776–1865*

(title of a work by this American writer in the series Cambridge
Studies in American Literature and Culture, published in the UK
by Cambridge University Press)

1995c: US
Malcolm Jones Jr
While [Zora Neale Hurston's] life makes her an easy candidate for
feminist sainthood, her abiding subject was not race or gender politics
but the American language.

('Telling Lies Above Suspicion', *Newsweek*, 27 February)

1995d: UK
Henry Porter
As must be obvious, the American language is not one language, but
many competing streams of invention.

('Back off, ease up, enjoy', in *The Guardian*, 6 April)

1995e: UK
The Prince of Wales has landed in hot water after an attack on the
American language at the launch of the British Council's new English
2000 initiative.

('Prince in row after Council launch speech', lead front-page
article in the *EFL Gazette*, London, April)

1995f: UK
Now more students say that Canadian English is much easier to
understand than heavily accented American, according to Leanne
Henwood of the English Language School at Humber College, Ontario.

('US misses out with accent on Canada', an article in the
EFL Gazette, London, May, p. 14)

1995g: UK
Richard Gunter

> It has been a long voyage – the Subject's [that is, the writer's] trip through the great sea of the American language.

> (contribution to the centennial publication of *PADS*, the journal of the American Dialect Society)

1995h: US
Mary Blume

> As an anglophile, why does he want the British to look as silly as France did during the Toubon effort? He says the official attempt to ban Americanisms was good for two reasons: instructions for machines and appliances should, for safety's sake, be in the language of the user and not in computerized American, and so should labor contracts.

> (report of an interview with Maurice Druon, the secretary of the Académie française, the *International Herald Tribune*, 15 July)

1995i: UK
Jonathon Green

> American has been the imperial language of the twentieth century, just as English was of the nineteenth. Yet even in democratic America there seems only to be room for a single 'privileged form'. Just as the non-middle class British dialects were pushed back to the linguistic margins, so has the language of another group that is perceived as marginal to mainstream society: a sub-set of American English, 'Black English', continues to fight for its position, but remains outside the standard.

> (*Chasing the Sun*, London: Cape, p. 379)

1995j: US (UK)
John Algeo

> Incidentally, neither book observes that in the second illustrative sentence above, British normally has 'write to a person' whereas American may have 'write a person,' that is, in American use the direct object of *write* can be either resultative (a letter) or dative (a recipient).

> (book review, *International Journal of Lexicography* 8:2)

1995k: Singapore
Anne Pakir

> Obviously, the powers that be would want to ensure that codification of norms should remain as that of those norms considered standard in the traditional English canon, mainly standard British and standard American.

> ('English in Singapore: The Codification of Competing Norms', in S. Gopinathan, Anne Pakir, Ho Wah Kam and Vanithamani Saravanan (eds.), *Language, Society and Education: Issues and Trends*, Singapore: Times Academic Press)

1996a: UK
Andrew Mayne and John Shuttleworth
> Here are eight short extracts from American. We'd like you to read
> through them carefully and note down anything that seems to you
> unacceptable as British English. For instance, it might be the spelling
> of *program* or the expression *stay home*... Can you speak 'American'?...
> Perhaps the strongest argument for saying that there's 'American' and
> there's 'English' is that the vocabulary of the two nations differs quite
> a lot.
>
> > (*The Language Book*, London: Hodder and Stoughton
> > [a British secondary school textbook])

1996b: UK
Philip Howard
> [Describing *The Holy Bible*, HarperCollins, 1996] Pity about the chapter
> and verse headings, which are hard to see. Pity about the language,
> which is American in a cassock.
>
> > (*The Times*, London, 6 December)

1996c: UK
> The Philippines, one of the largest English-speaking (or, rather,
> American-speaking) countries, hopes to exploit that advantage.
>
> > ('The coming global tongue', *The Economist*,
> > London, 21 December)

1997a: UK
> [of the writer Martin Amis] Welsh was not one of his fictional voices. But
> then nor, until now, was American. America and Americans have figured
> a lot in his dark comedies. And nobody caught earlier than he did how
> American was transforming English English.
>
> > ('In an American voice', *The Economist*, London, 4 October)

1997b: US
Alan Ryan
> [of the writer Christopher Lasch] His best-known book, *The Culture of
> Narcissism*, published in 1979, was a best-seller that added a much-
> needed phrase to the American language.
>
> > ('The Prophet', *The New York Review*, 6 November)

Panel 9.3 Citations of other terms used to identify national English languages

The three terms are listed in order of number of citations: *Australian 15, British 6, Canadian 1.*

(1) The terms *Australian* and *Australian language* used for Australian English

Both terms, though not so common as the American usages, have a significant depth in time, which indicates that, although they at first had a facetiously specific reference, they have since the Second World War become more serious and general. The existence and wide use of the syncopated joke form *Strine* suggests that the use of *Australian* to mean the usage of Australians has been relatively widespread. The letters *AND* indicate that the item is a citation from the *Australian National Dictionary*, Oxford University Press (Melbourne), 1988.

1891: Aus
M. Roberts
I tried to back the bullocks, but they scorned me utterly, in spite of the Australian language I used.

        (*Land-Travel and Sea-Faring*, p. 69, *AND* citation)

1902: Aus
The schoolboy reciting... to the inspector in 'perfect English' and then calling for the inspector's horse in pure Australian.

        (*Bulletin* (Sydney), 14 June, *AND* citation)

1915: Aus
Then he began to speak some pure Australian, and the language that came out of the hole in that driver's face heated the air for yards around.

        (*Honk* XI, 2/1, *AND* citation)

1916: Aus
English and French spoken; Australian understood.

        (a notice in Turkey, quoted in O. Hogue's *Trooper Bluegum at Dardanelles, AND* citation)

1920: Aus
He cursed them first of all in good round Australian.

        (*Huon Times* (Franklin), 30 April, *AND* citation)

1929: Aus
D. J. Hopkins
On her arrival in Sydney, my mother had some difficulty in making herself understood by the tradespeople. She did not know 'Australian'.

        (*Hop of 'Bulletin', AND* citation)

1945: Aus
Sidney James Baker
The Australian Language

(title of a book on Australian English by Sidney James Baker
(Currawong: Angus and Robertson), a New Zealand-born
journalist in Sydney, who modelled it on Mencken's
The American Language, New York: Alfred A. Knopf, 1919)

1969: Aus
L. Hadow
The other women of her age still spoke the tongue of their native
Jugoslavia... but... except in moments of excitement, of strain, of great
joy, Australian was the currency.

(*Full Cycle*, p. 101, *AND* citation)

1985: UK
Robert Burchfield
In Britain the Australian language tends to be judged through doubtless
unrepresentative forms of it carried abroad. Except for Patrick White's
work, Australian English is most likely to be encountered in Britain in
the amiable twitterings of popular entertainers like Rolf Harris or of
Barry Humphries... or in the dialogue of cinema or TV films.

(*The English Language*, Oxford University Press, p. 167)

1988: UK
David Crystal
Speakers of Australian, Indian, Jamaican or other Englishes can be
heard at almost any time, simply by turning on the radio or television, or
going to the cinema.

(*The English Language*, Harmondsworth: Penguin, p. 274)

1993a: Aus
Nicholas Hudson
Until recently, Australian was popularly seen as a vernacular with its
own colloquialisms and slang, not as a form of English with its own
vocabulary and idioms.

(from the entry 'Australianisms' in Nicholas Hudson's *Modern
Australian Usage*, Melbourne: Oxford University Press, p. 39)

1993b: Aus
Gordon Wilson
I write as a *user* of the Australian language; one who values our
Australian style as a legitimate prototype for a simplified international
English, particularly in S E Asia.

(letter to the editor of the newsletter *Australian Style*, 2.1,
Macquarie University, Sydney, December 1993, p. 12)

1995: UK (US)

Bryson explores the countless varieties of English, from American to Australian and Creole to Cockney, and exposes the perils of marketing foreign brands with names like *Pshitt* and *Super Piss.*

(description of the American writer Bill Bryson's book *The Mother Tongue: English and How It Got That Way*, in the *Softback Preview* (a book-club magazine-catalogue), London, January, p. 9)

1996a: UK
Malcolm Bradbury

Australian is a melting pot language on its own account and there are many forms of it. But part of its appeal is that it challenges the propriety of official English, which is seen as a language of empire, formality and command.

(quoted in 'Poms lose toffee-nosed tones to Aussie accent', in the *EL Gazette*, London, April 1996)

1996b: UK
Andrew Mayne and John Shuttleworth

Australian [chapter subtitle]
We're all quite familiar with the Australian accent, thanks to TV programmes like *Neighbours* – or we think we are! Here's a conversation in 'Australian', spelt as Australians would pronounce it. Can you understand what the conversation is about? Try saying it out loud. [There follows a list of items from the book *Let's Talk Strine* (Sydney: Ure Smith, 1965) by the pseudonymous Afferbeck Lauder ('Alphabetical Order'), the pseudonym of the writer Alistair Morrison.]

(*The Language Book*, London: Hodder and Stoughton, 1996 [school textbook])

1998: UK
Tom McArthur

There are now in the 1990s three clear-cut national standards, Standard Australian being buttressed by a comparable range of services to those that support Standard British and Standard American.

(*The English Languages*, Cambridge University Press, p. 5)

(2) *British* used to refer to British English

Compared with *American*, citations are few, probably because the majority of British nationals live in England and contrast something 'American' with something 'English', especially in terms of language. In addition, for citizens of the UK at large, the term *British language* seems unlikely to be used to refer to British English. However, the citations indicate that the concept has been launched.

1917: US
Fred Newton Scott

At a meeting in London University several years ago I had the pleasure of listening to speeches by eight well-known Englishmen. All used English, and good English too, but, phonetically regarded, there was as great a difference between the speech, say, of Mr. W. T. Stead and that of Sir John Cockburn, as could be heard on any university platform in America. Mr. Stead spoke precisely like an American from the Middle West – he might have been born in Chicago. The others spoke an unmistakable British, though all were easily intelligible.

('The Standard of American Speech', *The English Journal*,
6:1–15, January)

1958: Poland (US)
Margaret Schlauch

Their way of speaking [that is, the speech forms of immigrants to the New England colonies from 'old' England], transplanted to America, has remained closest to today's standard British.

(*The English Language in Modern Times*, Panstwowe Wydawnietwo Naukówe, Warsaw, p. 179. [A US academic working in Poland.])

1988: UK
David Crystal

There are many varieties of English spoken within [the Indian subcontinent], ranging from pidgin English to a standard English that is very close to British, including the use of Received Pronunciation.

(*The English Language*, Harmondsworth: Penguin, p. 258)

1990: US
John Algeo

Thus, the admirable *Complete Plain Words* of Sir Ernest Gowers comments on the increasing use of subjunctive verbs in present-day British.

('The Briticisms are coming! How British English is Creeping into the American Language', *Journal of English Linguistics*, 23:1, 2 (1990–1995). [Algeo uses the term extensively in contrast to *American.*])

1994: UK

[Headline] Translating into British
[The editor] Denys Parsons... has found a new source of work: translating American English into British English.

(news section of the magazine *Language International*, 6:2)

1995: Singapore
Anne Pakir

Obviously, the powers that be would want to ensure that codification of norms should remain as that of those norms considered standard in the traditional English canon, mainly standard British and standard American.

> ('English in Singapore: The Codification of Competing Norms',
> in S. Gopinathan, Anne Pakir, Ho Wah Kam and Vanithamani
> Saravanan (eds.), *Language, Society and Education: Issues and
> Trends*, Singapore: Times Academic Press)

1998: UK
Tom McArthur

Linguaphone chose, however, not to call the home variety 'British English', but left it unmarked, the implication being – intentional or not – that British is so obviously primary that it does not need further identification.

(*The English Languages*, chapter 2, Cambridge University Press, p. 37)

(3) *Canadian* used to refer to Canadian English

As yet hardly detectable.

1996: US

From Frostboil to Slob Ice, 'Canadian' stands apart [headline]
A new Canadian Dictionary of English, the first in more than a decade, was published this fall, and another, the Oxford Canadian Dictionary, is due out soon... To those who chart such things, there is little question that, despite British roots and American influence, Canadian has arrived.

> (article by Howard Schneider of the Washington Post service in
> the *International Herald Tribune*, 11 November)

Panel 9.4 A model of the Arabic languages

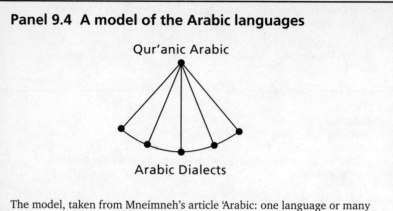

Qur'anic Arabic

Arabic Dialects

The model, taken from Mneimneh's article 'Arabic: one language or many languages?' (*Language International* 9:1, 1997) represents the national and regional varieties of Arabic, such as Egyptian Arabic and Yemeni Arabic, as located on the arc or rim of a circle, each linked to a a standardized high Arabic at the centre, derived from the language of the Qur'an and comparable to the position of World Standard English in the McArthur circle model (panel 4.8) and International English in the Görlach circle model (panel 4.10).

Index

Erasmus, Desiderius 106
ESL (English as a Second Language)
42–6, 104–5, 149
RP/Standard English taught 2,
104–5, 116, 129, 133, 149
Estuary English 117
Ethiopia 49, 54
European Bureau of Lesser Used
Languages 8, 139
European Society for the Study of
English (ESSE) 67, 76
European Union 34, 42
and Scots 8, 9, 139, 149, 216
evolutionary models of language 82,
89, 92

Falkland Islands 52, 53
family model of language 89–91,
182
Faroe Islands 49, 54, 90, 143
female models of language 89–90,
91–2, 98, 182
Fernando Po 44, 177
Fiji 51, 53
Finnish 42
foreign language, English as *see* EFL
Fowler, H.W. and F.G. 33–4, 72, 113,
220
fractured English 18–22
fragmentation of language 31, 58, 60,
66, 74, 106, 180–3
France 31, 32, 36, 106–7
Académie française 33, 79, 106,
211
see also French
franglais, Canadian 45
French xiv, 90, 203–4
creoles 40, 44, 164, 175, 204
18th-19th century cultural 38, 79,
167, 211
elements in 108, 175
and empire 30–1, 36, 92, 210
and English 17, 182, 189, 195, 204;
bilingualism 142–3; mixing 14,
45, 216
establishment of vernacular 106–7,
108
international status 32, 30–1, 38,

79, 167, 211
literature 108, 211
Norman 14, 17, 173–6, 189, 191
phases 82
pidgins 164
Québécois 32, 36, 40, 55, 148–9,
216
regulation 33, 79, 106, 211
in Romance family xvii, 203–4
and Scots 141, 146, 157
territories 36, 40, 41, 42, 47–8, 109,
186
Frenglish, Canadian 14, 45, 216
Frisian 90, 143
Friulian 204
Fulton, Henry 103, 104, 119

Gadarenes, Jesus in country of the
7–9, 212
Gaelic 40, 90, 109
Gaelic/English bilingualism 138,
145
Gaelic/English hybrids 43, 171–3,
175, 176, 216
see also under Ireland; Scotland
Gallego 90, 204
Gambia 49, 53, 55, 164, 177
Gardiner, Stephen 106
Geoffrey of Monmouth 185–6
geopolitical models 93–9
Georgia, USA 92, 171
German 36, 42, 90, 108, 143
High 24, 90, 187, 204
Low 90, 142, 143, 204
North 93, 204
West 84, 91, 98–9
Germanic 90, 93, 98–9, 138, 204
English as dialect of xvii, 72
Ghana 40, 49, 53, 55, 164, 177
Gibraltar 43, 49, 53
Glasgow 140
global English 86, 135
Görlach, Manfred 63, 24–6, 77, 174–5,
183
circle model of English 98, 101, 209
on pidgins and creoles 74, 205, 206
on Scots 150, 154
Gowers, Sir Ernest 34

similarities 88, 119, 156–7, 201,
202; prestige 109, 144–5
European Union recognition 8, 9,
149, 216
and French 141, 146, 157
historical development 9, 10, 88–9,
108, 138, 139, 141, 144, 146,
150, 215
hybridization with English 138, 140,
142, 147, 150
Lallans 152, 155
Latin influence 141, 146
literature 59, 139, 140, 150, 153
'Max und Moritz' in 24
Middle 215
and national identity 150
Older 141
orthography 139, 157–9
overseas influence 150
perceptions of status 148–50
pre-Union 104, 109, 141, 202
print tradition 7
status 7–8, 75, 138–42, 145–6, 150,
151–6, 204
Ulster Scots 10, 150
written language 147, 155; *see also*
literature *above*
Scott, Sir Walter 73
scripts 17, 109, 187, 210
Sea Island Creole *see* Gullah
second language, English as *see* ESL
Senegal 32
Serbian and Serbo-Croatian 90, 201
Seychelles 52, 53
Shaftesbury, 3rd Earl of 103–4, 119
Shakespeare, William; *The Tempest*
213
Shaw, George Bernard; *Pygmalion* 3
Shetlandic 25, 139
Sibbald, Sir Robert 147
Sicilian 204
Sierra Leone 40, 49, 53, 55
see also Krio
Singapore 32, 41, 93, 142, 175
English 6, 53, 55, 59, 75, 142;
hybrids 21–2, 216; official status
41, 51, 93, 142
Smith, Logan Pearsall 92, 122, 136

Smith, Thomas 106
social status
pronunciation and 116, 117, 118,
126, 129, 132, 134
varieties of language and xvi, 2–3, 6,
112, 140, 160–1; standard
115–18, 125, 126, 128–9, 131
socialism 114
Solomon Islands 52, 53
Pijin 44, 92, 165, 177
Somalia 49, 54
South Africa 41, 149
English 5, 41, 42, 50, 53, 55, 77,
117
Southron 9, 144, 147
Spain 44, 144, 145, 168
Spanglish 14, 45, 200–1, 202, 216
Spanish 33, 90, 108, 145, 195, 203–4
creoles 44, 92
diaspora language 30–1, 32, 36, 38,
39, 44, 47–8, 210
official status 42, 47–8
and Portuguese 144, 147
Spanish/English hybridization 14,
45, 150, 200–1, 202, 216
spelling *see* orthography
Sranan 10, 92, 162, 177
Sri Lanka 51, 53, 55
standard, linguistic 102–37
classical influence 79, 104–9
deviation from 110–11, 111–12,
197–200
education and spread of xiii–xiv, 32,
99, 133
high forms 110–12, 135
history 102–4, 110, 112, 119–35
Italian 88
Mandarin 128
in media 111–12, 127, 128, 132
in Middle Ages 105–6
orthography 109, 124, 127
print standard *see under* printing
use of term 119–35
written language as 109, 114, 126,
127, 128, 129–30, 131, 132, 224
see also under dialects
Standard English 58–9, 102–37
acrolect 6, 110–12